RECREATION

HAVING A GOOD TIME IN AMERICA

ISSN 1543-1593

RECREATION
HAVING A GOOD TIME IN AMERICA

Barbara Wexler

INFORMATION PLUS® REFERENCE SERIES
Formerly published by Information Plus, Wylie, Texas

GALE®

THOMSON

GALE

Detroit • New York • San Diego • San Francisco • Cleveland • New Haven, Conn. • Waterville, Maine • London • Munich

19977-S (handwritten)

THOMSON

GALE

Recreation: Having a Good Time in America

Barbara Wexler

Project Editor
Ellice Engdahl

Editorial
Paula Cutcher-Jackson, Kathleen Edgar,
Debra Kirby, Prindle LaBarge, Elizabeth Manar,
Charles B. Montney, Heather Price

Permissions
Debra J. Freitas

Product Design
Cynthia Baldwin

Composition and Electronic Prepress
Evi Seoud

Manufacturing
Keith Helmling

LIBRARY OF CONGRESS CATALOGING-IN-PUBLICATION DATA

ISBN 0-7876-5103-6 (set)
ISBN 0-7876-6074-4
ISSN 1543-1593

Printed in the United States of America
10 9 8 7 6 5 4 3 2 1

TABLE OF CONTENTS

CHAPTER 1

This chapter focuses on the most popular ways in which Americans spend their free time, including reading, personal computing/Internet use, sports and fitness, pets, hobbies, and volunteer work.

CHAPTER 2

Having fun can be expensive, and profitable. The increasing cost of recreation is discussed, as are sales trends for different segments of the recreation market, including consumer electronics (such as computers and DVD players), sporting goods and equipment, travel, toys, books, and collectibles.

CHAPTER 3

This chapter explores Americans' enduring love for the outdoors. It discusses the most popular forms of outdoor recreation; who participates, and why; newer forms of outdoor recreation, such as extreme sports; and the future of outdoor recreation.

CHAPTER 4

Americans spend billions of dollars each year on art- and media-related activities, such as going to movies, attending concerts and plays, visiting art and historical museums, and buying music and consumer electronics. This chapter explores how, where, and why. It also details trends in movie attendance, Internet use, record buying, and sales of televisions and other home electronics.

CHAPTER 5

This chapter focuses on participation and attendance trends in different individual and team sports, including America's most popular sports—baseball, basketball, and football—and many others, such as soccer, bowling, billiards/pool, tennis, and golf. Gender- and race-related differences in participation are also discussed.

CHAPTER 6

The history of gambling in the United States is as old as the country itself. This chapter traces gambling's history in America, from its humble beginnings in the late 1700s to the multibillion-dollar industry it is today, focusing on general trends and the many different types of gambling (casino, bingo and other charitable games, pari-mutuel wagering, lotteries, sports gambling, and Internet gambling).

CHAPTER 7

People's destinations and means of travel may vary, but one thing is clear: Americans love to travel. Discussed here are Americans' reasons for traveling; who travels; different types of trips (weekend excursions, cruises, ecotourism, cultural and heritage tourism); and the use of technology in making travel arrangements.

CHAPTER 8

As American society has changed, so has the role of recreation. Today, recreation serves many functions, such as building physical and emotional well-being, offering opportunities for socialization, and generating substantial profits. This chapter also explores important aspects of recreation in the United States, including the commercialization of professional sports and the "deification" of many professional athletes.

PREFACE

Recreation: Having a Good Time in America is one of the latest volumes in the Information Plus Reference Series. Previously published by the Information Plus company of Wylie, Texas, the Information Plus Reference Series (and its companion set, the Information Plus Compact Series) became a Gale Group product when Gale and Information Plus merged in early 2000. Those of you familiar with the series as published by Information Plus will notice a few changes from the 2001 edition. Gale has adopted a new layout and style that we hope you will find easy to use. Other improvements include greatly expanded indexes in each book, and more descriptive tables of contents.

While some changes have been made to the design, the purpose of the Information Plus Reference Series remains the same. Each volume of the series presents the latest facts on a topic of pressing concern in modern American life. These topics include today's most controversial and most studied social issues: abortion, capital punishment, care for the elderly, crime, the environment, health care, immigration, minorities, national security, social welfare, women, youth, and many more. Although written especially for the high school and undergraduate student, this series is an excellent resource for anyone in need of factual information on current affairs.

By presenting the facts, it is Gale's intention to provide its readers with everything they need to reach an informed opinion on current issues. To that end, there is a particular emphasis in this series on the presentation of scientific studies, surveys, and statistics. These data are generally presented in the form of tables, charts, and other graphics placed within the text of each book. Every graphic is directly referred to and carefully explained in the text. The source of each graphic is presented within the graphic itself. The data used in these graphics are drawn from the most reputable and reliable sources, in particular from the various branches of the U.S. government and from major independent polling organizations. Every effort has been made to secure the most recent information available. The reader should bear in mind that many major studies take years to conduct, and that additional years often pass before the data from these studies are made available to the public. Therefore, in many cases the most recent information available in 2003 dated from 2000 or 2001. Older statistics are sometimes presented as well, if they are of particular interest and no more-recent information exists.

Although statistics are a major focus of the Information Plus Reference Series they are by no means its only content. Each book also presents the widely held positions and important ideas that shape how the book's subject is discussed in the United States. These positions are explained in detail and, where possible, in the words of their proponents. Some of the other material to be found in these books includes: historical background; descriptions of major events related to the subject; relevant laws and court cases; and examples of how these issues play out in American life. Some books also feature primary documents, or have pro and con debate sections giving the words and opinions of prominent Americans on both sides of a controversial topic. All material is presented in an even-handed and unbiased manner; the reader will never be encouraged to accept one view of an issue over another.

HOW TO USE THIS BOOK

People have favorite activities that they enjoy doing during their free time, however much, or little, free time they have available. Most Americans enjoy watching television, reading, and spending time with friends and family, but beyond that their interests run in many directions. Some like to see movies in the theater or at home, others prefer gambling. Many Americans enjoy sports, but while some like to play basketball, others just like to watch, or prefer "extreme" sports such as mountain biking or bungee jumping. A huge entertainment industry has developed in the United States to meet these varied needs. This book presents the latest information on Americans' leisure activities and compares it with years past to highlight trends in how Americans use their free time. For example, watching movies at home is an increasingly popular way for Americans to spend an evening. Also, the number of weekend trips that Americans take has increased dramatically.

Recreation: Having a Good Time in America consists of eight chapters and three appendices. Each of the chapters is devoted to a particular aspect of recreation in the United States. For a summary of the information covered in each chapter, please see the synopses provided in the Table of Contents at the front of the book. Chapters generally begin with an overview of the basic facts and background information on the chapter's topic, then proceed to examine sub-topics of particular interest. For example, Chapter 5: Football, Baseball, Basketball, and Other Popular Sports begins with an overview of the most popular spectator and participatory sports in the United States. Differences between male and female sports enthusiasts are highlighted. The chapter then proceeds into more detailed examinations of some of the most popular participatory sports, including basketball, soccer, and bowling. Readers can find their way through a chapter by looking for the section and sub-section headings, which are clearly set off from the text. Or, they can refer to the book's extensive index, if they already know what they are looking for.

Statistical Information

The tables and figures featured throughout *Recreation: Having a Good Time in America* will be of particular use to the reader in learning about this topic. These tables and figures represent an extensive collection of the most recent and valuable statistics on recreation, as well as related issues—for example, graphics in the book cover how much Americans spend on different types of leisure activities; the number of Americans who gamble; the differences in the favorite leisure activities of Americans based on sex and income; and the impact of computers on recreation. Gale believes that making this information available to the reader is the most important way in which we fulfill the goal of this book: to help readers understand the issues and controversies surrounding recreation in the United States and reach their own conclusions.

Each table or figure has a unique identifier appearing above it, for ease of identification and reference. Titles for the tables and figures explain their purpose. At the end of each table or figure, the original source of the data is provided.

In order to help readers understand these often complicated statistics, all tables and figures are explained in the text. References in the text direct the reader to the relevant statistics. Furthermore, the contents of all tables and figures are fully indexed. Please see the opening section of the index at the back of this volume for a description of how to find tables and figures within it.

In addition to the main body text and images, *Recreation: Having a Good Time in America* has three appendices. The first is the Important Names and Addresses directory. Here the reader will find contact information for a number of government and private organizations that can provide further information on aspects of recreation. The second appendix is the Resources section, which can also assist the reader in conducting his or her own research. In this section, the author and editors of *Recreation: Having a Good Time in America* describe some of the sources that were most useful during the compilation of this book. The final appendix is the index. It has been greatly expanded from previous editions, and should make it even easier to find specific topics in this book.

ADVISORY BOARD CONTRIBUTIONS

The staff of Information Plus would like to extend their heartfelt appreciation to the Information Plus Advisory Board. This dedicated group of media professionals provides feedback on the series on an ongoing basis. Their comments allow the editorial staff who work on the project to continually make the series better and more user-friendly. Our top priorities are to produce the highest-quality and most useful books possible, and the Advisory Board's contributions to this process are invaluable.

The members of the Information Plus Advisory Board are:

- Kathleen R. Bonn, Librarian, Newbury Park High School, Newbury Park, California

- Madelyn Garner, Librarian, San Jacinto College—North Campus, Houston, Texas

- Anne Oxenrider, Media Specialist, Dundee High School, Dundee, Michigan

- Charles R. Rodgers, Director of Libraries, Pasco-Hernando Community College, Dade City, Florida

- James N. Zitzelsberger, Library Media Department Chairman, Oshkosh West High School, Oshkosh, Wisconsin

COMMENTS AND SUGGESTIONS

The editors of the Information Plus Reference Series welcome your feedback on *Recreation: Having a Good Time in America*. Please direct all correspondence to:

Editors
Information Plus Reference Series
27500 Drake Rd.
Farmington Hills, MI 48331-3535

ACKNOWLEDGMENTS

The editors wish to thank the copyright holders of material included in this volume and the permissions managers of many book and magazine publishing companies for assisting us in securing reproduction rights. We are also grateful to the staffs of the Detroit Public Library, the Library of Congress, the University of Detroit Mercy Library, Wayne State University Purdy/Kresge Library Complex, and the University of Michigan Libraries for making their resources available to us.

Following is a list of the copyright holders who have granted us permission to reproduce material in Recreation: Having a Good Time in America. *Every effort has been made to trace copyright, but if omissions have been made, please let us know.*

For more detailed source citations, please see the sources listed under each individual table and figure.

American Recreation Coalition: Table 1.10, Table 1.11

Consumer Electronics Association: Table 2.4, Table 2.5

Cruise Lines International Association: Figure 7.3, Figure 7.4, Figure 7.5, Table 7.2, Table 7.3, Table 7.4, Table 7.5, Table 7.6, Table 8.2

The Gallup Organization: Table 1.1, Table 1.2, Table 4.5, Table 5.1, Table 5.2, Table 5.7, Table 8.1

Harrah's Entertainment: Figure 6.3, Figure 6.4, Figure 6.5, Figure 6.6, Figure 6.7, Table 6.2, Table 6.3, Table 6.4, Table 6.5, Table 6.6, Table 6.7

Independent Sector: Figure 1.2, Table 1.15, Table 1.16

National Endowment for the Arts: Table 4.1, Table 4.2, Table 4.3, Table 4.4

National Indian Gaming Commission: Figure 6.1, Figure 6.2, Table 6.1

National Marine Manufacturers Association: Table 2.9

National Park Service: Figure 3.2, Figure 3.3, Table 3.2, Table 3.3

The NPD Group, Inc. and Toy Industry Association, Inc.: Table 2.6

Pew Internet and American Life Project: Table 1.3, Table 1.4

Pew Research Center for the People & the Press: Figure 1.1, Table 1.5, Table 1.6

Recreation Roundtable: Figure 3.1

Sporting Goods Manufacturers Association: Table 1.7, Table 1.8, Table 1.9, Table 1.12, Table 1.13, Table 1.14, Table 2.7, Table 2.8, Table 3.1, Table 5.3, Table 5.4, Table 5.5, Table 5.6

U.S. Bureau of Labor Statistics: Table 2.1, Table 2.2

U.S. Department of Commerce, Bureau of Economic Analysis: Table 2.3

U.S. Department of the Interior, Fish and Wildlife Service, and U.S. Department of Commerce, U.S. Census Bureau: Figure 2.1, Figure 2.2, Figure 2.3, Figure 3.4, Figure 3.5, Figure 3.6, Figure 3.7, Figure 3.8, Figure 3.9, Table 3.4, Table 3.5, Table 3.6, Table 3.7, Table 3.8, Table 3.9

U.S. Department of Transportation, Bureau of Transportation Statistics: Figure 7.1, Figure 7.2, Table 7.1

CHAPTER 1
HOW AMERICANS SPEND THEIR TIME

DEFINING LEISURE AND RECREATION

The word "leisure" comes from the Latin word *licere,* which means "to be allowed." Most Americans view leisure as something allowed after one's work is done: time that is free after required activities. Recreation, however, is a different matter. The *Oxford American Dictionary* defines recreation as "a process or means of refreshing or entertaining oneself after work by some pleasurable activity." Its Latin and French roots, which mean "restore to health" or "create anew," suggest rejuvenating of strength or spirit. While leisure activities are pastimes, recreational activities are intended to restore physical or mental health.

HOW MUCH FREE TIME?

In many international comparisons, Americans rank at or near the top of enjoying some of the highest standards of living in the world. Although the United States trails other countries in some significant measures of health and well-being, such as infant mortality and life expectancy, the world generally respects—even envies—the quality of life enjoyed by most Americans.

Americans do work hard. Although there has been no significant change since the 1970s in the number of hours of nonwork time available to Americans, public opinion surveys consistently report that Americans believe they have less free time today than in the past. Rushing and under stress, many report they do not get enough sleep each day, and most believe they do not have sufficient time for family and pleasurable activities. Some even consider themselves workaholics. Others believe they have filled their leisure hours with so much activity that it also becomes stressful, rather than restorative, rejuvenating, and relaxing.

A PERSONAL CHOICE

People who perform certain activities all day at a job often pursue dramatically different activities during their time off. For example, someone who sits behind a desk at work may choose a physically active pastime, such as recreational walking, the most popular participatory sport among both women and men since the early 1980s. Similarly, a person with a job that requires demanding physical labor may choose a more sedentary activity, such as playing computer games, reading, or painting. A person who lives in a flat region may go to the mountains to seek excitement, while someone living in the mountains might seek out a sandy ocean beach on which to relax.

Other people may enjoy one field so much that they perform that activity not only professionally, but also as a form of recreation. Some observers suggest that when workers derive less satisfaction from jobs where they have few opportunities to make meaningful contributions, recreation becomes even more important to personal happiness and satisfaction with life.

HOW DO AMERICANS LIKE TO SPEND THEIR LEISURE TIME?

A 2001 survey conducted by the Leisure Trends Group finds that nearly one-third of Americans said that reading was their favorite way to spend leisure time. Yet, when asked how they spent their leisure time during the previous day, twice as many survey respondents reported watching television rather than reading.

Other favorite ways to spend leisure time were spending time with family and friends (19.7 percent), seeing a movie (13.6 percent), shopping (12.9 percent), fishing (11.2 percent), traveling (9.8 percent), walking (8.9 percent), listening to the radio (8.2 percent), and spending time with kids (7.4 percent).

A comparison of how leisure time is spent versus the activities Americans claim are their favorite ways to spend leisure time suggests that they do not always get to spend their leisure time in ways that they like. For example,

TABLE 1.1

Leading ways to spend an evening, by age, December 2001

Top choices for way to spend an evening by age

	18–29	30–49	50–64	65+
Visiting with friends	19%	7	4	4
Staying home with family	13%	27	9	9
Watching TV/DVD/VHS	16%	23	33	38

SOURCE: Lydia Saad, "Top Choices for Way to Spend an Evening by Age," in "There's No Place Like Home to Spend an Evening, Say Most Americans," The Gallup Organization, January 10, 2002 www.gallup.com © 2002 The Gallup Organization, all rights reserved. Reprinted with permission.

housecleaning ranked eighth in the survey of how Americans spent leisure time but did not rank at all among the top ten favorite leisure-time activities!

FAVORITE WAYS TO SPEND AN EVENING

Americans enjoy spending time relaxing at home. A 2001 Gallup poll finds that Americans' favorite way to spend an evening is watching television (26 percent) or simply spending time with their families. Other favorite ways to spend an evening include reading (9 percent), resting and relaxing (9 percent), and socializing with friends (8 percent).

Americans seem to be homebodies. Although four out of five surveyed respondents reported eating out at least once a week, only 5 percent said that eating out was among their favorite ways to spend an evening. Young people aged eighteen to twenty-nine were more likely to prefer visiting with friends then remaining at home with family; however, even in this age group, the majority preferred to remain at home, staying with their families or watching television. (See Table 1.1.)

Among young adults, socializing with friends is named as the preferred way to spend an evening more often than watching television (19 percent compared to 16 percent). Interest in television increases with age and it is the preferred pastime for persons over age fifty. (See Table 1.1.) Interestingly, television has been the most popular way for Americans to spend an evening since 1960, based on previous Gallup polls that asked this same question.

READING

Reading is one of the top three leisure activities among Americans. A 2001 Gallup poll finds that while athletics was the most frequently named pursuit (33 percent) and crafts, such as sewing, knitting, woodwork, and model building, were named by 17 percent as a favorite activity, reading was mentioned by 12 percent of surveyed respondents.

The survey also finds that the overwhelming majority (84 percent) of Americans said they had read all or part of at least one book in the year preceding the survey. Many

TABLE 1.2

Method of selecting books to read, among adults who read in the past year, September 1999

WHICH OF THE FOLLOWING IS THE MAIN WAY YOU GENERALLY SELECT THE BOOKS YOU READ — [RANDOM ORDER: BASED ON A RECOMMENDATION FROM SOMEONE YOU KNOW; BY CHOOSING AN AUTHOR WHOSE BOOKS YOU LIKE; BASED ON BOOK REVIEWS YOU'VE READ; BY BROWSING A BOOKSTORE OR LIBRARY; BASED ON AN ADVERTISEMENT YOU'VE SEEN; BY BROWSING AN INTERNET SITE] OR DO YOU SELECT THEM ANOTHER WAY?

Based on 755 Form B respondents who read in past year; ± 4 percentage points

Based on a recommendation from someone you know	27%
By choosing an author whose books you like	27
Based on book reviews you've read	6
By browsing a bookstore or library	26
Based on an advertisement you've seen	3
Based on subject matter (vol.)	2
By browsing an Internet site	1
Other	7
No opinion	1
	100%

SOURCE: Darren K. Carlson, "Which of the following is the main way you generally select the books you read?" in "Poll Shows Continuing Strong American Reading Habits," The Gallup Organzation, October 4, 1999 www.gallup.com © 1999 The Gallup Organization, all rights reserved. Reprinted with permission.

surveyed respondents read regularly—30 percent read between one and five books per year, 16 percent said they read six to ten books, and four out of ten respondents read more than ten books during the year preceding the survey.

Choosing Books to Read

According to a 1999 Gallup poll, Americans preferred to read nonfiction. Of the Americans polled by Gallup, 46 percent said they read primarily nonfiction. Another 35 percent read mostly fiction, and 17 percent read both fiction and nonfiction equally. Among men, 51 percent preferred nonfiction, while only 41 percent of women preferred nonfiction. More older adults—persons thirty to sixty-four years old—preferred nonfiction than readers eighteen to thirty-nine years old.

Data collected by Ipsos-NPD report the sale of popular fiction by venue: large chain bookstores, small chain or independent bookstores, and Internet sales. In 1997 half of adult books sold were popular fiction and the proportion grew to 54 percent in 2000. Interestingly, consumers at large chain bookstores and those purchasing via the Internet bought a higher percentage of popular fiction books than customers of small chain and independent bookstores.

The Gallup poll finds that more than one-quarter of Americans choose their books based on recommendations from friends and a comparable proportion either choose a title by an author they like (27 percent) or browse the library or bookstore to select books (26 percent). Just 6 percent rely on book reviews they have read to help them select a book and just 1 percent browse Internet sites looking for books. (See Table 1.2.)

The Ipsos-NPD survey confirms that a growing proportion of consumers purchase books via the Internet. In 2000, Internet "etailers"—online vendors—made slightly more than 7 percent of all adult book sales, up from 5.4 percent in 1999. Consumers who buy books online are making purchases they have planned, rather than by browsing or making impulse purchases. In 2000, three-quarters of book purchases made on the Internet were planned.

In general, Americans' taste in books, as measured by market share, is relatively unchanged since 1991. Comparing market share figures from 1991 to 1998, researchers find just one category that has more than doubled in market share. Religious books made up 4.7 percent of the books sold in 1991. By 1998 the market share of religious books had grown to 9.9 percent. According to industry statistics published by the Association of American Publishers, this category continues to grow with net sales increasing 4.7 percent from 2000 to 2001.

COMPUTERS IN DAILY HOME USE

Personal computing has become an important leisure activity. The cost of buying a computer decreased significantly during the 1990s, and the growing affordability increased computer ownership. There is an expanding array of educational and entertainment software available, including a wide variety of games, financial programs, programs that teach foreign languages, and others that search the Internet.

By 2000 more than three-quarters of American public schools had access to the Internet. As an increasing proportion of schools gained access to the World Wide Web, there was a corresponding increase in students with the ability to use it. Students without Internet access in their homes or schools could go online at local public libraries. The 2000 Public Library Internet Study, conducted by the U.S. National Commission on Libraries and Information Science, an independent agency of the federal government, finds that nearly all (94.5 percent) libraries provide public access to the Internet. Library connectivity and public access services increased by more than 20 percent since 1998, when the previous survey reported that 73.3 percent of libraries offered public Internet access.

Internet Use Is the Norm

Use of the Internet continues to grow dramatically. A 1999 study by Media Research finds that 64 million American adults, or nearly one-third of the population over eighteen years of age, were using the Internet at least once a month. Another study using statistics from IntelliQuest finds that 83 million (40 percent) Americans over sixteen years of age were using the Internet in 1999. By 2002 the Pew Research Center for the People and the Press reports that nearly 113 million (60 percent) Americans had gone online. (See Table 1.3.)

TABLE 1.3

Internet activities of parents, 2002

About 59% of Americans (113 million) have gone online.[a] Here are the kinds of things they do:	Percent of those with Internet access
Send email	93%[a]
Use an online search engine to find information	85[c]
Do an Internet search to answer a question	80[e]
Search for a map or driving directions	79[e]
Look for info on a hobby	77[c]
Research a product or service before buying it	75[f]
Look for info about movies, books, or other leisure activities	73[b]
Check the weather	69[b]
Get news	66[a]
Get travel information	66[f]
Surf the Web for fun	65[c]
Look for health/medical information	64
Visit a government Web site	62
Buy a product	55[b]
Look up phone number or address	53[e]
Research for school or training	53[c]
Watch a video or audio clip	51[f]
Buy or make a reservation for travel	50[a]
Do any type of research for their job	49[c]
Get financial information	47[c]
Look for information about a job	47[b]
Send an instant message	46[a]
Look for political news/information	43[a]
Download other files such as games, videos, or pictures	41[e]
Check sports scores	38[g]
Listen to or download music online	37[f]
Listen to music online at a web site for a radio station, music store, recording artist, or music service	37[e]
Play a game	37[a]
Look for information about a place to live	36[b]
Bank online	32[a]
Search for information on the Internet about someone you know or might meet	28[b]
Share files from own computers such as music, video, pictures, computer games w/ others	28[e]
Download music files to your computer	26[e]
Chat in a chat room or in an online discussion	25[a]
Look for religious/spiritual information	25[c]
Look for weight loss or general fitness information	24[c]
Look for information about a mental health issue like depression or anxiety	23[a]
Use Internet to get photos developed/display photos	21[e]
Participate in an online auction	20[b]
Research your family s history or genealogy	20[f]
Look for information on something sensitive or embarrassing that you would rather not ask someone about	18[a]
Go online for news and info about the Republican and Democratic national conventions	16[g]
Visit an adult web site	14[e]
Create content for the Internet, such as helping build a web site, creating an online diary, or posting your thoughts online	13[a]
Buy or sell stocks, bonds, or mutual funds	13[b]
Make a phone call over the Internet	12[e]
Go to a dating Web site	10[a]
Visit an online support group	9[a]
Buy groceries online	8[g]
Make a donation to a charity online	7[a]
Take a class online for college credit	7[b]
Take any other class online	6[b]
Gamble	5[e]

The Pew Research Center for the People and the Press, in *The Internet News Audience Goes Ordinary* (1999), reports that the Internet audience is not only growing, but also increasingly resembles the population as a whole. Whereas well-educated, affluent men were once the greatest users of the Internet, people without college training, those with modest incomes, and women are using the Internet more and more. A Pew Internet and

TABLE 1.3

Internet activities of parents, 2002 [CONTINUED]

About 59% of Americans (113 million) have gone online.[a] Here are the kinds of things they do:	Percent of those with Internet access
Check e-mail on a hand-held computer	5[e]
Check email on a web-enabled cell phone	4[e]
Create a web log or "blog" that others can read online	3[a]
Check email on other messaging device	1[e]

[a]From the Pew Internet & American Life Project Survey, June-July 2002
[b]From the Pew Internet & American Life Project Survey, March-May 2002
[c]From the Pew Internet & American Life Project Survey, January 2002
[d]From the Pew Internet & American Life Project Survey, December 2001
[e]From the Pew Internet & American Life Project Survey, August-October 2001
[f]From the Pew Internet & American Life Project Survey, February-March 2001
[g]From the Pew Internet & American Life Project Survey, March-December 2000

SOURCE: "Internet Activities" in *Parents Online,* Pew Internet and American Life Project, Washington, DC, 2002 [Online] http://www.pewinternet.org/reports/chart.asp?img=Interne2.htm [accessed December 13, 2002]

American Life Project tracking survey conducted between March and May 2002 finds that almost one-quarter of persons with less than a high school education and 45 percent of high school graduates were online, compared to 82 percent of college graduates. Similarly, 38 percent persons with household incomes below $30,000 used the Internet, along with 65 percent of persons with incomes from $30,000 to $50,000 and 74 percent of those with incomes ranging from $50,000 to $75,000.

In *Counting on the Internet,* a 2002 report by the Pew Internet and American Life Project, researchers conclude that the popularity and reliability of the Internet as a source of information has raised Americans' expectations about the scope and availability of information online. Three-quarters of Internet users, 40 percent of whom had been online for more than three years, report positive experience in finding information about health care, government agencies, news, and shopping. Many users site the Internet as the first place they turn to for news and information.

According to Pew Internet and American Life Project surveys conducted during 2001 and 2002, nearly all persons with Internet access send e-mail (93 percent), 85 percent use online search engines to find information, 79 percent look for maps or driving directions, and more than three-quarters of users research products before they buy them and go online in pursuit of information about their hobbies. Other common uses include looking for weather forecasts (69 percent), getting news (66 percent), seeking travel information (66 percent), looking for health or medical information (64 percent), or simply surfing the Web for fun (65 percent). (See Table 1.3.)

The Pew Internet and American Life Project researchers estimate that 64 million Americans go online on an average day. Typical daily Internet activities include sending e-mail (46 percent), using a search engine to find information (29

TABLE 1.4

Survey of daily Internet activities, 2002

On an average day, about 60 million Americans go online. Here are the kinds of things they do on a typical day:	Percent of those with Internet access
Go online	53%[a]
Send email	46[a]
Use an online search engine to find information	29[c]
Get news	22[a]
Surf the Web for fun	22[c]
Look for info on a hobby	19[c]
Check the weather	17[b]
Do any type of research for their job	16[c]
Do an Internet search to answer a specific question	14[f]
Research a product or service before buying it	14[f]
Get financial information	13[c]
Look for info about movies, books, or other leisure activities	13[b]
Send an instant message	11[a]
Check sports scores	10[g]
Look for political news/information	9[a]
Research for school or training	9[c]
Visit a government Web site	8[a]
Bank online	8[a]
Play a game	7[a]
Watch a video or audio clip	7[f]
Listen to or download music online	6[f]
Get travel information	6[f]
Go online for news and info about the Republican and Democratic national conventions	5[g]
Look for health/medical information	5[a]
Chat in a chat room or in an online discussion	4[a]
Look for information about a job	4[b]
Share files from own computers such as music, video, pictures, computer games w/ others	4[e]
Download other files such as games, videos, or pictures	4[e]
Look up phone number or address	4[e]
Search for a map or driving directions	4[e]
Listen to music online at a web site for a radio station, music store, recording artist, or music service	4[e]
Create content for the Internet, such as helping build a web site, creating an online diary, or posting your thoughts online	3[a]
Buy a product	3[b]
Search for information on the Internet about someone you know or might meet	3[b]
Look for religious/spiritual information	3[c]
Look for weight loss or general fitness information	3[c]
Download music files to your computer	3[e]
Look for information about a place to live	3[b]
Go to a dating Web site	2[a]
Participate in an online auction	2[b]
Buy or make a reservation for travel	1[a]
Look for information about a mental health issue like depression or anxiety	1[a]
Gamble	1[e]
Buy groceries online	1[g]
Visit an online support group	1[a]
Use Internet to get photos developed/display photos	1[e]
Check email on a web-enabled cell phone	1[e]
Visit an adult web site	1[e]
Check e-mail on a hand-held computer	1[e]
Make a phone call over the Internet	1[e]
Buy or sell stocks, bonds, or mutual funds	1[b]
Check email on other messaging device	1[e]
Research your family's history or genealogy	1[f]
Take a class online for college credit	1[b]
Take any other class online	1[b]
Make a donation to a charity online	0[a]

percent), getting news (22 percent), checking the weather (17 percent), performing job-related research (16 percent), and conducting a search to answer a specific question (14 percent). Nearly one-quarter go online for recreation—that is, simply to surf the Web for fun. (See Table 1.4.)

TABLE 1.4

Survey of daily Internet activities, 2002 [CONTINUED]

On an average day, about 60 million Americans go online. Here are the kinds of things they do on a typical day:	Percent of those with Internet access
Look for information on something sensitive or embarrassing that you would rather not ask someone about	0[a]
Create a web log or "blog" that others can read online	0[a]

[a]From the Pew Internet & American Life Project Survey, June-July 2002
[b]From the Pew Internet & American Life Project Survey, March-May 2002
[c]From the Pew Internet & American Life Project Survey, January 2002
[d]From the Pew Internet & American Life Project Survey, December 2001
[e]From the Pew Internet & American Life Project Survey, August-October 2001
[f]From the Pew Internet & American Life Project Survey, February-March 2001
[g]From the Pew Internet & American Life Project Survey, March-December 2000

SOURCE: "Daily Internet Activities" in *Parents Online,* Pew Internet and American Life Project, Washington, DC, 2002 [Online] http://www.pewinternet.org/reports/chart.asp?img=Daily_A1.htm [accessed December 13, 2002]

FIGURE 1.1

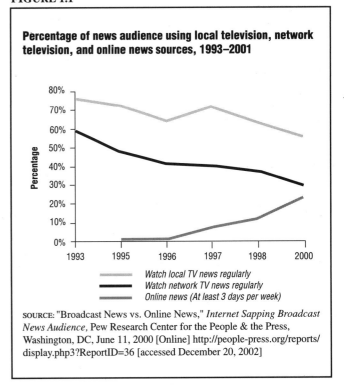

Percentage of news audience using local television, network television, and online news sources, 1993–2001

SOURCE: "Broadcast News vs. Online News," *Internet Sapping Broadcast News Audience,* Pew Research Center for the People & the Press, Washington, DC, June 11, 2000 [Online] http://people-press.org/reports/display.php3?ReportID=36 [accessed December 20, 2002]

LOGGING ON FOR NEWS. The Pew Research Center for the People and the Press compares patterns of viewing broadcast news on television to seeking news online and finds that from 1993 to 2000 reliance on regular broadcast news declined and regular use of online news sources had increased. (See Figure 1.1.) Younger adults, under age thirty, were more likely to go online at least once a week looking for news and less likely to have read a newspaper than adults over age thirty, however, adults aged thirty to forty-nine were the most likely to log on for daily news. (See Table 1.5.)

In addition to news, consumers are going online in search of stock market updates and financial advice. Although a Pew Research Center survey conducted in 2000 finds just 21 percent of the general public looked for stock market reports online, 28 percent of investors and nearly half of the active traders surveyed said they relied on the Internet for market updates. More than one-third of active traders sought investment advice online, while less than 20 percent relied on either television or newspapers for investment information. (See Table 1.6.)

ACCESSING MUSIC ONLINE. According to market research and forecasts conducted for the Recording Industry of America, 82 percent (141.1 million) are music consumers. An estimated 66 percent of music consumers (113.6 million) have Internet access at home or work and 17 percent of online music consumers (29.2 million) have high-speed Internet access from home that enables them to quickly download music, videos, and movies.

A survey conducted in May 2002 of 860 music consumers with Internet access finds that music purchases have declined among online consumers and that during 2002, half had downloaded music for free. The research reveals that the first impulse of many consumers, especial-

ly teens and young adults, when they hear a song they like is to download it for free. Nearly one-quarter of consumers who reported downloading music for free during 2002 said they did it at least once a week. The researchers conclude that there is a correlation between free downloading and music purchases—by more than two to one, consumers who download more report fewer music purchases.

Children, Teens, and College Students on the Internet

Almost half of all American children between the ages of two and twelve were projected to be online by 2002, according to the *1998 Jupiter Communications Consumer Content Report.* It was estimated that 18.8 million children under eighteen had access to home computers. Teens spent an average of 8.5 hours a week chatting and e-mailing on the Internet, and about 1.8 hours a week for school work.

According to the 2002 Pew Internet and American Life Project report *The Internet Goes to College,* college students are among the heaviest users of the Internet. This finding is not surprising since about one-fifth of current college students began using computers as young children and by age sixteen, all college students who responded to the survey had used computers, and most were Internet users. While only 59 percent of the general population has gone online, 86 percent of college students have gone online, and about half began using the Internet before they went to college.

College students are even more inclined to go online for recreation than the general population. Seventy-eight

TABLE 1.5

Patterns of news use by age, 2000

	Total %	<30 %	30–49 %	50+ %
Goes online	54	74	62	33
Online at least once a week for news	33	46	37	20
Online daily for news	15	17	18	10
Watched TV news yesterday	55	44	51	67
Read newspaper yesterday	46	29	43	58

Note: Based on total sample.

SOURCE: "Patterns of News Use By Age," *Internet Sapping Broadcast News Audience,* Pew Research Center for the People & the Press, Washington, DC, June 11, 2000 [Online] http://people-press.org/reports/display.php3? ReportID=36 [accessed December 20, 2002]

TABLE 1.6

Percentage of public using the Internet for finance and investment news, 2000

	General public %	All investors %	Active traders %
Main source for Stock market updates			
Newspapers	21	26	21
Television	37	30	24
Radio	4	4	1
Magazine	2	3	2
Internet	21	28	45
Other	7	8	7
Don't know	5	1	*
	100	100	100
Investment advice			
Newspaper	23	24	18
Television	26	21	19
Radio	3	3	2
Magazine	6	7	7
Internet	18	22	35
Broker/financial advisor (Vol.)	9	13	12
Other	8	7	5
Don't know	7	3	2
	100	100	100
(Percent of public	100%	46%	15%)

SOURCE: "Logging On for News, Advice," *Internet Sapping Broadcast News Audience,* Pew Research Center for the People & the Press, Washington, DC, June 11, 2000 [Online] http://people-press.org/reports/display.php3? ReportID=36 [accessed December 20, 2002]

percent of college students browse the Internet for fun, compared to 64 percent of all Internet users. Along with Internet surfing, 60 percent of college users have downloaded music files, 72 percent check their e-mail at least once a day, and typically about one-quarter of college students use instant messaging to chat with friends each day. Although only 10 percent of college students said they use the Internet principally for entertainment, 42 percent report that they use the Internet primarily to communicate socially and nearly three-quarters of students said most of their online communication is with their friends.

Computer Use Among Older Adults

According to a 2002 report from the U.S. Department of Commerce, older adults are the fastest-growing segment of Internet users. Persons over age sixty are rapidly dispelling myths about their reluctance to embrace new technology, as they surf the Web in record numbers. Although there were an estimated 3.7 million older adult Internet users in 2001, researchers predict explosive growth in the population of older users, with a projected 17.3 million older adults online in 2005.

Computers have been readily integrated into the lives of older adults in many settings, ranging from nursing homes to senior recreation centers. For older adults who are homebound as a result of illness or disability, Internet access can offer opportunities to socialize, contact friends and family, and purchase food and other necessities without leaving their homes.

SPORTS AND FITNESS ACTIVITIES ARE IMPORTANT TO MANY AMERICANS

Like tastes in food, fashion, and music, American exercise habits have undergone significant shifts. Participation in sports and other fitness activities are important to many Americans. The Sporting Goods Manufacturers Association (SGMA) in *Sports Participation in America,*

2002 Edition describes facts about the 86.1 million Americans who are frequent sports participants and the 83.6 million occasional participants, along with Americans' preoccupation with fitness and trends in fitness activity:

• Participation in team sports increased between 1998 and 2001.

• More people are participating in camping, hiking, and mountaineering, while hunting and fishing have declined in popularity.

• Recreational activities that are considered enjoyable continue to attract enthusiasts—there are an estimated 93.6 million recreational swimmers, 84.2 million recreational walkers, and 52.9 million recreational bicyclists.

• The most popular sport in America is bowling, with 55.5 million participants.

• Treadmills are the fitness equipment most frequently purchased and free weight training is the most popular fitness activity.

• Extreme sports experienced explosive growth between 1990 and 2001—participation in in-line skating skyrocketed by 453 percent and snowboarding grew by 224 percent.

The SGMA report also concludes that Americans prefer noncompetitive sports and fitness activities that are less intense and low key. Of the top twenty most popular

TABLE 1.7

Top 30 most popular sports, 2002

Sport	# of Participants (Millions)
1. Recreational swimming [1]	93.6
2. Recreational walking [2]	84.2
3. Bowling [3]	55.5
4 Recreational bicycling [4]	52.9
5. Free weights [5]	45.4
6. Freshwater fishing (not including fly fishing) [6]	43.5
7. Tent camping [7]	43.5
8. Treadmill exercise [8]	41.6
9. Billiards/pool [11]	39.3
10. Basketball [10]	38.7
11. Stretching [12]	38.1
12. Day hiking [9]	36.9
13. Fitness walking [13]	36.4
14. Running/jogging [14]	34.9
15. Golf [15]	29.4
15. Calisthenics [18]	29.4
17. Stationary cycling [17]	28.7
18. Inline skating [16]	26.0
19. Weight/resistance machines [19]	25.9
20. Darts [21]	19.5
21. RV camping [20]	19.1
22. Soccer [24]	19.0
23. Abdominal machine/device [23]	18.7
24. Softball (regular) [25]	17.7
25. Ice skating [26]	16.8
26. Hunting (shotgun/rifle) [29]	16.7
26. Touch football [not ranked in 2000]	16.7
28. Horseback riding [27]	16.6
29. Scooters (non-motorized) [not ranked in 2000]	15.8
30. Fitness swimming [not ranked in 2000]	15.3

[ ] = Ranking in 2000

SOURCE: "Top 30 Most Popular Sports" in "Sports and Activities That Dominate U.S. Participation," in *Superstudy of Sports Participation,* Sporting Goods Manufacturer's Association, North Palm Beach, FL, 2002 www.SGMA.com

TABLE 1.8

Most popular sports for males based on "frequent" participation, 2001

Activity	Year 2001
1. Basketball (25+ days/year)	13,216,000
2. Freshwater fishing (15+ days/year)	9,472,000
3. Free weights: dumbbells (100+ days/year)	8,085,000
4. Free weights: barbells (100+ days/year)	7,566,000
5. Calisthenics (100+ days/year)	7,519,000
6. Stretching (100+ days/year)	7,296,000
7. Golf (25+ days/year)	6,596,000
8. Billiards/pool (25+ days/year)	6,515,000
9. Running/jogging (100+ days/year)	6,302,000
10. Fitness walking (100+ days/year)	5,993,000
11. Weight/resistance machines (100+ days/year)	5,113,000
12. Baseball (25+ days/year)	5,093,000
13. Soccer (25+ days/year)	5,004,000
14. In-line skating (25+ days/year)	4,582,000
15. Hunting (shotgun/rifle) [15+ days/year]	4,496,000

SOURCE: "Most Popular Sports for Males Based on "Frequent" Participation (Age 6 and Older)" in "Men and Fitness: a Strong Link," in *Superstudy of Sports Participation,* Sporting Goods Manufacturer's Association, North Palm Beach, FL, 2002 www.SGMA.com

TABLE 1.9

Most popular sports for women based on "frequent" participation, 2001

(Age 6 and older)

Activity	Year 2001
1. Fitness walking (100+ days/year)	10,818,000
2. Stretching (100+ days/year)	10,041,000
3. Treadmill exercise (100+ days/year)	6,120,000
4. Basketball (25+ days/year)	5,135,000
5. Day hiking (15+ days/year)	4,273,000
6. Free weights: Hand weights (100+ days/year)	4,243,000
7. In-line skating (25+ days/year)	4,213,000
8. Bowling (25+ days/year)	4,200,000
9. Soccer (25+ days/year)	4,113,000
10. Running/jogging (100+ days/year)	4,042,000
11. Calisthenics (100+ days/year)	3,673,000
12. Recreational vehicle camping (15+ days/year)	3,421,000
13. Fishing (freshwater/other) [15+ days/year]	3,303,000
14. Weight/resistance machines (100+ days/year)	3,284,000
15. Court volleyball (25+ days/year)	3,244,000

SOURCE: "Most Popular Sports for Women Based on "Frequent" Participation (Age 6 and older)," in "Diversity That's the Name of the Game for American Women," in *Superstudy of Sports Participation,* Sporting Goods Manufacturer's Association, North Palm Beach, FL, 2002 www.SGMA.com

sports listed in Table 1.7, basketball is the only team sport Americans named as a favorite. Basketball claimed 38.7 million participants, while soccer had 19 million, softball had 17.7 million, and touch football had 16.7 million.

AMERICA'S MOST POPULAR SPORTS

The SGMA determines the top thirty most popular sports in America based on the number of participants. (See Table 1.7.) Recreational swimming had the most participants, with 93.6 million persons participating at least once during 2001. Not far behind in numbers of participants during 2002 was recreational walking with 84.2 million. Other popular sports in 1999 included bowling (55.5 million), recreational bicycling (52.9 million), freshwater fishing (43.5 million), tent camping (43.5 million), and exercising on a treadmill (41.6 million).

Gender and Age Influence Sports and Fitness Choices

Athletically inclined men seem to prefer fitness activities. Seven out of the top fifteen most popular sports for male participants emphasized fitness rather than competition or team sports. (See Table 1.8.) Of the fitness-related activities, exercising with free weights was most popular, followed by calisthenics, stretching, running/jogging, fitness walking, and exercising using weight/resistance machines.

Women who participate in sports and fitness activities seek variety rather than favoring a single sport or fitness activity. Fitness walking, stretching, and treadmill exercise were the most popular activities among women who frequently engaged in athletics. (See Table 1.9.) Female fitness enthusiasts also favored team sports, such as basketball, soccer, and court volleyball, as well as outdoor activities, such as hiking, recreational vehicle camping, and fishing.

TABLE 1.10

Top outdoor activity choices by age group

18–29 year olds
1. Swimming
2. Walking
3. Pleasure driving
4. Fishing
5. Bicycling (on road)
6. Campground camping
7. Hiking
8. Motorcycling/snowmobiling
9. Backpacking/wilderness
10. Wildlife viewing
11. Hunting
12. Motorboating
13. Golf
14. Birdwatching
15. Off-road bicycling
16. Horseback riding
17. Skiing
18. Canoeing/kayaking
19. RV camping

30–44 year olds
1. Walking
2. Swimming
3. Pleasure driving
4. Fishing
5. Bicycling (on road)
6. Hiking
7. Campground camping
8. Wildlife viewing
9. Backpacking/wilderness
10. Birdwatching
11. Motorboating
12. Golf
13. Motorcycling/snowmobiling
14. RV camping
15. Hunting
16. Canoeing/kayaking
17. Skiing
18. Horseback riding
19. Off-road bicycling

45–59 year olds
1. Walking
2. Pleasure driving
3. Swimming
4. Fishing
5. Hiking
6. Birdwatching
7. Wildlife viewing
8. Bicycling/wilderness
9. Campground camping
10. Backpacking/wilderness
11. Golf
12. Motorboating
13. RV camping
14. Motorcycling/snowmobiling
15. Hunting
16. Canoeing/kayaking
17. Horseback riding
18. Off-road bicycling
19. Skiing

60+ year olds
1. Walking
2. Pleasure driving
3. Birdwatching
4. Fishing
5. Wildlife viewing
6. Swimming
7. Golf
8. Hiking
9. Motorboating
10. RV camping
11. Bicycling (on road)
12. Campground camping
13. Hunting
14. Backpacking/wilderness
15. Skiing
16. Motorcycling/snowmobiling
17. Canoeing/kayaking
18. Horseback riding
19. Off-road bicycling

SOURCE: "Top Activity Choices By Age Group," in *Outdoor Recreation in America 2001*, American Recreation Coalition, Washington, DC, 2001

TABLE 1.11

Outdoor activities with the largest variation in adult participation in households with and without children aged 0–17

Activity	Percentage of adults participating from households with kids 0–17	Percentage of adults participating from households without kids 0–17
Golf	43	56
Birdwatching	36	63
Walking	44	56
Bicycling (on road)	56	43
Horseback riding	56	44

SOURCE: "Kids Make a Difference!" in *Outdoor Recreation in America 2001*, American Recreation Coalition, Washington, DC, 2001

Among adults in all but the youngest age group of eighteen to twenty-nine, walking was the top-ranked activity choice. Eighteen- to twenty-nine-year-olds preferred swimming to walking and activities such as birdwatching and recreational vehicle camping were lower on their list than for the older age groups. (See Table 1.10.) Participation also varied depending on whether the adults' households included children. Adults with children aged zero to seventeen favored on-road bicycling and horseback riding, activities in which children can also participate, over golf and bird-watching, activities that children are less likely to enjoy. Not surprisingly, adults in households without children reported greater participation in golf and bird-watching. (See Table 1.11.)

Popular Sports for Children and Seniors

America's love of sports and fitness is not bounded by age. The SGMA studied recreational activities that were "frequent" among youths aged six to seventeen during 2001. Active American children and teens enjoyed both team and individual sports: three of the top four most popular activities were basketball, soccer, and baseball. (See Table 1.12.) Young people also enjoyed fitness activities such as running and jogging. Calisthenics, stretching, and outdoor recreation, such as skating, riding scooters, freshwater fishing, and skateboarding, were also among the top ten most popular pursuits.

Many of America's older adults (over age fifty-five) have embraced exercise as a strategy for enhancing health and wellness and the 2001 SGMA survey finds seniors were frequent participants in recreational and fitness activity. Ten of the fifteen most popular sports among physically active older adults were low-impact or no-impact activities, such as fitness walking, stretching, golf, treadmill exercise, and recreational vehicle camping. (See Table 1.13.)

Retired Americans are often thought of as spending their leisure time playing golf. In fact, the SGMA survey supports this stereotype to some extent. During 2001, 3.2 million seniors played golf twenty-five days or more per year. Other popular frequent leisure activities for seniors include bowling (1.8 million), stretching (4.3 million), fishing (1.7 million), and working out with free weights (1.5 million).

GROWING ENTHUSIASM FOR EXTREME SPORTS. An increasing number of Americans are seeking challenge, thrills, and fitness by participating in extreme sports, such as snowboarding, skateboarding, wakeboarding, and rock climbing. In 2002 in-line skating attracted the most participants, followed by skateboarding, paintball, artificial wall climbing, and snowboarding. (See Table 1.14.)

PETS—COMPANIONSHIP, PLEASURE, AND WELL-BEING

Pets often provide more than recreation for their owners—they may become companions and family members, and most pet owners report that their pets bring pleasure to their life. Many pet owners, wanting to extend their pets'

TABLE 1.12

Most popular sports for youth based on "frequent" participation, 2001

(Ages 6 - 17)

Activity	Year 2001
1. Basketball (25+ days/year)	11,287,000
2. Soccer (25+ days/year)	7,692,000
3. In-line skating (25+ days/year)	7,482,000
4. Baseball (25+ days/year)	4,719,000
5. Scooter riding (52+ days/year)	4,469,000
6. Freshwater fishing (15+ days/year)	3,712,000
7. Running/jogging (100+ days/year)	3,340,000
8. Calisthenics (100+ days/year)	3,327,000
9. Stretching (100+ days/year)	3,169,000
10. Skateboarding (52+ days/year)	3,144,000
11. Court volleyball (25+ days/year)	3,032,000
12. Touch football (25+ days/year)	2,614,000
13. Slow-pitch softball (25+ days/year)	2,466,000
14. Billiards/pool (25+ days/year)	2,151,000
15. Tent camping (15+ days/year)	1,918,000

SOURCE: "Most Popular Sports for Youth Based on "Frequent" Participation (Ages 6-17)," in "Top Sports for American Youth," in *Superstudy of Sports Participation,* Sporting Goods Manufacturer's Association, North Palm Beach, FL, 2002 www.SGMA.com

TABLE 1.13

Most popular sports for seniors based on "frequent" participation, 2001

Activity	Year 2001
1. Fitness walking (100+ days/year)	5,545,000
2. Stretching (100+ days/year)	4,252,000
3. Golf (25+ days/year)	3,231,000
4. Treadmill exercise (100+ days/year)	2,910,000
5. Recreational vehicle camping (15+ days/year)	2,048,000
6. Bowling (25+ days/year)	1,822,000
7. Freshwater fishing [15+ days/year]	1,744,000
8. Stationary cycling: Upright Bike [Regular] (100+ days/year)	1,697,000
9. Free weights: Hand Weights (100+ days/year)	1,508,000
10. Calisthenics (100+ days/year)	1,254,000
11. Free weights: dumbbells (100+ days/year)	1,239,000
12. Day hiking (15+ days/year)	1,147,000
13. Weight/resistance machines (100+ days/year)	986,000
14. Aquatic exercise (100+ days/year)	809,000
15. Abdominal machine/device (100+ days/year)	730,000

SOURCE: "Most Popular Sports for Seniors Based on "Frequent" Participation (Age 55 and Older)" in "Seniors Balance Fun and Fitness," in *Superstudy of Sports Participation,* Sporting Goods Manufacturer's Association, North Palm Beach, FL, 2002 www.SGMA.com

TABLE 1.14

Most popular extreme sports, 2001

Sport	# of Participants (participated at least once in 2001)
1. In-line skating	26,022,000
2. Skateboarding	12,459,000
3. Paintball	7,678,000
4. Artificial wall climbing	7,377,000
5. Snowboarding	6,797,000
6. Mountain biking	6,189,000
7. Trail running	5,773,000
8. BMX bicycling	3,668,000
9. Wakeboarding	3,097,000
10. Roller hockey	2,733,000
11. Mountain/rock climbing	1,819,000
12. Boardsailing/windsurfing	537,000

SOURCE: "Most Popular Extreme Sports in the USA," in *Superstudy of Sports Participation,* Sporting Goods Manufacturer's Association, North Palm Beach, FL, 2002 www.SGMA.com

lives and improve their health, are willing to spend large amounts on veterinary care; some purchase health insurance for their pets. Some even send their pampered pets to day camps and spas and make arrangements for the care of their pets' in the event of their own illness or death.

The numbers of dog and cat owners are almost equal. According to the American Pet Products Manufacturers Association's *2001–2002 National Pet Owners Survey,* there are about 68 million owned dogs in the United States and 73 million owned cats. Four out of ten households (40 million) own at least one dog, and three out of ten (34 million) own at least one cat. Seven out of ten owned dogs and eight out of ten owned cats are spayed or neutered.

Twenty percent of owned cats and dogs were adopted from animal shelters. Sixty-three percent of owners have just one dog, while half of cat-owning households have one cat and the remaining half own two or more. On average, dog owners spent more than cat owners on veterinary expenses during the twelve months preceding the survey— dog owners spent $196, while cat owners averaged $104.

Pets Are More Than Companions, They Can Contribute to Health and Wellness

Research conducted during the late 1990s found that pet ownership was related to better health. At first, it was believed that the effects were simply increased well-being—the obvious delight of hospital and nursing home patients petting puppies, watching kittens play, or viewing fish in an aquarium clearly demonstrated pets' abilities to calm frayed nerves and make people smile.

A study published in the *Journal of the American Geriatrics Society* (vol. 47, no. 3, March 1999) finds that

attachment to a companion animal is linked to maintaining or slightly improving the physical and psychological well-being of older adults. Following nearly 1,000 older adults for one year, Parminder Raina et al. find that pet owners are more satisfied with their physical health, mental health, family relationships, living arrangements, finances, and friends.

Other research reveals the specific health benefits of human interaction with animals. Several researchers observe that petting dogs and cats actually lowers blood pressure. The physiological mechanisms responsible for these health benefits are as yet unidentified, however, some researchers think that pets connect people to the natural world, enabling them to focus on others, rather than simply themselves. Other investigators observe that dog

TABLE 1.15

Volunteering, 2000

Percentage of adults who volunteered	44%
Total number of adult volunteers	83.9 million
Average weekly hours per volunteer	3.6 hours
Annual hours volunteered	15.5 billion hours
Estimated hourly value of volunteer time*	$15.40 per hour
Total dollar value of volunteer time	$239.2 billion
Percentage of adults asked to volunteer	50%
Percentage of adults who volunteered when asked	63%

* The hourly value of volunteered time is updated yearly by INDEPENDENT SECTOR and is based on the average hourly wage for nonagricultural workers, as published in The Economic Report of the President (2001 Edition), increased by 12% to estimate fringe benefits.

SOURCE: "Volunteering in the United States, 2000," in *Giving and Volunteering in the United States 2001*, Independent Sector, Washington, DC, 1999

owners walk more than persons without dogs and credit pet owners' improved health to exercise. Nearly everyone agrees that the nonjudgmental affection pets offer boosts health and wellness.

HOBBIES

A hobby is an activity or pastime that is performed primarily for pleasure, rather than for business. Hobbies were once the mainstay of leisure time. While this sort of activity still exists, industry observers believe it is less popular, seeming to have been surpassed by collecting, a profit-motivated activity.

Some of the most common hobbies are cross-stitching/embroidering, crocheting, quilting, knitting, cake decorating, model train collecting, wreath making, art/drawing, photography, gardening, studying genealogy, floral arranging, woodworking, and solving crossword puzzles. Children and teens often enjoy playing board games, drawing/painting and sculpting, playing musical instruments, and card collecting.

The Hobby Industry Association, an industry trade group, in *2001 HIA Nationwide Craft and Hobby Consumer Usage and Purchases Study,* finds that 76 percent of surveyed households reported that at least one member of the household engaged in a craft or hobby, an increase from 70 percent in 2000. Craft and hobby participants are often married, have children, are better educated, and have higher household incomes than noncrafters.

Cross-stitching/embroidering was the most popular craft activity (19 percent), followed by home decor painting (15 percent), scrapbooking/memory crafts (13 percent), floral arranging (13 percent), and crocheting (12 percent). Participation for specific crafts and hobbies increased across the board from 2000 to 2001, with 5 percent more respondents reporting interest and involvement in needlecrafts and floral craft projects.

Collecting as Recreation

Collectors devote time, energy, and often considerable resources to amassing, compiling, and organizing their collections. Along with more common pursuits, such as stamp and coin collecting, there are individuals and groups devoted to collecting everything imaginable, from pricey antique automobiles, celebrity autographs, and memorabilia from events such as the 1939 World's Fair, to toys, action figures, and favors distributed with children's meals at fast food restaurants.

Research conducted in the late 1990s described giftware and collectible purchasers as middle- to working-class high school graduates, with household incomes under $30,000. Those aged eighteen to thirty-four spent about $21 per purchase, while those over age fifty-five spent just $15. The largest number of purchasers (36 percent) spent less than $30 on the last gift they purchased, 28 percent spent $30 to $49, and 30 percent spent $50 or more.

Unity Marketing's most recent research shows that 40 percent of U.S. households are involved with collectibles and characterizes today's collector as "younger, smarter, more affluent and shops in a much wider range of retail venues than yesterday's collector." While collectors have traditionally been female, men are now emerging as collectors, attracted by online auction sites such as eBay.

VOLUNTEER WORK

Many Americans spend their leisure time in volunteer work helping others. The Independent Sector (IS), in its most recent national survey report *Giving and Volunteering in the United States 2001,* finds that an estimated 44 percent of adults older than twenty-one (83.9 million) volunteered approximately 15.5 billion hours during 2000. (See Table 1.15.)

To better appreciate the importance and magnitude of participation in volunteering, it is helpful to translate volunteer time into paid hours of labor. The volunteer workforce during 2000 represented the equivalent of more than 9 million full-time employees providing labor worth more than $239 billion. (See Table 1.15 and Table 1.16.)

Who Volunteers?

The IS survey finds that volunteers to formal organizations contributed more than twenty-four hours of service per month. There were no differences in the number of hours volunteers contributed based on their experience, religious attendance, household giving patterns, age, gender, race, or ethnicity. The researchers conclude that the amount of time an individual chose to devote to volunteering was essentially independent of any distinguishing characteristics.

Half of those who volunteered had been asked to do so and the study finds that individuals who were asked to

TABLE 1.16

Number of volunteers, hours, and dollar value, 1987–2000

Volunteer indicator	2000*	1998	1995	1993	1991	1989	1987
Civilian noninstitutional population 18 years old or older (March 1988, 1990, 1992, 1994, 1996, 1999, in millions)	N/A	197.1	190.5	187.1	184.4	180.9	176.7
Volunteers (percentage of population)	44%	55.5%	48.8%	47.7%	51.1%	54.4%	45.3%
Volunteers (in millions)	83.9	109.4	93.0	89.2	94.2	98.4	80.0
Average weekly hours per volunteer	3.6	3.5	4.2	4.2	4.2	4.0	4.7
Average annual hours per volunteer	N/A	182.0	218.4	218.4	217.6	208.0	244.4
Annual hours volunteered (in billions)	N/A	19.9	20.3	19.5	20.5	20.5	19.6
Annual hours volunteered, excluding informal volunteering (in billions)	15.5	15.8	15.7	15.0	15.2	15.7	14.5
Full-time equivalent employment, excluding informal volunteering, at 1,700 hours per year per employee (in millions)	9.1	9.3	9.2	8.8	9.0	9.2	8.8
Dollar value of a volunteer hour	$15.40	$14.30	$12.84	$12.13	$11.58	$10.82	$10.06
Total assigned dollar value of volunteer time, excluding informal volunteering (in billions)	$239.2	$225.9	$201.5	$182.3	$176.4	$169.6	$149.0

Dollar value of a volunteer hour in other years: $7.46 (1980); $8.12 (1981); $8.60 (1982); $8.98 (1983); $9.32 (1984); $9.60 (1985); $9.81 (1986); $10.39 (1988); $11.21 (1990); $11.84 (1992); $12.45 (1994); $13.23 (1996); $13.73 (1997); $14.30 (1998); $14.83 (1999); $15.40 (2000); $16.05 (2001).

*All volunteering numbers for 2000 are for individual adults aged 21 or older. All other years, 1989 to 1998, include individual adults aged 18 or older. Other significant changes were also introduced in the 2001 *Giving and Volunteering* survey, including survey methodology, which makes comparison to prior years difficult.

SOURCE: "Volunteers: Number, Hours, and Dollar Value: 1987–2000," in *Giving and Volunteering in the United States 2001*, Independent Sector, Washington, DC, 2002 [Online] http://www.independentsector.org/programs/research/volunteer_time.html [accesed January 8, 2003]

volunteer were considerably more likely to do so (63 percent) than those who had not been asked (25 percent). (See Figure 1.2.) Women were somewhat more likely to volunteer (46 percent) than men (42 percent).

What Do Volunteers Do?

The IS survey finds that the most popular volunteer activity involved providing direct service, such as serving food, making repairs, visiting people or providing companionship, or providing transportation. Fund-raising was another popular volunteer activity, along with giving advice or counseling, and organizing an event.

FIGURE 1.2

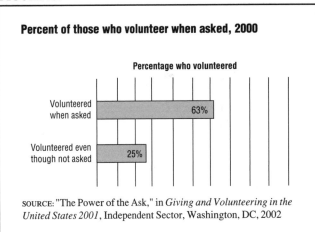

Percent of those who volunteer when asked, 2000

SOURCE: "The Power of the Ask," in *Giving and Volunteering in the United States 2001*, Independent Sector, Washington, DC, 2002

CHAPTER 2

THE COST OF HAVING FUN

CONSUMER EXPENDITURES FOR RECREATION

Americans are always finding new ways to spend their free time and money. In good economic times, people generally have more discretionary income to spend on leisure and recreation. The U.S. Bureau of Labor Statistics reports that in 2001 Americans spent an average of $1,953 on entertainment, slightly more than the $1,863 that was spent in 2000. (See Table 2.1.) Persons aged thirty-five to forty-four spent the most on entertainment ($2,464), and those over seventy-five, the least ($707). (See Table 2.2.)

Data from the Bureau of Economic Analysis, a division of the U.S. Department of Commerce, show that consumers steadily increased their total spending on entertainment events each year from 1997 through 2001. (See Table 2.3.) Americans spent $29.4 billion in 2001 to see performing arts, movies, and spectator sports.

In 2001 Americans spent a total of $593.9 billion on recreation, up from $564.7 billion in 2000. Almost one-fifth of those dollars ($105.6 billion) was spent on video and audio goods, including musical instruments and computer goods. Toys and sports supplies accounted for $66.7 billion, and $60.8 billion was spent on personal transportation (including boats and pleasure aircraft), sports, and photographic equipment. (See Table 2.3.)

Spending for Computers Surges

Although total expenditures for various forms of entertainment increased between 1997 and 2001, most goods and services experienced incremental or gradual growth. Examples of goods and activities that sustained modest increases were books and maps, gardening supplies (flowers, seeds, and potted pants), admissions to spectator amusements, and clubs and fraternal organizations. (See Table 2.3.)

More dramatic increases occurred in two categories related to computer use. In 1997, $25.9 billion was spent on computers, peripherals, and software; by 2001 Ameri-

cans spent $32.9 billion for computers and software. Similarly, spending for video and audio goods, including musical instruments and computer goods rose from $83.7 billion in 1997 to $105.6 billion in 2001.

CONSUMER ELECTRONICS

An explosion of technology has changed the consumer electronics industry. Digital technology has made

TABLE 2.1

Annual expenditures of all consumer units and percent changes, Consumer Expenditure Survey, 1999–2001

Item	1999	2000	2001	Percent change 1999–2000	Percent change 2000–2001
Number of consumer units (000's)	108,465	109,367	110,339		
Income before taxes[1]	$43,951	$44,649	$47,507		
Average age of reference person	47.9	48.2	48.1		
Average number in consumer unit:					
Persons	2.5	2.5	2.5		
Earners	1.3	1.4	1.4		
Vehicles	1.9	1.9	1.9		
Percent homeowner	65	66	66		
Average annual expenditures	$36,995	$38,045	$39,518	2.8	3.9
Food	5,031	5,158	5,321	2.5	3.2
At home	2,915	3,021	3,086	3.6	2.2
Away from home	2,116	2,137	2,235	1.0	4.6
Housing	12,057	12,319	13,011	2.2	5.6
Apparel and services	1,743	1,856	1,743	6.5	-6.1
Transportation	7,011	7,417	7,633	5.8	2.9
Health care	1,959	2,066	2,182	5.5	5.6
Entertainment	1,891	1,863	1,953	-1.5	4.8
Personal insurance and pensions	3,436	3,365	3,737	-2.1	11.1
Other expenditures	3,868	4,001	3,939	3.4	-1.5

[1]Income values are derived from "complete income reporters" only.

SOURCE: "Annual expenditures of all consumer units and percent changes, Consumer Expenditure Survey, 1999-2001" *Consumer Expenditures in 2000,* U.S. Bureau of Labor Statistics, Washington, DC, 2000

TABLE 2.2

Average annual expenditures and characteristics, Consumer Expenditure Survey, 2000

Item	All consumer units	Under 25	25-34	35-44	45-54	55-64	65 and over	65-74	75 and over
Number of consumer units (in thousands)	109,367	8,306	18,887	23,983	21,874	14,161	22,155	11,538	10,617
Consumer unit characteristics:									
Income before taxes[1]	$44,649	$19,744	$45,498	$56,500	$58,889	$48,108	$25,220	$29,349	$20,563
Income after taxes[1]	41,532	18,813	42,665	52,626	54,149	44,109	23,890	27,553	19,759
Age of reference person	48.2	21.3	29.8	39.5	49.4	59.1	75.0	69.4	81.2
Average number in consumer unit:									
Persons	2.5	1.9	2.9	3.3	2.7	2.1	1.7	1.9	1.5
Children under 18	.7	.4	1.1	1.3	.6	.2	.1	.1	(²)
Persons 65 and over	.3	(²)	(²)	(²)	(²)	.1	1.3	1.4	1.3
Earners	1.4	1.3	1.5	1.7	1.8	1.4	.4	.6	.2
Vehicles	1.9	1.1	1.8	2.2	2.4	2.2	1.5	1.8	1.1
Percent distribution:									
Housing tenure:									
Homeowner	66	12	46	69	75	81	80	82	77
With mortgage	39	7	39	56	53	40	16	23	9
Without mortgage	27	5	7	13	22	41	63	59	68
Renter	34	88	54	31	25	19	20	18	23
Average annual expenditures	$38,045	$22,543	$38,945	$45,149	$46,160	$39,340	$26,533	$30,782	$21,908
Food	5,158	3,213	5,260	6,092	6,295	5,168	3,652	4,178	3,077
Food at home	3,021	1,643	2,951	3,484	3,657	3,071	2,448	2,760	2,106
Cereals and bakery products	453	238	429	531	560	441	376	414	334
Cereals and cereal products	156	90	167	190	180	140	123	133	112
Bakery products	297	148	263	341	380	301	253	281	222
Meats, poultry, fish, and eggs	795	437	770	918	970	832	626	727	515
Dairy products	325	175	317	383	377	321	275	310	236
Fruits and vegetables	521	253	488	552	626	558	495	529	457
Other food at home	927	541	946	1,101	1,124	918	676	779	563
Food away from home	2,137	1,569	2,309	2,607	2,638	2,097	1,205	1,418	971
Alcoholic beverages	372	392	431	420	417	371	211	261	155
Housing	12,319	7,109	13,050	15,111	14,179	12,362	8,759	9,671	7,766
Shelter	7,114	4,574	7,905	8,930	8,297	6,587	4,597	5,114	4,034
Owned dwellings	4,602	634	4,142	6,433	5,964	4,780	3,043	3,619	2,418
Mortgage interest and charges	2,639	386	2,888	4,302	3,558	2,278	793	1,179	375
Property taxes	1,139	176	755	1,246	1,471	1,462	1,175	1,272	1,070
Maintenance, repairs, insurance, other expenses	825	72	499	884	935	1,040	1,075	1,168	973
Rented dwellings	2,034	3,618	3,514	2,067	1,614	1,123	1,140	952	1,344
Other lodging	478	322	248	430	719	685	413	543	272
Utilities, fuels, and public services	2,489	1,248	2,341	2,810	2,857	2,756	2,198	2,438	1,937
Natural gas	307	102	273	350	344	341	310	318	301
Electricity	911	444	826	1,009	1,045	1,048	834	921	740
Fuel oil and other fuels	97	21	58	97	109	113	137	151	121
Telephone services	877	589	950	1,018	1,007	909	620	720	511
Water and other public services	296	91	234	336	352	345	298	328	264
Household operations	684	226	871	896	583	542	661	498	839
Personal services	326	154	641	542	147	93	215	99	340
Other household expenses	358	72	230	354	435	449	446	399	498
Transportation	7,417	5,189	8,357	8,702	8,827	7,842	4,397	5,797	2,875
Vehicle purchases (net outlay)	3,418	2,628	4,139	3,996	3,863	3,623	1,904	2,631	1,114
Cars and trucks, new	1,605	1,061	1,845	1,724	1,690	2,097	1,076	1,447	673
Cars and trucks, used	1,770	1,547	2,217	2,198	2,128	1,508	823	1,173	441
Other vehicles	43	⁴20	77	74	45	⁴18	⁴5	⁴10	(⁵)
Gasoline and motor oil	1,291	947	1,341	1,577	1,592	1,349	735	958	491
Other vehicle expenses	2,281	1,397	2,482	2,677	2,868	2,375	1,374	1,766	947
Public transportation	427	216	395	451	505	495	385	442	322
Health care	2,066	504	1,256	1,774	2,200	2,508	3,247	3,163	3,338
Entertainment	1,863	1,091	1,876	2,464	2,231	1,955	1,069	1,403	707
Personal care products and services	564	345	576	644	682	569	426	479	368
Reading	146	57	118	151	178	179	148	166	128
Education	632	1,257	585	615	1,146	380	108	149	63

possible a new array of products. The difference between information management and consumer electronics is beginning to blur. According to projections by the Consumer Electronics Association (CEA), Americans were expected to spend nearly $99 billion on consumer electronics in 2003, an increase of 3.5 percent over 2002. (See Table 2.4.) The average American household spends about $1,000 per year on consumer electronic products.

America Goes Digital

According the CEA, digital products were the fastest-growing segment of the industry. In some cases,

TABLE 2.2

Average annual expenditures and characteristics, Consumer Expenditure Survey, 2000 [CONTINUED]

Item	All consumer units	Under 25	25-34	35-44	45-54	55-64	65 and over	65-74	75 and over
Tobacco products and smoking supplies	319	237	310	427	376	349	163	223	99
Miscellaneous	776	322	804	852	927	824	661	761	553
Cash contributions	1,192	189	648	1,003	1,537	1,301	1,828	2,022	1,618
Personal insurance and pensions	3,365	1,216	3,614	4,570	4,795	3,838	939	1,379	460
Life and other personal insurance	399	54	242	412	549	587	378	514	230
Pensions and Social Security	2,966	1,162	3,373	4,158	4,246	3,252	561	865	231

[1] Components of income and taxes are derived from "complete income reporters" only.
[2] Value less than 0.05.
[3] Value less than 0.5.
[4] Data are likely to have large sampling errors.
[5] No data reported.

SOURCE: Adapted from "Table 3. Age of reference person: Average annual expenditures and characteristics, Consumer Expenditure Survey, 2000" *Consumer Expenditures in 2000*, U.S. Bureau of Labor Statistics, Washington, DC, 2000

TABLE 2.3

Personal consumption expenditures on recreation, 1997–2001

		1997	1998	1999	2000	2001
86	**Recreation**	**456.6**	**489.1**	**526.5**	**564.7**	**593.9**
87	Books and maps (d.)	26.3	28.2	30.8	33.2	35.1
88	Magazines, newspapers, and sheet music (n.d.)	29.1	31.0	32.5	34.2	35.2
89	Nondurable toys and sport supplies (n.d.)	53.2	56.5	60.4	62.7	66.7
90	Wheel goods, sports and photographic equipment, boats, and pleasure aircraft (d.)	42.8	46.2	50.4	55.3	60.8
91	Video and audio goods, including musical instruments, and computer goods (d.)	83.7	90.3	98.1	106.3	105.6
92	Video and audio goods, including musical instruments (d.)	57.9	61.6	66.7	71.8	72.7
93	Computers, peripherals, and software (d.)	25.9	28.7	31.4	34.5	32.9
94	Radio and television repair (s.)	4.0	4.1	4.1	4.1	4.2
95	Flowers, seeds, and potted plants (n.d.)	15.3	15.9	16.7	17.5	18.5
96	Admissions to specified spectator amusements	22.1	23.4	25.0	27.1	29.4
97	Motion picture theaters (s.)	6.3	6.9	7.6	7.8	8.7
98	Legitimate theaters and opera, and entertainments of nonprofit institutions (except athletics)(s.)	8.6	8.7	8.9	9.9	10.6
99	Spectator sports (s.)	7.1	7.7	8.5	9.5	10.1
100	Clubs and fraternal organizations (s.)	14.6	14.9	15.9	16.7	17.3
101	Commercial participant amusements (s.)	52.8	57.3	63.0	68.4	73.3
102	Pari-mutuel net receipts (s.)	3.6	4.3	4.5	4.7	4.8
103	Other (s.)	109.1	117.0	125.1	134.4	142.9

Note: Consumer durable goods are designated (d.), nondurable goods (n.d.), and services (s.).

SOURCE: "Table 2.4. Personal Consumption Expenditures by Type of Expenditure [Billions of dollars]" in *National Income and Products Accounts Tables*, U.S. Department of Commerce, Bureau of Economic Analysis, Washington, DC, August 2002

digital units outsold analog models. Stand-alone digital videodisc (DVD) players were the fastest-growing technology, present in about 30 percent of U.S. homes in 2002. Digital wireless phones offer mobile access to the Internet. Digital television provides dramatically better picture quality, new ways to store and manipulate information, and the potential for interactivity. Digital audio offers new ways to deliver and store musical recordings. Furthermore, the new technology permits consumer electronic devices to be smaller, sleeker, lighter, and more portable.

Video

A telephone survey conducted by the CEA finds that U.S. households have growing numbers of video products. In 2002, 98 percent of households had color television (TV), and more than two-thirds had color TV with stereos. Up 2 percent since 1999, in 2002, 94 percent of homes had videocassette recorders (VCRs). While just 3 percent of households had DVD players in 1999, by June 2002 nearly 30 percent of homes had DVD players. Direct-to-home satellite systems also grew in popularity—in June 1999, 12 percent of homes had satellite

TABLE 2.4

Total factory sales of consumer electronics, 1998–2001, estimated 2002, and projected 2003

(millions of dollars)

	1998	1999	2000	2001	Est. 2002	Proj 2003
Analog direct-view color TV	6,122	6,199	6,503	5,130	5,138	5,037
Analog projection TV	1,577	1,632	1,481	1,060	824	537
Digital TV sets and displays	43	295	1,426	2,648	4,830	5,689
Monochrome TV	23	20	15	15	12	9
LCD TV	67	61	107	101	106	111
Plasma TV	-	-	-	116	400	629
TV/VCR combinations	831	1,014	968	790	613	572
Videocassette players	21	15	14	5	4	2
VCR decks	2,409	2,333	1,869	1,058	774	631
Camcorders	2,144	2,448	2,838	2,236	2,315	2,228
Laserdisc players	10	3	3	-	-	-
Direct to home satellite systems	733	957	790	1,175	1,077	920
Personal video recorders	na	46	77	144	77	147
Separate component DVD players	421	1,099	1,717	2,097	2,275	2,332
TV/PC combinations	323	357	686	748	638	552
Set-top Internet access devices	80	145	193	195	196	173
Total	**14,805**	**16,625**	**18,686**	**17,517**	**19,279**	**19,569**
Home & portable audio products						
Rack audio systems	200	148	84	42	23	18
Compact audio systems	1,557	1,695	1,776	1,357	1,128	1,079
Separate audio components	1,565	1,530	1,545	1,261	1,279	1,217
Home theater-in-a-box	224	229	331	794	1,118	1,312
Portable equipment	2,146	1,987	2,155	1,847	1,368	1,267
MP3 players	-	100	80	100	182	219
Home radios	300	348	351	326	314	293
Total	**5,992**	**6,036**	**6,323**	**5,727**	**5,412**	**5,405**
Mobile electronics						
Aftermarket autosound	1,859	2,070	2,169	2,098	2,256	2,307
Mobile video & navigation	-	-	273	293	627	864
Wireless telephones	6,000	6,066	8,995	8,651	8,835	8,882
Family radio services	180	306	418	461	347	336
Pagers	550	660	750	790	810	729
Aftermarket vehicle security	213	205	218	266	265	266
Radar detectors	160	165	170	170	134	170
Factory installed autosound	2,540	2,610	2,700	2,850	2,950	3,127
Total	**11,502**	**12,082**	**15,693**	**15,580**	**16,225**	**16,681**
Home information products						
Cordless telephones	1,745	1,808	1,764	1,960	1,659	1,818
Corded telephones	489	483	386	294	239	206
Telephone answering devices	1,104	1,044	994	1,062	1,103	1,009
Caller ID devices	92	64	54	35	29	19
Fax machines	647	455	386	349	297	242
Personal word processors	280	240	240	97	36	13
Personal computers	16,640	16,390	16,400	12,960	11,523	11,011
Computer printers	4,188	4,500	5,116	5,245	4,829	4,842
Aftermarket computer monitors	1,076	1,148	1,222	1,425	1,208	1,873
Modems/fax modems	1,305	1,460	1,564	1,564	1,365	1,749
Digital cameras	519	1,207	1,825	1,972	2,685	3,037
Other computer peripherals	1,212	1,440	1,950	2,150	2,365	2,507
Computer software	3,450	3,930	4,480	5,062	5,265	5,581
Total	**32,747**	**34,168**	**36,380**	**34,176**	**32,603**	**33,905**
Blank media						
Blank audio cassettes	248	208	162	129	121	104
Blank video cassettes	639	590	351	357	342	326
Blank computer media	700	900	1,200	1,550	1,600	1,800
Total	**1,587**	**1,698**	**1,713**	**2,036**	**2,063**	**2,230**
Accessories & batteries						
Electronic accessories	1,178	1,398	1,356	1,378	1,500	1,635
Batteries	2,963	3,620	4,943	4,590	4,960	4,590
Total	**4,141**	**5,018**	**6,299**	**5,968**	**6,460**	**6,225**
Electronic gaming						
Electronic gaming hardware	1,980	2,250	2,700	3,250	3,750	3,375
Electronic gaming software	4,480	5,100	5,850	6,725	7,725	9,270
Total	**6,460**	**7,350**	**8,550**	**9,975**	**11,475**	**12,645**
Home security	**1,520**	**1,660**	**1,750**	**1,820**	**1,965**	**2,122**
Grand Total	**78,753**	**84,636**	**95,394**	**92,799**	**95,481**	**98,783**

SOURCE: "Total Factory Sales of Consumer Electronics," in *U.S. Consumer Electronics Sales & Forecasts: 1998–2003*, Consumer Electronics Association, Arlington, VA, October 2002

TABLE 2.5

Household penetration of consumer electronic products, June 1999–June 2002

(Based on Telephone Surveys Conducted by CEA)

	June 1999	Jan. 2000	June 2000	Jan. 2001	June 2001	Jan. 2002	June 2002
All television	98%	98%	98%	98%	98%	98%	98%
Color TV	98%	98%	98%	98%	98%	98%	98%
VCR decks	92%	93%	94%	94%	94%	94%	94%
Monochrome TV	44%	43%	42%	41%	40%	40%	39%
Color TV with stereo	64%	65%	67%	69%	70%	69%	69%
Camcorder	35%	36%	38%	39%	40%	42%	43%
Projection TV	14%	14%	15%	15%	15%	15%	16%
All LCD TV	11%	11%	12%	12%	12%	12%	13%
TV/VCR combinations	17%	18%	20%	21%	22%	22%	22%
DVD player	3%	5%	7%	15%	21%	25%	29%
Direct to home satellite	12%	13%	15%	16%	16%	18%	20%
Mobile electronics							
Electronic car alarm	29%	29%	30%	30%	31%	31%	31%
Wireless telephones	48%	51%	55%	59%	63%	64%	66%
Pager	36%	37%	39%	40%	41%	41%	41%
Car CD player	24%	26%	27%	28%	29%	33%	40%
Home office products							
Corded phone	96%	96%	96%	96%	96%	96%	96%
All CD including CD-ROM	71%	72%	74%	75%	76%	77%	78%
Telephone answering device	73%	74%	76%	77%	77%	78%	78%
Cordless phone	77%	78%	80%	81%	81%	81%	81%
Personal computers	52%	54%	56%	58%	59%	60%	60%
Computer printers	47%	49%	51%	54%	56%	57%	57%
Computer with CD-ROM	48%	51%	53%	57%	59%	60%	60%
Digital camera	5%	7%	12%	18%	20%	22%	25%
Multi-line phone	20%	21%	22%	23%	23%	23%	23%
Modem or fax/modem	47%	51%	54%	55%	55%	56%	56%
Home fax machines	11%	11%	11%	12%	12%	12%	12%
Caller ID equipment	23%	25%	26%	27%	28%	28%	28%
Audio products							
Home radios	98%	98%	98%	98%	98%	98%	98%
Separate component systems	57%	57%	57%	57%	57%	57%	57%
Home CD players	56%	56%	57%	57%	57%	57%	57%
Rack or compact audio system	41%	42%	42%	43%	43%	43%	43%
CD boombox	35%	37%	38%	39%	39%	40%	41%
Personal portable CD player	24%	26%	27%	28%	30%	33%	36%
Home theater system	20%	21%	22%	23%	24%	25%	27%

SOURCE: "U.S. Household Penetration of Consumer Electronics Products," in *U.S. Consumer Electronics Sales & Forecasts:1998–2003,* Consumer Electronics Association, Arlington, VA, October 2002

systems and by June 2002, 20 percent of households had satellite systems. (See Table 2.5.)

Audio

Similarly, the CEA reports that between June 1999 and June 2002, more American households acquired audio products. The number of households with personal portable compact disc players increased by 12 percent, and 7 percent more households boasted home theater systems. (See Table 2.5.)

Video Games

According to a study by the NPD Group, a marketing information company, video game retail sales exceeded $6 billion in the first ten months of 2002, representing a 25 percent increase over the same period in 2001. The industry anticipated a record $10 billion in sales in 2002, exceeding the $9.4 billion in total sales during 2001. Table 2.6 shows that the $9.4 billion spent on video games

in 2001 represented a 43 percent increase over 2000. In addition, because of technology developments, sales of all home entertainment devices, which include TV set-top boxes, handheld computers, and gaming consoles, are expected to increase dramatically. The International Data Corporation, a research organization, predicts sales of home entertainment devices will increase from 11 million sold in 1999 to 89 million by 2004.

SPORTING GOODS SALES

Sports Apparel

Americans have become very aware of their personal health and fitness. Some Americans who take part in physical fitness activities, such as jogging or walking, or who play active sports, such as softball or skiing, often feel they need highly specialized apparel and equipment, and others want to dress as if they are professional players. According to the Sporting Goods Manufacturers Association (SGMA), manufacturers' sales (the wholesale value) of all sports

TABLE 2.6

Toy industry sales, 2001 vs 2000

Ranked on percentage change
Sales reflect total US industry[1]
(Preliminary volumes in millions)

	2001	2000	% Change
Action figures/accessories	$1,618	$1,187	36%
Building/construction	$882	$722	22%
Ride-ons	$773	$664	17%
Infant/preschool	$3,154	$2,772	14%
Arts & crafts	$2,630	$2,357	12%
Dolls/accessories	$3,061	$2,835	8%
Vehicles	$2,821	$2,624	8%
Models/accessories	$281	$266	6%
All other toys	$2,703	$2,681	1%
Learning/exploration	$464	$491	−6%
Games/puzzles	$2,237	$2,492	−10%
Plush	$2,031	$2,336	−13%
Pretend play	$479	$565	−15%
Trading cards/accessories	$318	$440	−28%
Sports	$1,528	$2,135	−29%
Total traditional toy industry	$24,979	$24,568	2%
Video games	$9,409	$6,581	43%
Total toy industry	$34,388	$31,149	10%

[1]This annual analysis process reflects the most current data available; as a result, some 2000 figures may have been restated.

SOURCE: "2001 VS 2000 State of the Industry," The NPD Group, Inc., Port Washington, NY, and Toy Industry Association, Inc., New York, NY [Online] http://www.toy-tia.org/industry/statistics/soi02.htm [accessed December 13, 2002]

apparel totaled $21.3 billion in 2001. (See Table 2.7.) The SGMA observes that "active" sports apparel sales did not grow, but "total" sports apparel sales increased. The SGMA interprets this finding as an indication that many sports apparel purchases were not for active participation in sports, but were for fashion or comfort.

SGMA research confirms that only 20 percent of sports apparel purchases were made with the intention of using it exclusively to play sports. More than half of sports apparel consumers used their clothing for multiple purposes: exercise and sports, recreational activities, and everyday use. Only 15 percent of men and 7 percent of women cited athletic competition as the primary reason for buying sports apparel. Sports apparel was worn to work by 57 percent of buyers. Almost 30 percent of buyers reported they wore sports apparel to work on "casual Fridays."

Athletic Footwear

According to the SGMA, the U.S. wholesale value of manufacturers' shipments of athletic footwear sales reached $9.2 billion in 2001, up 2 percent from 2000. (See Table 2.8.) Running shoes accounted for nearly 30 percent of the wholesale athletic footwear market. The SGMA observes that only 20 percent of all pairs of athletic shoes were intended primarily for use in sports or exercise.

According to data from the National Sporting Goods Association (NSGA), retail sales of athletic footwear rose

4 percent during the six-month period from October 2000 through March 2001. Retail sales for the period totaled $6.8 billion, compared to $6.5 billion for the same period the previous year. The average retail price paid for athletic shoes in 2001 was $40.17, slightly less than the $40.32 spent in 2000.

The NSGA reports that more females (53.8 percent) purchased athletic shoes during 2000 than males did (46.2 percent). Consumers under age fourteen (26.6 percent) and ages forty-five to sixty-five (23.2 percent) made nearly half of all athletic footwear purchases, however, purchases by older adults (persons age sixty-five and older) grew from 7.8 percent in 2000 to 9.4 percent in 2001.

Sports Equipment

The SGMA reports that sports equipment sales were essentially unchanged from 2000 ($17.4 billion) to 2001 ($17.3 billion). In 2001 the largest amount of wholesale revenue came from exercise equipment and machines ($3.6 billion). Golf equipment had nearly $2.6 billion in sales. Camping gear rose to $1.7 billion and firearms/hunting declined from $1.9 billion in 2000 to $1.8 billion in 2001. Fishing also increased in sales during 2001 (5 percent), with about $1 billion in wholesale sales. (See Table 2.7.)

In team sports, the three largest categories of sales during 2001 were baseball/softball ($440 million), basketball ($395 million), and soccer ($230 million). (See Table 2.7.)

Exercise Equipment

The SGMA finds that by 2000 adults in half of all American households owned at least one piece of exercise equipment, and it was used regularly in two out of three of those households. During 2001 the wholesale value of home exercise equipment sold was close to $3 billion.

Owners of fitness equipment were about equally male and female. Those twenty-five to thirty-four owned 24 percent of the equipment, thirty-five to forty-four, 23 percent, fifty-five and over, 22 percent, forty-five to fifty-four, 18 percent, and eighteen to twenty-four, 13 percent. The most frequently owned equipment was free weights, followed by treadmills and stationary bikes.

Research conducted by the NSGA finds that in 2001 more females (52 percent) than males (39 percent) purchased fitness equipment. Nearly one-third of purchases were made by consumers aged thirty-one to forty-four, 29 percent were made by persons aged forty-five to sixty-four, and 22 percent of exercise equipment purchases were made by adults aged twenty-five to thirty-four.

Industry observers attribute the strength of the exercise and fitness market to the growing number of older Americans who want to stay healthy and fit. This trend is expected to continue as an aging U.S. population, intent on lifetime fitness, drives the market.

TABLE 2.7

Sporting Goods Manufacturer's Association recreation market report, 2001

U.S. WHOLESALE VALUE OF ANNUAL MANUFACTURERS SHIPMENTS ($MILLIONS)

Category	2001	2000
Sports Equipment		
Archery	$250	$250
Paintball	225	195
Total baseball/softball	**440**	**440**
Gloves & mitts	110	110
Baseballs	64	64
Softballs	29	33
Bats	180	162
Batting gloves	37	40
Protective/other	20	31
Total basketball	**395**	**385**
Basketballs/accessories	215	210
Backboards	180	175
Billiards	230	240
Bowling	220	220
Total camping	**1,697**	**1,680**
Tents	284	282
Coolers/chests	291	289
Sleeping bags	170	177
Jugs/containers	88	85
Backpacks (exc. daypacks)	77	77
Other	787	770
Total Exercise	**3,610**	**3,655**
Exercise - consumer	2,910	2,905
Treadmills	925	925
Aero gliders	130	180
Ski machines	150	180
Home gyms	290	280
Exercise cycles	205	200
Free weights	170	160
Exercise benches	150	140
Stair climbing machines	80	100
Ab machines	160	135
Consumer	650	605
Exercise - institutional	700	750
Firearms & hunting	1,800	1,900
Footballs & sets	125	120
Total golf	**2,590**	**2,524**
Balls	780	760
Clubs	1,300	1,266
Others	510	498
Ice skates & hockey	$235	$235
Inline roller skates only	175	195
Inline accessories	55	60
Optical goods	530	505
Racquetball	23	25
Skateboards	130	125
Scuba & skin diving	265	295
Snow skiing, alpine	269	265
Running	$2,709	$2,610
Snowboards	215	230
Soccer	230	220
Table tennis	17	17
Total tennis	**234**	**238**
Balls	77	78
Racquets	107	109
Other	50	51
Volleyball (balls, sets)	70	70
Water sports - ski equip.	120	135
Other water sports equip.	300	380
Fishing	1,000	960
Miscellaneous (e.g. lawn games, darts, indoor games, boxing, cricket, field hockey, gymnastics, handball, lacrosse, martial arts, paddleball, polo, rugby, sleds, toboggans, track & field, squash)	250	255
Team/institutional (not listed above)	1,535	1,505
TOTAL SPORTS EQUIPMENT	**$17,270**	**$17,356**
Sports apparel		
Activewear:		
Tops	13,360	13,495
Socks	1,170	1,530
Swimwear	1,490	1,320
Sweatshirts	1,115	1,435
Outerwear/jackets	915	975
Pants/slacks	485	905
Shorts	740	815
Sweatpants/shorts	535	580
Underwear	325	335
Accessories (caps, hats, etc.)	475	380
Sport/exercise bras	135	190
Total activewear	**$20,745**	**$21,960**
Team uniforms	525	525
TOTAL SPORTS APPAREL	**21,270**	**22,485**
Athletic footwear		
Snow skiing, X-country	35	32
Basketball	1,665	1,490
Cross-training/fitness	1,300	1,335
Athleisure	605	585
Walking	720	725
Other sport (golf, football, etc.)	595	610
Hiking	413	440
Tennis	330	270
Aerobic	143	150
Sport sandals	212	225
Recreational boots	478	540
TOTAL ATHLETIC FOOTWEAR	**$9,170**	**$8,980**
TOTAL SPORTING GOODS EQUIPMENT, SPORTS APPAREL, & ATHLETIC FOOTWEAR	**$47,710**	**$48,821**
Recreational transport		
Bicycles & accessories	2,520	$2,800
Pleasure boats & motors	8,094	7,635
Recreational vehicles (except motor homes)	6,095	6,298
Personal watercraft	537	588
TOTAL RECREATIONAL TRANSPORT	**$17,246**	**$17,321**
TOTAL SPORTS EQUIPMENT, SPORTS APPAREL, ATHLETIC FOOTWEAR, AND RECREATIONAL TRANSPORT INDUSTRIES	**$64,956**	**$66,142**

SOURCE: "SGMA Recreation Market Report—2001" in *Recreation Market Report*, Sporting Goods Manufacturer's Association, North Palm Beach, FL, 2002 www.SGMA.com

TABLE 2.8

Wholesale value of athletic footwear shipments, 2000–01

(In millions)

	2001	2000
Running	$2,709	$2,610
Basketball	1,665	1,490
Cross-training/fitness	1,300	1,335
Athleisure	605	585
Walking	720	725
Other sport (golf, football, etc.)	595	610
Hiking	413	440
Tennis	330	270
Aerobic	143	150
Sport sandals	212	225
Recreational boots	478	540
Total athletic footwear	**$9,170**	**$8,980**
Total sporting goods equipment, sports apparel, & athletic footwear	**$47,710**	**$48,821**

SOURCE: Adapted from "U.S. Wholesale Value of Annual Manufacturers Shipments," in *SGMA Recreation Market Report,* Sporting Goods Manufacturer's Association, North Palm Beach, FL, 2002 www.SGMA.com

Recreational Transport Expenses

The SGMA reports that wholesale recreational transport sales, which include bicycles, pleasure boats/motors, recreational vehicles, and snowmobiles, totaled $17.2 billion in 2001. Sales for pleasure boats and motors grew from $7.6 billion in 2000 to $8.1 billion in 2001. (See Table 2.7.)

The National Marine Manufacturers Association (NMMA) estimates that in 2001 69.5 million Americans participated in recreational boating. Americans owned about 1.7 million sailboats and approximately 2.4 million miscellaneous craft, such as canoes and rowboats. In 2001 the average cost of a jet boat was $18,405, an inboard cruiser averaged a hefty $341,945, while canoes averaged just $549 each. (See Table 2.9.) The NMMA estimates that Americans spent more than $25.6 billion on retail expenditures for boating in 2001, up from $19.3 billion in 1997.

TRAVEL COSTS

Travel and tourism is the largest services export industry in the United States. It is also the third largest retail sales category and one of America's largest employers. An estimated 7.9 million U.S. residents work in the travel and tourism industry, resulting in $174 billion in payroll in 2001. The Travel Industry Association of America (TIA) calculates that in 2001 one out of every eighteen people in the U.S. civilian labor force was employed as a result of direct travel spending in the United States.

Although the travel industry was one of the nation's hardest hit industries following the events of September 11, 2001, an economic downturn, and subsequent periods of economic uncertainty, domestic and international travelers spent an estimated $555.2 billion in 2001. International travel accounted for $73.1 billion and international visitors spent $18 billion traveling in the United States in 2001. This spending generated more than $98.8 billion in tax revenues for federal, state, and local governments.

The TIA finds that travel sales on the Internet have risen dramatically from about $12 million in 1997 to $64 million in 2002. Forty-two percent of online travel planners said they did all or most of their travel planning online during 2002, up from 29 percent who performed much or most of their travel planning online the previous year. During 2002 more than 39 million people booked travel using the Internet, an increase of 25 percent from 2001.

In 2002 airline tickets were the most frequently purchased travel products online, accounting for 77 percent of all online travel booking, followed by accommodations at 57 percent and rental cars at 37 percent. About a quarter of online travel planners purchased tickets for cultural events, and 21 percent bought travel packages. Nearly one-third of online travel planners reported spending $2,500 or more in 2002 on travel booked online.

The TIA predicts that tourism will continue to grow. By 2004 total domestic person trips are expected to exceed 1.07 billion, up from 998 million in 2000. Fifty-three million international travelers are expected to visit the United States, up from 51 million in 2000. Total travel expenses are expected to increase from $570.5 billion in 2000 to $588.6 billion in 2004.

AMUSEMENT PARK EXPENDITURES

Americans have always enjoyed amusement parks and attractions, such as Busch Gardens, Disneyland, and Six Flags. Big amusement parks and theme parks featuring children's rides, roller coasters, and water slides have existed in the United States since the early years of the twentieth century. According to the International Association of Amusement Parks and Attractions, in 2001 the U.S. amusement park industry had 319 million visitors and receipts of $9.6 billion, up from $9.1 billion in 1999.

SPENDING ON TOYS AND CRAFTS

Buying and playing with toys is a popular activity in the United States. In the past, the toy industry considered children zero to fourteen as their prime audience. Today, the prime toy-purchasing years are zero to ten years of age. The grandparent/older-adult market accounts for 14 percent of toy purchases. The Toy Industry Association (TIA) reports that in 2001 U.S. toy imports totaled $15.1 billion, primarily from China, Japan, and Mexico; the United States exported approximately $939 million worth of toys to other nations.

The United States is the largest market for toys in the world, followed by western Europe, Asia, and Japan. U.S. toy sales in 2001 rose to $34 billion, up from $31 billion in 2000. (See Table 2.6.) While some toys may sell very

TABLE 2.9

Number and value of boats sold, 1999–2001

	1999		2000		2001	
Outboard boats:						
Total units sold	230,200		241,200		224,400	
Retail value	$	1,988,928,000	$	2,306,577,000	$	2,338,023,600
Average unit cost	$	8,640	$	9,563	$	10,419
Outboard motors:						
Total units sold	331,900		348,700		299,000	
Retail value	$	2,602,096,000	$	2,901,881,400	$	2,508,012,000
Average unit cost	$	7,840	$	8,322	$	8,388
Boat trailers:						
Total units sold	168,000		158,500		135,900	
Retail value	$	190,008,000	$	184,494,000	$	179,931,600
Average unit cost	$	1,131	$	1,164	$	1,324
Inboard boats-runabouts:						
Total units sold	12,100		13,600		13,700	
Retail value	$	308,429,000	$	366,438,400	$	435,153,100
Average unit cost	$	25,490	$	26,944	$	31,763
Inboard boats-cruisers						
Total units sold	7,000		8,000		8,100	
Retail value	$	1,799,420,000	$	2,272,432,000	$	2,769,754,500
Average unit cost	$	257,060	$	284,054	$	341,945
Sterndrive boats:						
Total units sold	79,600		78,400		74,100	
Retail value	$	2,054,476,000	$	2,253,843,200	$	2,264,570,100
Average unit cost	$	25,810	$	28,748	$	30,561
Canoes						
Total units sold	121,000		111,800		105,800	
Retail value	$	67,034,000	$	64,508,600	$	58,084,200
Average unit cost	$	554	$	577	$	549
Personal water craft:						
Total units sold	106,000		92,000		83,000	
Retail value	$	771,044,000	$	720,176,000	$	658,107,000
Average unit cost	$	7,274	$	7,828	$	7,929
Jet boats:						
Total units sold	7,800		7,000		6,000	
Retail value	$	132,678,000	$	123,641,000	$	110,430,000
Average unit cost	$	17,010	$	17,663	$	18,405
Sailboats:						
Total units sold	21,200		22,200		26,200	
Retail value	$	589,360,000	$	740,900,000		N/A
Average unit cost	$	27,800	$	33,374		N/A

SOURCE: "The Boating Market," in *Boating 2001*, National Marine Manufacturers Association, Chicago, IL, 2001 [Online] http://www.nmma.org/facts/boatingstats/2001/files/boatingmarket.asp?bhcp=1 [accessed January 6, 2003]

well one year and then disappear the next year, other toys sell very well year to year. These enduringly popular best-sellers are the basis of the toy business and include games, such as Monopoly and Chutes and Ladders, and preschool and infant toys, such as trains and plush stuffed animals.

In 2001 the leader in toy sales was video games ($9.4 billion). Other strong sellers were infant/preschool toys ($3.2 billion), dolls/accessories ($3.1 billion), vehicles ($2.8 billion), miscellaneous (all other toys) toys ($2.7 billion), arts and crafts for children ($2.6 billion), games/puzzles ($2.2 billion), plush stuffed toys ($2.0 billion), and action figures/accessories ($1.6 billion). (See Table 2.6.)

Spending on crafts and hobbies grew by 11 percent in 2001, up from $23 billion in 2000 to $25.7 billion in 2001. Needlecrafts, painting and finishing supplies, floral crafts, and general crafts all experienced increased sales.

SPENDING ON BOOKS

According to Ipsos-NPD, a market research firm that researches trends in book purchasing, consumers spent about $12.8 billion to purchase 1.62 billion print books in 2001, a 2 percent increase from the $12.6 billion spent on books during 2000. Many other people borrowed books from libraries, purchased used books, and shared, loaned, or passed books on to friends or family.

Ipsos-NPD reports that the percentage of adult and children's books sold was relatively unchanged from 2000 to 2001, but the teen book market experienced a slight increase, with sales increasing from 1.9 percent in 2000 to 2.2 percent in 2001. Although J. K. Rowling's wildly popular *Harry Potter* children's books are considered by industry experts to have reinvigorated children's book sales, a dip in the population of children under age

FIGURE 2.1

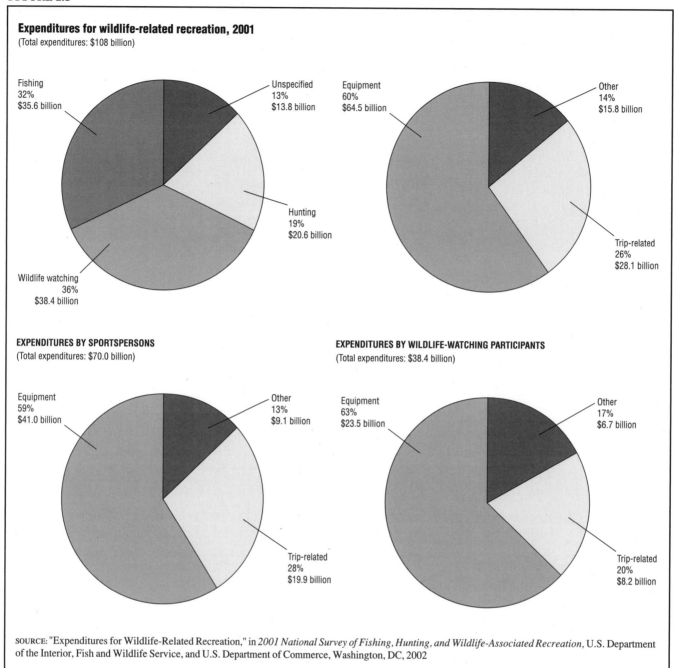

Expenditures for wildlife-related recreation, 2001
(Total expenditures: $108 billion)

Fishing
32%
$35.6 billion

Unspecified
13%
$13.8 billion

Hunting
19%
$20.6 billion

Wildlife watching
36%
$38.4 billion

Equipment
60%
$64.5 billion

Other
14%
$15.8 billion

Trip-related
26%
$28.1 billion

EXPENDITURES BY SPORTSPERSONS
(Total expenditures: $70.0 billion)

Equipment
59%
$41.0 billion

Other
13%
$9.1 billion

Trip-related
28%
$19.9 billion

EXPENDITURES BY WILDLIFE-WATCHING PARTICIPANTS
(Total expenditures: $38.4 billion)

Equipment
63%
$23.5 billion

Other
17%
$6.7 billion

Trip-related
20%
$8.2 billion

SOURCE: "Expenditures for Wildlife-Related Recreation," in *2001 National Survey of Fishing, Hunting, and Wildlife-Associated Recreation,* U.S. Department of the Interior, Fish and Wildlife Service, and U.S. Department of Commerce, Washington, DC, 2002

fourteen offset some of the gains realized by this resurgence of interest in children's books.

Furthermore, consumers are purchasing more children's books than they have in recent years. However, during 2001 and 2002 a higher percentage of children's books were purchased at discounted prices at dollar stores and through special markets (book fairs, book clubs, and mail order) than at bookstores. From January to June 2001 bookstores accounted for 16 percent of children's book purchases, while dollar stores and special markets combined accounted for 42 percent of sales. During the first half of 2002, 17 percent of children's books were pur-

chased at bookstores and 41 percent at dollar stores and through special markets.

During 2001 adult trade paperback sales increased by 1.3 percent, after increases of a scant 0.6 percent in 2000 and 3.3 percent in 1999; however, the 2001 increase barely kept pace with U.S. population growth. Although a slightly higher percentage of households made book purchases during 2001 (56.5 percent) than in 2000, consumers shopped less frequently for books during 2001 than they had during 1999 and 2000.

Industry experts attribute the slow growth in sales to the high price of hardcover books and a major shift in the

FIGURE 2.2

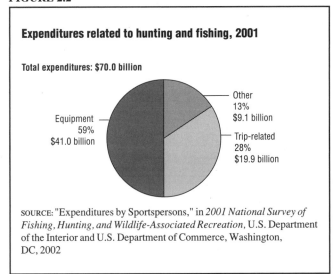

Expenditures related to hunting and fishing, 2001

Total expenditures: $70.0 billion

Equipment
59%
$41.0 billion

Other
13%
$9.1 billion

Trip-related
28%
$19.9 billion

SOURCE: "Expenditures by Sportspersons," in *2001 National Survey of Fishing, Hunting, and Wildlife-Associated Recreation,* U.S. Department of the Interior and U.S. Department of Commerce, Washington, DC, 2002

FIGURE 2.3

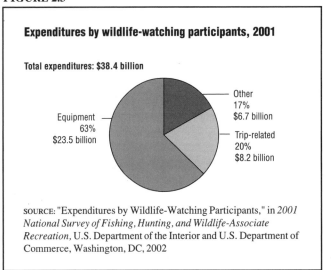

Expenditures by wildlife-watching participants, 2001

Total expenditures: $38.4 billion

Equipment
63%
$23.5 billion

Other
17%
$6.7 billion

Trip-related
20%
$8.2 billion

SOURCE: "Expenditures by Wildlife-Watching Participants," in *2001 National Survey of Fishing, Hunting, and Wildlife-Associate Recreation,* U.S. Department of the Interior and U.S. Department of Commerce, Washington, DC, 2002

way consumers purchase books. Ipsos-NPD reports that bookstores accounted for one out of every three books purchased in 2001. Increasingly, purchases are being made on the Internet and through book clubs, mail order, book fairs, and used bookstores, rather than at traditional retail bookstores.

COSTS OF WILDLIFE-RELATED RECREATION

Many Americans enjoy participating in recreation that involves wildlife. Fishing and hunting remain among the most popular forms of recreation in the United States, and increasing numbers of people enjoy watching, photographing, and feeding wild animals and birds. According to the U.S. Fish and Wildlife Service, more than 82 million U.S. residents fished, hunted, and observed wildlife in 2001.

The U.S. Department of the Interior's *2001 National Survey of Fishing, Hunting, and Wildlife-Associated Recreation* finds that, in 2001 Americans spent more than $108 billion on wildlife-related recreation. Fishing accounted for approximately 32 percent of that expense, wildlife-watching activities, 36 percent, and hunting, 19 percent. (Another 13 percent was unspecified.) (See Figure 2.1.) Of the expenditure by sportspersons, 59 percent was for equipment, 28 percent was trip related, and 13 percent was other. (See Figure 2.2.)

Americans who enjoyed watching wildlife spent an estimated $38.4 billion in 2001. Of that amount, 63 percent was for equipment, 20 percent was trip related, and 17 percent was other (such as magazines, membership dues, and contributions to conservation or wildlife-related organizations). (See Figure 2.3.) Although the number of participants has declined somewhat, those who do participate spend more—on more expensive equipment—than previously.

Expenditures by wildlife recreationists, including funds generated by licenses and taxes on fishing and hunt-

ing equipment, finance many conservation efforts throughout the United States. The U.S. Fish and Wildlife Service calls wildlife recreationists "the Nation's most ardent conservationists" because they not only underwrite conservation efforts, but they also take the time to introduce children and adults to the pleasures of the outdoors and wildlife.

BUYING COLLECTIBLES

By the end of the 1990s, collectibles, the most dynamic category of giftware, accounted for $5.45 billion of the $20.86 billion giftware market. This category grew at an annual rate of more than 10 percent and represented 26 percent of total giftware sales. Industry observers credit the "cocooning trend," with its emphasis on the importance of the home as a place of leisure and entertainment, as a prime driver of increasing sales of collectibles. They also cite the investment value of collectibles and the concept of "family collecting" as fueling sales growth as baby boomers find collecting a satisfying way to spend time with their children.

Although interest in collectibles remains high, the industry has not remained as prosperous. Unity Marketing, in its *Collectibles Industry Report, 2002,* reports that the collectibles industry revenues declined 9 percent in 2001 to $6.5 from $7.1 billion in 2000. The figurine and sculpture category, which is the industry's largest, saw sales decline by 20 percent during 2001. Industry observers attribute the decline to the events of September 11, 2001, and the subsequent sluggish economy.

PAYING TO TAKE A RISK

Weekend daredevils may encounter a variety of insurance problems, depending on the pastime and the danger involved. People who participate in extreme sports and high-risk recreational pursuits may find themselves forced to pay high rates for insurance coverage or be unable to get such coverage at all. When approached by persons who participate in risky activities, insurance companies may decline to insure them, exclude accidents related to the dangerous activity, postpone coverage until after a specific event, or require a physical examination to renew such a policy. In some cases, they may deem the activity and relative risk as negligible or slight and offer the policy at no additional cost.

Some insurance companies have added questions about high-risk behaviors to their applications for prospective policyholders. Participation in extreme sports can add hundreds or thousands of dollars in annual premiums. Pursuits that involve great speed—auto, motorcycle, and boat racing—tend to make insurers most apprehensive. Disability insurers are more likely than other carriers to reject such high-risk applicants than other types of carriers. Disability claims have increased sharply, with some insurers losing money and others leaving the business.

Sports associations sometimes step in to provide insurance when other carriers will not. The Professional Association of Diving Instructors offers certified scuba divers medical insurance. The U.S. Hang Gliding Association has a $1 million liability policy to cover a glider who sails into bystanders. The American Motorcycle Association offers its racers some medical coverage and accidental death and dismemberment insurance.

THE COST OF A NIGHT OUT

A survey conducted by a Philadelphia-based online dating service in 2000 compared the cost of a date—dinner and a movie—in various cities in the United States. New York was the most expensive city with an average cost of $135, followed by Chicago ($128) and San Francisco ($124). Las Vegas was the least expensive of the fourteen major cities ranked, with dinner and a movie averaging just $74. When the cost of a baby-sitter is added to the cost of an evening out, the price may be prohibitive for many American families. The high cost of an evening out is considered one of the market forces driving the booming business of video and DVD movie rentals.

Family outings can also be quite expensive. Although admission to the zoo is free, a day at the St. Louis Zoo for a family of four will cost about $85 without any purchases at the gift shop. Theme park admission fees have increased dramatically over the years: in 1955 a family of four (two parents and two children) was admitted to Disneyland for just $8, in 2000 the same family paid $144. In 2003 admission for two adults and two children to Six Flags Magic Mountain in California cost $140, admission to Hershey Park in Pennsylvania was $130, and entrance to Colorado's Hyland Hills Water World was $100.

CHAPTER 3
OUTDOOR RECREATION

THE LURE OF THE OUTDOORS

Americans love the outdoors. Millions of Americans spend their free time participating in outdoor activities. Surveys by the Sporting Goods Manufacturers Association (SGMA) find that recreational walking, swimming, and bicycling are the most popular outdoor activities. Other popular outdoor activities include freshwater fishing, tent camping, and day hiking.

Not only do many Americans participate in recreational swimming and bicycling, they do so with great frequency. Roper Starch Worldwide, in *Outdoor Recreation in America, 2000,* an annual national survey of recreation patterns, reports increasing rates of participation. (See Figure 3.1.) For example, the study shows that more than three-quarters of Americans (78 percent) engage in outdoor recreation at least once a month and this number has risen steadily since 1997. Along with increases in the percentage of Americans who participated in recreational walking (up 15 percent from 1999) during 2000, more people engaged in outdoor photography, driving for pleasure, and bird-watching.

America's love of the outdoors is increasing. An SGMA survey finds that four of the five most popular sports were outdoor activities (recreational swimming, walking, bicycling, and freshwater fishing). (See Table 3.1.) Indeed, if tent camping and day hiking are considered, then six of the top ten sports during 1999 were outdoor activities.

In its 2002 edition of the annual report *Outdoor Recreation in America,* the SGMA observes that for most Americans, participation in outdoor activities, even when these activities are among their favorite things to do, is infrequent and often associated with vacation, travel, or summer camp. With increasingly busy lives, many Americans do not take time to reconnect to the natural world and participate in outdoor activities. For example, the SGMA report cites a University of Michigan Institute for Social Research Study that finds that the time children aged 9–12 spent outdoors per day declined by 60 percent between 1981 and 1997, from nearly 2 hours to 47 minutes.

Still, many Americans do find the time to pursue outdoor activities and the SGMA report offers statistics and insight about outdoor enthusiasts including:

- Tent campers (43.5 million) outnumber recreation vehicle (RV) campers 2 to 1; however, there are more frequent RV campers (6.3 million) than frequent tent campers (5.7 million)

- Although overall participation in fishing has declined since 1990, there are more than 53 million freshwater, fly, and saltwater anglers in the United States and there are more frequent participants—people who fish 15 or more days per year—in freshwater fishing than there were in 1990

- More than two-thirds (70 percent) of mountain bikers are less than 53 years old and 40 percent have been involved in mountain biking for 3 years or less

- Participation in trail running has increased by 11.5 percent since 1998 and trail runners averaged 47 days of participation during 2001—the most days devoted to any outdoor activity

- Boaters who sail have the highest average annual household income ($76,800) of any sport and the oldest average age of male participants (40.1 years)

- Females prefer day hiking and males favor overnight hiking

- When asked to compare camping, hiking, bicycling, and fishing, parents named camping their favorite outdoor family experience

FIGURE 3.1

How often Americans participated in outdoor recreation, 1994–2000

PERCENT SAYING THAT THEY PARTICIPATE

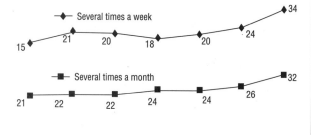

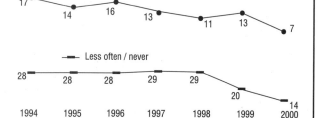

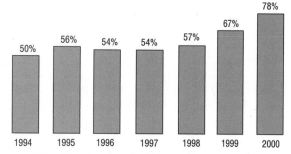

RECREATION PARTICIPATION RATES: AT LEAST ONCE A MONTH

SOURCE: "How Often Americans Participate in Outdoor Recreation" and "Recreation Participation Rates: At Least Once a Month," in *Outdoor Recreation in America 2000: Addressing Key Societal Concerns,* Recreation Roundtable, Washington, DC, September 2000 [Online] http://www.funoutdoors.com/Rec00/ [accessed January 9, 2003]

TABLE 3.1

Number of participants who participated in sports "frequently," 1998–99

(in thousands of people)

Activity	1998	1999	Percent change 98 - 99
Fitness	49,124	49,204	0.0%
Team sports	25,042	24,799	- 1.0%
Racquet sports	6,451	5,561	-13.8%
Recreational	30,928	28,757	- 7.0%
Outdoors	61,994	64,743	+ 4.4%
Winter	13,077	13,218	+ 1.1%
Water sports	5,288	3,313	-18.4%
Cardio equipment	17,279	17,288	0.0%
Strength equipment	18,920	20,424	+ 8.0%
Strength training	26,673	25,757	+ 0.3%
Cardio exercise	45,759	44,369	- 3.0%

SOURCE: "Frequent Participants," in "Avid Sports Participants Profiled in New Report," Sporting Goods Manufacturer's Association, North Palm Beach, FL, June 2000 www.SGMA.com

The decline in frequency of participation was most pronounced among persons aged 18–29 and 30–45, and participation also declined from 43 percent to 31 percent among high-income Americans. Furthermore, households with children and persons who identified themselves as "Internet accessors" experienced sharper declines in participation than the general public.

Half of the surveyed participants viewed the quality of recreation opportunities as essentially unchanged, but golfers, wildlife viewers, boaters, and hunters were more likely to believe opportunities had improved. Motorcyclists and snowboarders were less positive about perceived changes in recreation opportunities, but off-road bicyclists were the least optimistic with one in five reporting diminished opportunities.

Of the surveyed participants, 38 percent described their political affiliation as Democrat, while 32 percent said they were Independent and 26 percent were Republican. Nearly half (47 percent) of downhill skiers said they were Republican, compared to 20 percent who identified themselves as Democrat. Hunters were twice as likely to be Republican (38 percent) as Democrat (19 percent); however, a high percentage were Independent. Motorboaters were 38 percent Republican and 25 percent Democrat and "RVers" had a similar distribution—38 percent Republican and 30 percent Democrat. More Republicans than Democrats participated in motorcycling/snowboarding (35 percent versus 23 percent) and golf (35 percent versus 31 percent).

Downhill skiers reported the highest median household income ($67,000), followed by golfers ($58,000), hikers ($57,000), RVers ($55,000) and off-road bicyclists ($56,000). Bird-watchers reported the highest median age—49—while off-road bicyclists had a median age of 32.

WHO ENGAGES IN OUTDOOR ACTIVITY AND WHY?

A 2001 survey about outdoor recreation prepared by the Recreation Roundtable finds that the percent of American adults participating frequently in outdoor activities declined from 78 percent in 2000 to 70 percent in 2001, however, there was an increase in the percentages of Americans participating in 20 of 37 activities. The greatest growth in participation during the 12 months preceding the survey was in wildlife viewing, hiking, running, jogging, and motorboating.

A Family Affair

Recreation often starts with the family. Many Americans began the recreational activities they enjoy as adults when they were children. Parents who emphasized and participated in outdoor activities raised children who were more likely to become participants in and supporters of outdoor activities. The activities with the highest participation by adults with children include bicycling (56 percent), horseback riding (56 percent), "RVing" (54 percent), camping in a campground (54 percent), swimming (51 percent), motorcycling/snowmobiling (51 percent), motorboating (49 percent), fishing (49 percent), hiking (48 percent), and downhill skiing (48 percent).

Outdoor Recreation Is Fun

There are many reasons that Americans give for participating in outdoor recreation. Many people value the social aspects—bonding with family and friends—as well as improved health and fitness. Others are drawn to outdoor activities by their love of nature. But the number one reason given by Americans in a 1999 Roper survey was "to have fun" (83 percent). The second most popular motivation for engaging in outdoor activities was for relaxation (80 percent).

VISITING THE GREAT OUTDOORS

National and State Parks

One of the best ways to enjoy the outdoors is to visit the nation's National Park System (NPS). Since Congress established Yellowstone National Park as the first national park in 1872, the United States has created a system of national parks occupying millions of acres of land. Today, the 80-million-acre park system encompasses more than 385 parks, monuments, preserves, memorials, historic sites, recreational areas, seashores, and other units spread from Alaska, to the U.S. Virgin Islands, to American Samoa. In addition to providing recreation for almost 300 million visitors each year, the NPS preserves habitats that range from arctic tundra to tropical rain forest and protects many thousands of North American plant and animal species. (See Table 3.2.)

The park system is administered by the National Park Service, a Department of Interior agency that supervises about 2 dozen nationally significant scenic, natural, scientific, historical, or archaeological sites. Established in 1916, the park service employs more than 12,000 permanent personnel and almost twice as many temporary or seasonal workers. More than 120,000 volunteers spent vacation time working for the park service in 2001, donating more than 4 million hours of service.

The NPS includes national parks, such as Yosemite National Park in California and Yellowstone National Park, mostly in Wyoming; national monuments, such as

TABLE 3.2

Recreation visits to National Park Service areas by type of area, 2001

Areas administrated by type	Recreation visits	Areas reporting visits	Areas administered
International Historic Site	0	0	1
National Battlefield	1,578,131	10	11
National Battlefield Park	2,260,199	3	3
National Battlefield Site	0	0	1
National Historic Site	10,109,574	70	77
National Historical Park	26,292,964	36	40
National Lakeshore	3,469,258	4	4
National Memorial	26,462,172	28	28
National Military Park	5,667,987	9	9
National Monument	21,842,404	67	74
National Park	64,083,237	56	57
National Parkway	34,366,307	4	4
National Preserve	1,740,382	15	17
National Recreation Area	48,333,109	17	18
National Reserve	68,165	1	2
National River	4,431,108	4	5
National Scenic Trail	0	0	3
National Seashore	18,706,770	10	10
National Wild & Scenic River	814,496	5	10
Parks (Other)	9,947,663	9	11
NPS TOTAL	**279,873,926**	**348**	**385**

SOURCE: "Table 1. 2001 Recreation Visits by Type of Area," *National Park Service Statistical Abstract 2001*, National Park Service, Denver, CO, 2001

the Washington Monument and the Lincoln Memorial in Washington, D.C.; and national commemorative sites, such as the Gettysburg battlefield in Pennsylvania, the Vicksburg battlefield in Mississippi, and the Ellis Island Immigration Museum in New York. The NPS also includes some lakes, rivers, and seashores. (See Table 3.2.)

Of the sites administered by the NPS, 10 accounted for more than 40 percent of all 2001 visits. (See Table 3.3.) Slightly more than half of all visitors were baby boomers (ages 35–54), about one-quarter were young adults (ages 18–34), and the balance (22 percent) were older adults (over age 55).

Camping enables visitors to stay overnight in the national parks; during 2001 nearly 3.5 million tent campers, close to 3 million RV campers, and about 2 million backcountry campers stayed on NPS grounds. (See Figure 3.2.) Not surprisingly, park visitation was greatest in the summer months, peaking at about 42.5 million visitations in July, and lowest in January (11.5 million). (See Figure 3.3.)

In addition, many millions more visited national forests or lands administered by the Bureau of Land Management for car or motorcycle tours, hunting, fishing, boating, and winter recreational activities. Others traveled to state parks and recreation areas.

Rails to Trails

Many railways around the country have been abandoned by the railroads. Almost every state has turned some of that acreage into public trails for hiking, jogging,

TABLE 3.3

Recreation visits to National Park Service areas by state, 2000–01

State	Visits 2000	Visits 2001	Percent change	State	Visits 2000	Visits 2001	Percent change
Alabama	608,394	555,147	−8.8%	Nebraska	181,229	182,611	0.8%
Alaska	2,025,934	2,055,152	2.5%	Nevada	6,647,299	6,430,872	−3.3%
Arizona	11,525,818	10,988,475	−4.7%	New Hampshire	37,030	37,550	1.4%
Arkansas	2,243,965	2,318,599	2.4%	New Jersey	5,541,529	5,631,953	1.6%
California	34,410,505	32,554,774	−5.4%	New Mexico	1,766,079	1,843,650	4.4%
Colorado	5,807,033	5,597,641	−3.6%	New York	18,532,586	16,621,375	−10.3%
Connecticut	15,910	17,643	10.9%	North Carolina	21,068,081	21,333,633	1.3%
Dist of Columbia	28,801,619	28,801,922	0.0%	North Dakota	484,242	502,440	3.8%
Florida	8,914,714	8,923,251	0.1%	Ohio	3,585,692	3,393,066	−5.4%
Georgia	6,022,686	6,087,065	1.1%	Oklahoma	1,808,354	2,091,766	15.7%
Guam	155,789	149,865	−3.8%	Oregon	831,394	869,174	4.5%
Hawaii	5,184,536	4,764,088	−8.1%	Pennsylvania	8,326,184	8,073,440	−3.0%
Idaho	437,473	425,692	−2.7%	Puerto Rico	1,086,104	1,281,528	18.0%
Illinois	367,968	392,214	6.6%	Rhode Island	56,240	51,816	−7.9%
Indiana	2,108,500	2,010,602	−4.6%	South Carolina	937,688	1,583,410	68.9%
Iowa	270,378	263,486	−2.5%	South Dakota	3,772,167	3,635,275	−3.6%
Kansas	116,220	128,654	10.7%	Tennessee	8,348,808	7,815,318	−6.4%
Kentucky	3,851,514	3,367,362	-12.6%	Texas	5,878,012	5,401,275	−8.1%
Louisiana	895,470	969,370	8.3%	Utah	8,843,646	8,343,133	−5.7%
Maine	2,469,238	2,516,551	1.9%	Vermont	46,289	26,350	−43.1%
Maryland	3,179,601	3,394,440	6.8%	Virgin Islands	802,939	790,316	−1.6%
Massachusetts	10,250,764	9,845,682	−4.0%	Virginia	24,028,901	24,605,608	2.4%
Michigan	1,638,863	1,567,850	−4.3%	Washington	7,275,528	7,217,400	−0.8%
Minnesota	597,544	542,266	−9.3%	West Virginia	1,942,282	2,099,083	8.1%
Mississippi	7,006,366	6,859,139	−2.1%	Wisconsin	366,628	314,387	−14.2%
Missouri	5,338,809	5,353,407	0.3%	Wyoming	5,754,332	5,617,976	−2.4%
Montana	3,696,401	3,629,186	−1.8%				
NPS TOTAL						279,873,926	−2.1%

SOURCE: "Table 2. 2001 Recreation Visits by State," *National Park Service Statistical Abstract 2001*, National Park Service, Denver, CO, 2001

FIGURE 3.2

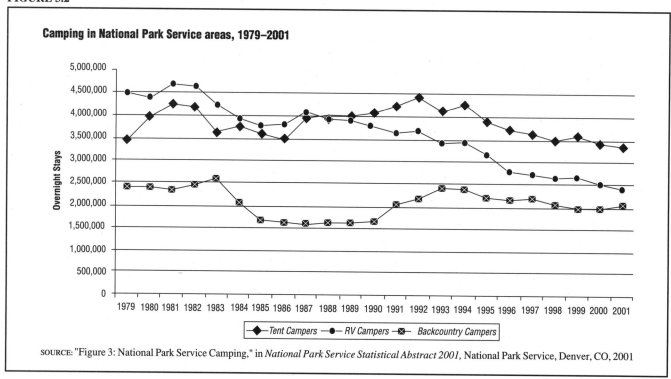

Camping in National Park Service areas, 1979–2001

SOURCE: "Figure 3: National Park Service Camping," in *National Park Service Statistical Abstract 2001*, National Park Service, Denver, CO, 2001

biking, and even horseback riding. According to the Washington, D.C.-based nonprofit Rails-to-Trails Conservancy (RTC), the 10 states that have done the most con-verting of trail mileage are Wisconsin (1,226 miles), Minnesota (1,174), Michigan (1,081), Pennsylvania (705), Iowa (495), Washington (440), New York (433), Maine

FIGURE 3.3

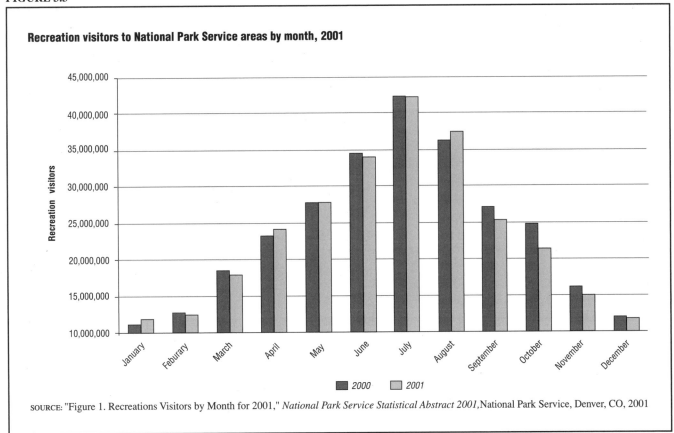

Recreation visitors to National Park Service areas by month, 2001

SOURCE: "Figure 1. Recreations Visitors by Month for 2001," *National Park Service Statistical Abstract 2001,* National Park Service, Denver, CO, 2001

(410), Illinois (367), and West Virginia (289). During 2002, working in cooperation with state and local agencies, the RTC helped to launch several projects in California, including bicycle and pedestrian trails.

BOATING

The National Marine Manufacturers Association (NMMA) estimates that 69.5 million Americans participated in recreational boating in 2001, fewer than the 72.3 million in 2000. Almost 17 million boats were in use, and nearly 6 million people water-skied, down from 6.7 million in 2000. Almost 13 million Americans were registered boaters. Michigan (1,000,049), California (904,863), Florida (840,684), Minnesota (812,247), Texas (626,761), and Wisconsin (573,920) led in the number of registered boaters in 2000.

Americans own about 1.7 million sailboats and approximately 2.5 million miscellaneous craft, such as canoes and rowboats. The NMMA estimates that Americans spent about $26 billion on retail expenditures for boating in 2001, up from $25 billion in 2000.

GARDENING

According to the National Gardening Association (NGA), in 2001 more than three-fourths (85 million) of U.S. households had at least one gardener, up from 72 mil-

lion in 1994. Gardening participation varies from year to year, based on home ownership rates, the number of sunny days during the growing season, and portrayals of gardening in the media. Gardening offers an array of health benefits. It provides an ideal form of moderate exercise, and tilling the soil can soothe jagged nerves, relieve stress, and reconnect people to the natural, seasonal rhythms of the earth. Surveyed gardeners report that they gardened for the pleasure of being outdoors, the aesthetic pleasure gardening provides, the relaxation, and the exercise.

The exercise benefits of gardening vary—some activities burn as many as 250 calories in a half-hour. Strenuous tasks such as mowing with a push mower, mixing compost into the soil, using heavy power tools, and chopping wood are as vigorous as tennis, jogging, and weight lifting. More sedate activities, such as watering the lawn, trimming shrubs with power tools, raking, or riding a power mower, burn fewer calories but still offer opportunities to bend, stretch, and strengthen joints.

Flower gardening is more popular than vegetable gardening in the United States, with 4 out of 10 households growing flowers, compared to 3 out of 10 raising vegetables. Householders aged 35–54 (51 percent) were most likely to live in a flower-gardening household; middle-aged and older households were more likely to grow vegetables. On average, 31 percent of all households grew vegetables. The NGA predicts that the huge number of

TABLE 3.4

Participants in wildlife-related recreation by participant's state of residence, 2001

(Population 16 years old and older. Numbers in thousands)

Participant's state of residence	Population	Total participants		Sportspersons		Wildlife-watching participants	
		Number	Percent of population	Number	Percent of population	Number	Percent of population
United States, total	**212,298**	**82,302**	**39**	**37,805**	**18**	**66,105**	**31**
Alabama	3,427	1,323	39	726	21	965	28
Alaska	454	320	70	205	45	241	53
Arizona	3,700	1,296	35	437	12	1,107	30
Arkansas	1,999	1,038	52	621	31	778	39
California	25,982	6,873	26	2,486	10	5,491	21
Colorado	3,215	1,518	47	679	21	1,213	38
Connecticut	2,536	996	39	331	13	883	35
Delaware	599	220	37	94	16	170	28
Florida	12,171	3,857	32	2,158	18	2,856	23
Georgia	6,096	1,932	32	1,136	19	1,326	22
Hawaii	916	195	21	114	12	126	14
Idaho	972	507	52	306	31	388	40
Illinois	9,244	3,148	34	1,507	16	2,492	27
Indiana	4,558	2,179	48	914	20	1,786	39
Iowa	2,201	1,212	55	580	26	983	45
Kansas	2,017	942	47	491	24	735	36
Kentucky	3,121	1,547	50	703	23	1,264	40
Louisiana	3,306	1,326	40	829	25	840	25
Maine	1,005	607	60	256	26	520	52
Maryland	4,078	1,546	38	571	14	1,311	32
Massachusetts	4,837	1,726	36	521	11	1,493	31
Michigan	7,587	2,950	39	1,325	17	2,424	32
Minnesota	3,688	2,388	65	1,437	39	1,993	54
Mississippi	2,111	851	40	533	25	579	27
Missouri	4,206	2,010	48	1,076	26	1,612	38
Montana	699	438	63	279	40	362	52
Nebraska	1,266	623	49	308	24	498	39
Nevada	1,454	439	30	194	13	334	23
New Hampshire	954	506	53	175	18	450	47
New Jersey	6,300	1,993	32	669	11	1,694	27
New Mexico	1,337	595	45	256	19	471	35
New York	14,201	3,990	28	1,493	11	3,524	25
North Carolina	5,918	2,330	39	982	17	1,884	32
North Dakota	483	228	47	170	35	135	28
Ohio	8,645	3,407	39	1,513	17	2,768	32
Oklahoma	2,587	1,308	51	730	28	1,042	40
Oregon	2,630	1,545	59	611	23	1,286	49
Pennsylvania	9,303	4,169	45	1,648	18	3,522	38
Rhode Island	765	280	37	96	13	242	32
South Carolina	3,080	1,375	45	674	22	1,079	35
South Dakota	559	326	58	176	31	251	45
Tennessee	4,317	2,109	49	903	21	1,706	40
Texas	15,445	4,515	29	2,745	18	3,088	20
Utah	1,554	736	47	468	30	572	37
Vermont	479	319	67	125	26	287	60
Virginia	5,471	2,535	46	970	18	2,168	40
Washington	4,516	2,537	56	932	21	2,234	49
West Virginia	1,447	694	48	353	24	517	36
Wisconsin	4,059	2,489	61	1,141	28	2,159	53
Wyoming	377	223	59	138	37	172	46

Note: Detail does not add to total because of multiple responses. U.S. totals include responses from participants residing in the District of Columbia, as described in the statistical accuracy appendix.

SOURCE: "Table 50. Participants in Wildlife-Related Recreation by Participant's State of Residence: 2001," in *2001 National Survey of Fishing, Hunting, and Wildlife-Associated Recreation,* U.S. Department of the Interior and U.S. Department of Commerce, Washington, DC, 2002

baby boomer households entering the prime gardening ages will likely boost the overall number of flower-gardening households by 17 percent and vegetable-gardening households by 18.5 percent by 2010.

For many older adults, gardening is an enjoyable way to incorporate exercise and creativity into their lives. For others, it is therapeutic. Hospitals; assisted-living facilities; nursing homes; and adult day care, retirement, and recre-ation centers offer programs ranging from botany classes and garden clubs to horticultural therapy (gardening as a means of helping to heal illness and promote well-being).

WILDLIFE AS RECREATION

America is a huge country with many millions of square miles of natural wilderness and a rich tradition of enjoying nature. Many Americans find wildlife-associated recreation

TABLE 3.5

Wildlife watching participants, days, and expenditures, 1996–2001

(U.S. population 16 years old and older. Numbers in thousands)

	1996		2001[1]		1996–2001
	Number	Percent	Number	Percent	percent change
Wildlife watching, total	**62,868**	**100**	**66,105**	**100**	**5**
Residential	60,751	97	62,928	95	4*
Observe wildlife	44,063	70	42,111	64	−4*
Photograph wildlife	16,021	25	13,937	21	−13*
Feed wild birds or other wildlife	54,122	86	53,988	82	0
Visit public parks or areas	11,011	18	10,981	17	0
Maintain plantings or natural areas	13,401	21	13,072	20	−2*
Nonresidential	23,652	38	21,823	33	−8*
Observe wildlife	22,878	36	20,080	30	−12
Photograph wildlife	12,038	19	9,427	14	−22
Feed wildlife	9,976	16	7,077	11	−29
Days, nonresidential	313,790	100	372,006	100	19*
Observing wildlife	278,683	89	295,345	79	6*
Photographing wildlife	79,342	25	76,324	21	−4*
Feeding wildlife	89,606	29	103,307	28	15*
Wildlife-watching expenditures, total (2001 dollars)	**$29,062,524**	**100**	**$33,730,868**	**100**	**16***
Trips	10,250,604	35	8,162,439	24	−20*
Equipment	16,785,440	58	23,616,982	70	41
Wildlife-watching equipment	8,783,405	30	6,850,971	20	−22*
Auxiliary equipment	853,374	3	716,900	2	−16*
Special equipment	7,148,661	25	16,049,111	48	125
Other	2,026,480	7	1,951,447	6	−4*

[1] All 2001 expenditures are adjusted to make them comparable to 1991 estimates.
*Not different from zero at the 5 percent level.

SOURCE: "1996–2001 Wildlife Watching Participants, Days, and Expenditures," *2001 National Survey of Fishing, Hunting, and Wildlife-Associated Recreation*, U.S. Department of the Interior and U.S. Department of Commerce, Washington, DC, 2002

a source of immense pleasure, and some of the most popular recreational activities involve wildlife and wild terrain.

According to data gathered by the U.S. Departments of the Interior and Commerce, more than 30 percent of Americans were involved in wildlife-related recreation activities in 2001 and participation has increased by 5 percent since 1996. (See Table 3.4 and Table 3.5.) Participation varies by state, with Alaska (70 percent) reporting the highest proportion of participants. Other states with high levels of participants include Vermont (67 percent), Minnesota (65 percent), Montana (63 percent), Oregon (59 percent), Wyoming (59 percent), South Dakota (58 percent), Washington (56 percent), Iowa (55 percent), New Hampshire (53 percent), Arkansas (52 percent), Idaho (52 percent), and Oklahoma (51 percent). (See Table 3.4.)

Not surprisingly, states with ample opportunities for wildlife recreation—observing wildlife, photographing, and feeding birds or other wildlife—report higher levels of participation than states better known for other environmental attractions. For example, Hawaii, which is better known for its beaches, hotels, and resorts, reports that just 21 percent of its population engages in wildlife recreation. Similarly, Nevada, with its urban tourism attracting employees and visitors to the cities of Las Vegas and Reno, reports that just 30 percent of its residents participate in wildlife recreation. (See Table 3.4.)

National Survey

The mission of the U.S. Fish and Wildlife Service (FWS) is to conserve and enhance the nation's fish, wildlife, and habitat. For conservation efforts to be effective, the FWS needs to know how people use fish and wildlife resources. Since 1955 the FWS has conducted a periodic survey of fishing, hunting, and wildlife-related recreation. The 2001 FWS survey and report is the tenth such study conducted to determine how often recreationists participate and how much they spend on their activities.

The most recent report, the *2001 National Survey of Fishing, Hunting, and Wildlife-Associated Recreation* (U.S. Department of the Interior, Fish and Wildlife Service, and U.S. Department of Commerce, Washington, DC, 2002), finds that more than 82 million Americans participated in some form of wildlife-related activity in 2001.

During 2001, according to the survey, 34.1 million people in the United States fished, 13 million hunted, and 66.1 million enjoyed other forms of wildlife-watching recreation, including photographing or feeding animals. Among anglers, hunters, and nonconsumptive participants (those who do not capture or kill the animals or fish), many of those who participated in one activity often engaged in the other activities as well. For example, in 2001 more than two-thirds (71 percent) of hunters also fished, and more than one-quarter (27 percent) of anglers hunted.

FIGURE 3.4

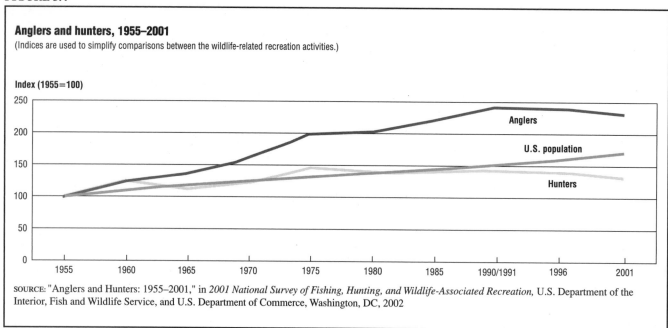

Anglers and hunters, 1955–2001

(Indices are used to simplify comparisons between the wildlife-related recreation activities.)

SOURCE: "Anglers and Hunters: 1955–2001," in *2001 National Survey of Fishing, Hunting, and Wildlife-Associated Recreation,* U.S. Department of the Interior, Fish and Wildlife Service, and U.S. Department of Commerce, Washington, DC, 2002

FIGURE 3.5

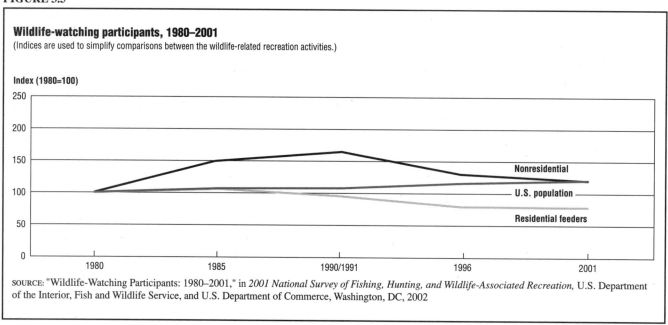

Wildlife-watching participants, 1980–2001

(Indices are used to simplify comparisons between the wildlife-related recreation activities.)

SOURCE: "Wildlife-Watching Participants: 1980–2001," in *2001 National Survey of Fishing, Hunting, and Wildlife-Associated Recreation,* U.S. Department of the Interior, Fish and Wildlife Service, and U.S. Department of Commerce, Washington, DC, 2002

Trends

People are enjoying wildlife-related activities as much as ever. The number of anglers in 2001, 34.1 million, decreased only slightly since 1996, when there were 35.2 million anglers. The number of hunters, 13 million, also dropped from 14 million in 1996. Despite these declines, trends reveal that the number of anglers outpaced U.S. population growth at a rate of 2 to 1 from 1955 to 2001. Although the number of hunters increased by 31 percent during the same period, this rate of growth did not keep pace with U.S. population growth. (See Figure 3.4.)

Participation in wildlife watching grew to 66.1 million in 2001, from 62.9 million in 1996. The percentage of people who took trips away from their homes to observe, feed, or photograph wildlife fell by 19 percent from 1980 (the first year it was measured) to 2001. The number of people who enjoyed these activities within one mile of their homes (62.9 million) increased by 4 percent from 1996. (See Table 3.5 and Figure 3.5.)

Expenditures

In 2001 Americans spent about $108 billion, representing about 1 percent of the gross domestic product, on

TABLE 3.6

Anglers by gender and age, 2001

Total, both sexes	**34.1 million**
Male	25.2 million
Female	8.9 million
Total, all ages	**34.1 million**
16 and 17	1.3 million
18 to 24	2.9 million
25 to 34	6.6 million
35 to 44	9.0 million
45 to 54	6.9 million
55 to 64	4.2 million
65 and older	3.1 million

SOURCE: "Anglers—by Gender and Age," in *2001 National Survey of Fishing, Hunting, and Wildlife-Associated Recreation*, U.S. Department of the Interior, Fish and Wildlife Service, and U.S. Department of Commerce, Washington, DC, 2002

FIGURE 3.6

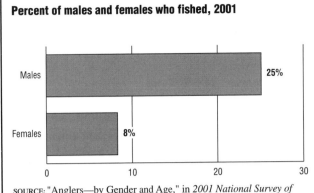

Percent of males and females who fished, 2001

SOURCE: "Anglers—by Gender and Age," in *2001 National Survey of Fishing, Hunting, and Wildlife-Associated Recreation*, U.S. Department of the Interior, Fish and Wildlife Service, and U.S. Department of Commerce, Washington, DC, 2002

wildlife-related recreation. Fishing accounted for approximately 32 percent of that expenditure, wildlife-watching activities, 36 percent, and hunting, 19 percent. (Another 13 percent was unspecified.) (See Figure 2.1 in Chapter 2.) Of the money spent, 59 percent was for equipment, 28 percent was trip-related, and 13 percent fell into the "other" category.

Who Participates in Wildlife Sports?

In 2001 the greatest number of wildlife enthusiasts lived in California, Texas, New York, Florida, and Illinois. (See Table 3.4.) The greatest percentage and the largest number of anglers and hunters were between the ages of 25 and 54. (See Table 3.6.) The majority of anglers and hunters were male: 74 percent of the anglers and 91 percent of the hunters. Of those who watched wildlife, 54 percent were female, while 34 percent of all women watched wildlife at their residences. (See Figure 3.6 and Table 3.7.)

Most hunters (96 percent) were white, 2 percent were black, and 2 percent were other races. Among anglers, 93 percent were white, 5 percent were black, 1 percent were Asian, and 1 percent were other races. Among those who participated in nonresidential wildlife-watching activities, 95 percent were white, 3 percent were black, 1 percent were Asian, and 1 percent were other races.

Among anglers, 35 percent had a high school education, 27 percent had 1 to 3 years of college, and 26 percent had 4 years of college or more. Only 12 percent had fewer than 12 years of school. Among hunters, 38 percent had a high school diploma, 26 percent had 1 to 3 years of college, 22 percent had 4 years of college or more, and only 14 percent had fewer than 12 years of school. For those who enjoyed wildlife-watching activities, 27 percent had a high school diploma, 27 percent had 1 to 3 years of college, and 37 percent had 4 or more years of college. Only 8 percent had less than a high school education.

TABLE 3.7

Residential wildlife-watching participants by gender and age, 2001

(In millions)

Total, both sexes	**62.9**
Male	28.8
Female	34.1
Total, all ages	**62.9**
16 and 17	1.5
18 to 24	2.7
25 to 34	8.1
35 to 44	14.1
45 to 54	13.9
55 to 64	10.1
65 and older	12.5

SOURCE: "Residential Participants-by Gender and Age," *2001 National Survey of Fishing, Hunting, and Wildlife-Associated Recreation*, U.S. Department of the Interior and U.S. Department of Commerce, Washington, DC, 2002

Hunting

In 2001, 13 million Americans 16 years and older enjoyed hunting a variety of game animals within the United States. In order of preference, hunters sought big game (deer, elk, bear, and wild turkey), small game (squirrels, rabbits, pheasants, quail, and grouse), migratory birds (doves, ducks, and geese), and other animals (groundhogs, raccoons, foxes, and coyotes). Hunters spent $20.6 billion on trips and equipment during 2001. (See Table 3.8.) Collectively, they hunted 228 million days and took 200 million trips.

People living in the west north central states were most likely to hunt (12 percent), while residents of the Pacific states (2 percent) and the New England (4 percent) and middle and south Atlantic states (5 percent each) were least likely. (See Figure 3.7.) Nearly all (95 percent) hunted within their resident state; only 2.1 million hunted out of state.

TABLE 3.8

Total hunters and hunting days, trips, and expenditures, 2001

Hunters	**13.0 million**
Big game	10.9 million
Small game	5.4 million
Migratory bird	3.0 million
Other animals	1.0 million
Days	**228 million**
Big game	153 million
Small game	60 million
Migratory bird	29 million
Other animals	19 million
Trips	**200 million**
Big game	114 million
Small game	46 million
Migratory bird	24 million
Other animals	15 million
Expenditures	**$20.6 billion**
Big game	10.1 billion
Small game	1.8 billion
Migratory game	1.4 billion
Other animals	0.2 billion
Unspecified	7.1 billion

Detail does not add to total because of multiple responses and nonresponse.

SOURCE: "Total Hunting," in *2001 National Survey of Fishing, Hunting, and Wildlife-Associated Recreation,* U.S. Department of the Interior, Fish and Wildlife Service, and U.S. Department of Commerce, Washington, DC, 2002

Animal rights advocates have criticized hunters as wanton, unfeeling killers. Hunters and hunters' organizations are working to counter this negative image by teaching ethics to hunters, actively promoting the contributions that hunters make to conservation, and defending hunting as a time-honored American tradition. The campaign to improve hunting's reputation coincided with state initiatives to restrict specific types of hunting, such as the baiting of bears in Michigan and Washington and airborne hunting of wolves in Alaska.

Fishing

In 2001 more than 34 million U.S. residents enjoyed a variety of fishing activities throughout the United States. Collectively, anglers fished 557 million days and took 437 million fishing trips. Freshwater species were fished for by 84 percent of anglers, while saltwater fish were fished for by 26 percent. (There was some overlap due to the anglers who fished for both.) Anglers spent $35.6 billion on fishing-related expenses during the year. Of that amount, 41 percent was trip-related, 48 percent went for equipment, and 11 percent was for other expenses.

Wildlife-Watching Activities

Wildlife-watching activities, including observing, feeding, and photographing wildlife, continue to be popular in the United States. These activities are termed either "residential" (within a mile of one's home) or "nonresidential" (at least 1 mile from home). In 2001, 31 percent (66.1 million) of the American population 16 years and older enjoyed watching wildlife. Each participant spent an average of $738 for a total of $38.4 billion. Of the total spent, 61 percent was for equipment, 21 percent was trip-related, and 17 percent went for other expenses.

Among the nearly 63 million people who enjoyed wildlife-watching activities in their own communities (residential), 82 percent fed birds, 64 percent observed wildlife, 21 percent photographed wildlife, and 17 percent visited public areas, such as parks, within 1 mile from of their homes. Another 20 percent maintained plantings for wildlife or natural areas for the primary purpose of benefiting wildlife. Among those who took trips away from home for the primary purpose of observing, feeding, or photographing wildlife, 30 percent observed, 14 percent photographed, and 11 percent fed the animals. (See Table 3.5.)

Residents from the west north central (41 percent), east south central (34 percent), and New England (36 percent) states were most likely to enjoy local wildlife activities. (See Figure 3.8.) Residents of the mountain (15 percent) and west north central states (14 percent) were most likely to travel to participate in wildlife activities. (See Figure 3.9.) Almost equal proportions of males and females enjoyed wildlife-watching activities. (See Table 3.7 and Table 3.9.)

Whale Watching

Whale watching became increasingly popular during the 1990s. The whales support an industry pouring millions of dollars into many coastal economies. The Whale and Dolphin Conservation Society, based in Bath, England, reports that each year more than 9 million people in 65 countries go on whale-watching expeditions, and the number of people is growing by 10 percent each year. Two-thirds of whale watching is done in the United States. Worldwide, the activity annually generates more than $500 million in revenue.

Whale watching in the United States generates an estimated $45 million in direct revenue and more than $175 million in associated business. In southern New England alone, tourists pay more than $25 million each year to visit whales in their natural environment. Humpback, fin, minke, and, occasionally, orca or pilot whales frequent these waters, and the highly endangered North Atlantic right whale can sometimes be seen.

The California gray whale, now removed from the endangered species list, is the star of the West Coast's whale-watching industry. Commercial whale-watching vessels also serve as forums for educational outreach and scientific research.

"Canned Hunting"

During the 1990s a controversial form of commercial exploitation of wildlife, known as "canned hunting,"

FIGURE 3.7

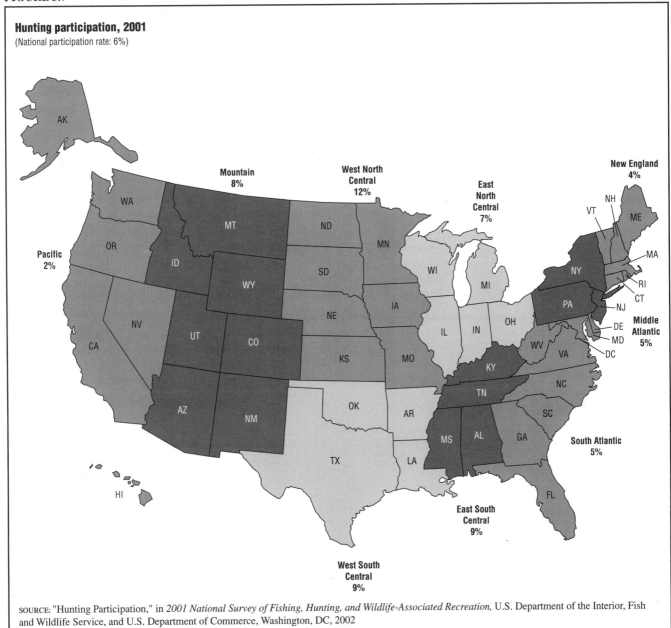

Hunting participation, 2001

(National participation rate: 6%)

SOURCE: "Hunting Participation," in *2001 National Survey of Fishing, Hunting, and Wildlife-Associated Recreation*, U.S. Department of the Interior, Fish and Wildlife Service, and U.S. Department of Commerce, Washington, DC, 2002

swept across the country. Beginning in Texas, canned hunting now occurs in most states. A 2001 Humane Society investigation estimates that there may be as many as several thousand canned-hunting facilities across more than twenty-five states.

In a canned hunt, the "hunter" pays a set fee and steps into an enclosure where an animal—boar, ram, bear, lion, tiger, zebra, buffalo, rhinoceros, or antelope—is confined. The hunter then kills the animal with the weapon of his or her choice. The animals are easily cornered. Some have been domesticated or raised in facilities where they have become friendly to humans, even walking up to them.

No federal laws restrict canned hunts, although in late 2001 Senator Joseph Biden, a Democrat from Delaware, introduced legislation that would make it illegal to "knowingly transfer, transport, or possess in interstate or foreign commerce a confined exotic mammal for the purposes of allowing the killing or injuring of that animal for entertainment" or for the collection of a "trophy." California, Connecticut, Georgia, Indiana, Maryland, Massachusetts, Montana, Nevada, North Carolina, New Jersey, Oregon, Rhode Island, Washington, Wisconsin, and Wyoming ban in-state canned-hunt ranches. Investigations reveal that zoos across the nation have sold animals they consider surplus either directly to canned-hunt facilities or to dealers who sell animals to auctions patronized by canned-hunt organizers. Some pressure has been exerted on zoos to acknowledge their responsibility for the animals they discard.

FIGURE 3.8

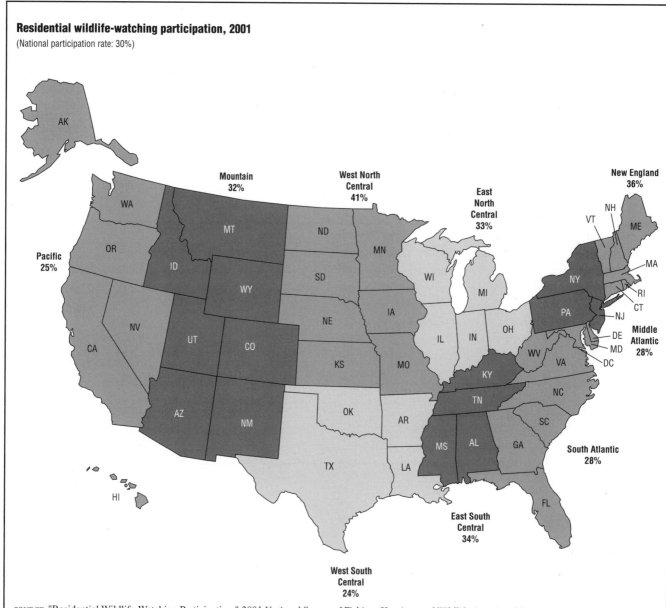

Residential wildlife-watching participation, 2001

(National participation rate: 30%)

SOURCE: "Residential Wildlife-Watching Participation," *2001 National Survey of Fishing, Hunting, and Wildlife-Associated Recreation,* U.S. Department of the Interior and U.S. Department of Commerce, Washington, DC, 2002

MOTORCYCLING—CHANGING TIMES

Motorcycling is not only a means of transportation, but also a popular recreational activity. The Motorcycle Industry Council reports that motorcycle sales increased 10.7 percent during 2002, promising industry revenues in excess of the $6.4 billion in retail sales in 2001. During 2001 on-road motorcycles made up more than 52 percent of the market and off-road machines made up 31 percent. Scooters and dual-purpose machines accounted for the rest. Among the on-road models, cruisers continued to lead the market with more than 50 percent of unit sales. Sport bikes came in second with more than 20 percent of on-road sales. Regionally, the South accounts for most motorcycle sales, followed by the West, the Midwest, and the East.

The Motorcycle Owner—A Profile

In 1980 the average age of registered motorcyclists was 26; by 1990, 32; and by 1998, 38. In 1980 the average motorcycle owner earned $17,500 per year; by 1990, $33,100; and in 1999, $45,000. According to J.D. Powers and Associates, a market research firm, the typical profile of a new motorcycle buyer is a 42-year-old man with a median income of $67,000.

Today, the industry increasingly caters to aging baby boomers with disposable incomes and a "yen" for adventure. Manufacturers have introduced a line of bigger, safer, and more expensive machines with plenty of extras—wide-body, big-windshield cruising bikes—

FIGURE 3.9

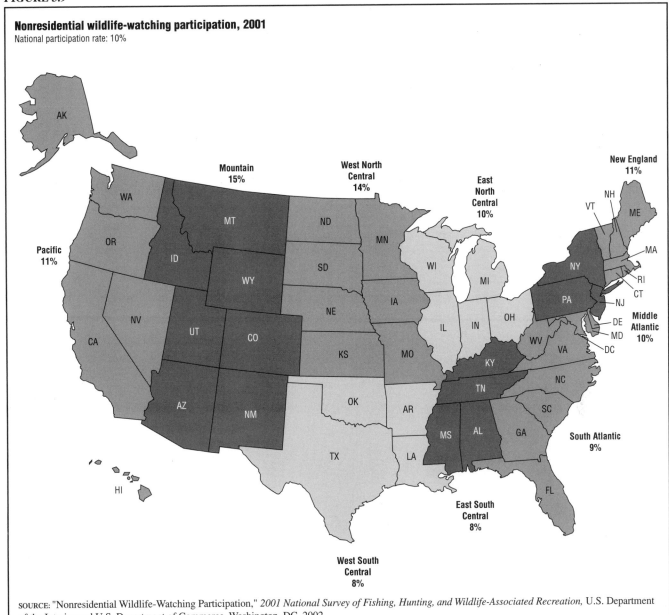

Nonresidential wildlife-watching participation, 2001
National participation rate: 10%

SOURCE: "Nonresidential Wildlife-Watching Participation," *2001 National Survey of Fishing, Hunting, and Wildlife-Associated Recreation,* U.S. Department of the Interior and U.S. Department of Commerce, Washington, DC, 2002

aimed at customers more interested in comfort than performing daredevil acrobatics.

One out of four motorcycles sold today is sold to a woman. Very expensive bikes are reviving the industry. The recovery of Harley-Davidson from the edge of bankruptcy was based on marketing to older, more affluent consumers looking for excitement in their lives.

RECREATIONAL VEHICLES

Recreational vehicles (RVs) include a variety of vehicles, such as motor homes, travel trailers, folding camping trailers, truck campers, and van conversions. Motor homes and vans are motorized, while the others must be towed or mounted on other vehicles. There are approxi-

mately 7.2 million RVs in the United States—1 in every 12 vehicle-owning households. There are an estimated 30 million RV enthusiasts, including renters of RVs.

RV owners cite freedom, flexibility, comfort, family appeal, affordability, and versatility as the reasons they choose to purchase RVs. Sports enthusiasts value the ability of bringing snowmobiles, motorcycles, and bicycles with them for their outdoor adventures. Fans of this type of vehicle claim that family vacations in a RV improve family relationships and communication. A survey conducted by Harris Interactive during 2001 finds that families with two or more children were likely buyers of RVs.

According to a 2001 study conducted by the University of Michigan, RV ownership has increased 7.8 percent

TABLE 3.9

Nonresidential wildlife-watching participants by gender and age, 2001

(In millions)

Total, both sexes	**21.8**
Male	11.4
Female	10.4
Total, all ages	**21.8**
16 and 17	0.7
18 to 24	1.4
25 to 34	3.8
35 to 44	5.7
45 to 54	5.0
55 to 64	2.9
65 and older	2.4

SOURCE: "Nonresidential Participants-by Gender and Age," *2001 National Survey of Fishing, Hunting, and Wildlife-Associated Recreation,* U.S. Department of the Interior and U.S. Department of Commerce, Washington, DC, 2002

during the past 4 years and has grown by 42 percent over the past 21 years. The annual retail value of RV shipments is nearly $10 billion.

Who Owns RVs?

The University of Michigan study describes the typical RV owner as a 49-year-old married man with an annual household income of $56,000. RV owners are likely to be home owners and they tend to spend their disposable income on travel, averaging 4,500 miles during 28–35 days of travel per year. Though 10 percent of RVs are owned by persons over age 55, nearly 9 percent are owned by baby boomers; and this group of 35–54-year-olds is considered the fastest-growing segment of the RV market.

Shifting U.S. demographics—the aging of baby boomers—will likely add to the growth of the RV industry. Increasing numbers of single people, especially women, are also taking to the road in RVs. The University of Michigan study projects that out of all households, 15 percent will own an RV by 2010, outpacing the projected 10 percent growth in U.S. households.

AMUSEMENT AND THEME PARKS AND CIRCUSES

Theme and amusement parks, in general, enjoyed growth in attendance in the 1990s. According to the Economic Consulting Services of Newport Beach, California, attendance at the nation's top 50 parks increased 3.6 percent annually, to almost 161 million people. Most of the observed growth, however, was due to the opening of new parks, such as Universal Studios and Disney's MGM Studio, both in Florida, and Six Flags Fiesta Texas in San Antonio. Overall attendance increases obscure the diminishing popularity of theme parks, especially among middle-aged and older adults.

Many adults may be wearying of the very things that give young adults such a thrill: high-tech, action-packed adventure. In addition, theme parks are becoming increasingly expensive to attend. Estimated per capita expenditures at the nation's top 50 parks grew dramatically—72 percent—from 1987 to 1997; in 1997 the average visitor spent $33.82.

Though several theme parks, including SeaWorld California, Six Flags Great Adventure in New Jersey, Las Vegas's Adventuredome at the Circus Circus Hotel and Casino, and Paramount's Kings Island in Ohio, reported increases, attendance at most amusement parks declined during 2001, according to data compiled by Amusement Business, an organization that tracks industry news. Reduced attendance is attributed to an economic downturn, the September 11, 2001, terrorist attacks, and declining consumer confidence.

Disney theme parks suffered losses, including a 9 percent decline in attendance at Epcot, a 12 percent decline at California's Disneyland Park, and a 4 percent drop in attendance at the Magic Kingdom, traditionally the most visited theme park in the United States. California Adventure, Disney's new theme park, attracted a disappointing 5 million visitors during its first year of operation despite widespread promotion and discounted entry fees.

Universal's Orlando experienced a 15 percent drop and attendance at Universal Studios Orlando was down 10 percent. SeaWorld Orlando suffered a 2 percent decline and attendance at Universal Studios Hollywood was down 9 percent.

Because children are generally accompanied by adults to theme parks, the parks are seeking novel ways to appeal to adult visitors. The parks of the future will likely anticipate the needs and preferences of their older customers. They will feature fewer thrill rides and place greater emphasis on serene, comfortable surroundings, such as fountains, seats, and garden settings.

Similarly, parks are expected to cater to families' preferences for wholesome pastimes, rather than competitive or violence-oriented activities. Legoland, a Carlsbad, California, park that debuted in 1998, invites visitors to build structures with plastic blocks and appeals to families seeking lively, creative recreation.

Ringling Brothers Comes to Town

According to company spokesperson Susannah Smith, Ringling Brothers Circus, the "Greatest Show on Earth," plays to more people than any other live show—11 million people a year—and appears within 100 miles of 87 percent of the American population. Each of Ringling's 2 touring groups travels to more than 90 cities during a 2-year run.

Ringling presents a new show each year and arrives at approximately the same time in the same location to hometowns across America. This history, frequency, and consistency have made Ringling an enduring family tradition for many Americans.

In January 2001 Feld Entertainment, the world's largest producer of live family entertainment, created a campaign to update Ringling's brand and fine-tune its marketing after analyzing customers and the marketplace. To stimulate ticket sales, Ringling targeted both parents and children. The new campaign was launched in the New York City area on February 5, 2001, and included print, television, radio, outdoor, and transit advertising.

THRILL CHASING—EXTREME SPORTS

Growing numbers of people are participating in high-risk recreational activities. Young adults dominate the thrill seekers, but older people are jumping in as well. Skydiving, hang gliding, rock climbing, mountaineering, bungee jumping, white-water rafting, and other extreme sports are all showing huge increases in participation.

The U.S. Parachute Association (USPA) reports that its membership was over 34,000 at the end of 2001 and growing. Between 130,000 and 150,000 people skydive every year. The USPA reports that most sky divers are younger men, but the numbers of women and older people are growing rapidly; the 40-plus group is the fastest-growing. More than 25 percent of members are in their 40s, while nearly 12 percent are aged 50–59 and 3.5 percent are aged 60 and older.

The American Mountain Guides Association reports a membership of more than 1,000 in 2002, with steady growth. Mountain climbing has become so popular that getting away from the crowd can be difficult. Some mountain climbers have reported scaling remote peaks only to find other climbers there. Even on Mount Everest, the tallest mountain in the world, a number of teams might be active on the slopes at any one time. Participation is growing; and rock-climbing gyms have sprung up around the country. Women can excel at climbing because flexibility and balance can be more important in this sport than muscle bulk.

One explanation for the rising popularity of extreme sports is the heightened awareness of them created by the media. Movies and advertising often feature mountain climbers or sky divers in dramatic, breathtaking scenes. In addition, many participants report a life affirming "adrenaline rush," and some experts suggest that extreme sports enthusiasts enjoy the appearance of living on the edge. Impulsive, energetic, and eager to "break the rules," they long to perform extraordinary feats. Industry experts call these people "experiencers."

Easily bored and always seeking new thrills, advocates of extreme sports continue to search for new challenges. Skydiving now has new forms, including sky surfing, free flying, and aerial ballet, for those who think simply jumping from 15,000 feet is too easy. Bungee jumping now includes bridge, aerial, structure, and earth jumping.

Others believe that the improved safety of extreme sports as a result of technological advances and training has stimulated this growth. Equipment is well-engineered to ensure that bungee cords and parachutes are almost certainly not likely to fail; and modern sports medicine can prepare participants with conditioning programs and exercises and assist them in recovering after mishaps.

Selling Excitement

Advertisers of products such as sport utility vehicles (which are largely targeted to Generation Xers, who account for most experiencers), have discovered that they must sell excitement: their products must be perceived as fun items for "breaking the rules."

Sports manufacturing industry experts predict that the popularity of extreme sports will grow as young adults' earnings continue to rise. Furthermore, traditional obstacles to participation, such as gender and age, are rapidly disappearing because Americans remain physically active longer.

THE FUTURE OF OUTDOOR RECREATION

According to the middle-series projections of the U.S. Census Bureau, the total population of the United States will increase 54 percent between 1990 and 2050. Most of the growth, however, will be among the older ages and minorities, neither of which have historically high rates of participation in active sports. A rapidly increasing share of young adults will be black, Hispanic, or Asian. In general, minorities have less discretionary income than whites, especially older whites.

Steve Murdock of Texas A&M University, in *An American Challenge: Population Change and the Future of the United States* (1996), predicts that bird-watching is the only outdoor activity in which participation will increase faster than the rate of population growth. According to Murdock, walking, one of the most frequently enjoyed outdoor activities, will also likely increase by more than 50 percent. The participation of blacks, Hispanics, and other minorities will increase rapidly in every sport because these races will dominate younger cohorts who traditionally have the highest sports-participation rates. Young minorities, however, have fewer financial resources; and the slowest-growing sports, such as backpacking and tennis, appeal primarily to the young and affluent. In view of these demographic changes, the long-term status of any sport, Murdock contends, will likely depend on the number of minority participants.

CHAPTER 4
THE ARTS AND MEDIA

ATTENDING ARTS ACTIVITIES

More Americans are attending arts activities. The National Endowment for the Arts (NEA) *1997 Survey of Public Participation in the Arts* finds that half of the American adult population, or 97 million people, attended at least one of seven arts activities: jazz performances, classical music concerts, operas, musical plays, plays, ballets, or art museums. In contrast, in 1992 only 41 percent of adults participated in the arts.

Visiting art museums was a popular activity. An estimated 35 percent of adults visited an art museum at least once in the year preceding the survey, followed by musical plays (25 percent), nonmusical plays (16 percent), classical music concerts (16 percent), jazz performances (12 percent), ballets (6 percent), and operas (5 percent). (See Table 4.1.) The average person visited art museums more than three times a year, for a total of 225 million visits.

In addition, a number of related arts activities had high participation rates. Two-thirds of surveyed participants said they had read literature such as plays, poetry, and short stories, and nearly half had visited a historic park or arts and crafts fair. (See Table 4.2.)

In general, attendance at various arts events was highest among whites, except for jazz performances—which blacks attended in greater proportions—and opera and art museums, which drew a higher proportion of Asians. People between the ages of forty-five and fifty-four were

TABLE 4.1

Attendance at arts events, 1997

Arts activity	Persons		Attendances / visits	
	Percent of adults participating at least once in last 12 months	Number of adults attending/visiting in millions[1]	Average number of visits per attender	Total number of visits in millions
Attended				
Jazz performance	11.9%	23.3	3.1	72.2
Classical music	15.6	30.5	2.9	88.5
Opera performance	4.7	9.2	1.8	16.5
Musical play	24.5	47.9	2.2	105.4
Non-musical play	15.8	30.9	2.5	77.3
Ballet	5.8	11.3	1.7	19.3
Other dance[2]	12.4	24.3	2.6	63.1
Visited				
Art museum	34.9	68.3	3.3	225.3
Historic park	46.9	91.7	4.1	376.1
Art/craft fair	47.5	92.9	2.6	241.6
Read				
Literature[3]	63.1	123.4	NA[4]	NA[4]

[1] The number of attenders was computed by multiplying the attendance rate by 195.6 million: the U.S. resident noninstitutionalized population, 18 years of age and over in 1997.
[2] "Other dance" refers to dance other than ballet, including, for example, modern, folk and tap.
[3] "Literature" refers to reading plays, poetry, novels or short stories.
[4] No frequency information was obtained for reading literature.

SOURCE: Jack Faucett Associates, Inc., "Table 1. Attendance at Arts Events: 1997," in *1997 Survey of Public Participation in the Arts: Summary Report,* Research Division Note # 39, National Endowment for the Arts, Washington, DC, December 1998

TABLE 4.2

Attendance rates at arts events, by demographic group, 1997

(In percent. For persons 18 years old and over. Excludes elementary and high school performances. Based on the 1997 household survey Public Participation in the Arts. Data are subject to sampling error.)

Item	Attendance at least once in the prior 12 months at -								
	Jazz perfor-mance	Classical music perfor-mance	Opera	Musical play	Non-musical play	Ballet	Art museum	Historic park	Reading literature[1]
Total	12	16	5	25	16	6	35	47	63
Sex:									
Male	13	14	4	22	15	4	34	48	55
Female	11	17	5	27	17	8	36	46	71
Race:									
Hispanic	7	8	3	16	10	5	29	33	50
White	12	18	5	27	17	7	36	51	65
African American	16	10	2	22	16	4	31	37	60
American Indian	11	9	5	15	5	1	22	42	56
Asian	10	16	7	20	18	4	42	44	69
Age:									
18 to 24 years old	15	16	5	26	20	7	38	46	70
25 to 34 years old	13	11	4	23	13	5	37	49	61
35 to 44 years old	14	14	4	26	15	7	37	52	64
45 to 54 years old	13	20	6	29	20	7	40	54	66
55 to 64 years old	9	16	5	23	14	5	30	45	58
65 to 74 years old	8	18	4	24	15	5	28	37	59
75 years old and over	4	14	3	15	13	4	20	25	61
Education:									
Grade school	2	2	-	6	3	2	6	13	29
Some high school	3	4	2	13	7	2	14	27	46
High school graduate	7	8	2	16	9	4	25	41	58
Some college	15	18	5	28	19	7	43	56	72
College graduate	21	28	10	44	28	11	58	67	80
Graduate school	28	45	14	50	37	14	70	73	86
Income:									
$10,000 or less	5	4	2	12	10	2	16	23	45
$10,001 to $20,000	6	8	2	12	7	3	20	29	53
$20,001 to $30,000	8	10	2	17	10	4	26	39	62
$30,001 to $40,000	11	13	3	21	16	5	32	50	62
$40,001 to $50,000	11	15	5	23	15	6	37	52	64
$50,001 to $75,000	16	22	8	32	20	8	46	62	72
$75,001 to $100,000	23	26	6	41	27	10	55	65	75
Over $100,000	27	35	13	51	32	13	60	69	76

[1] Includes novels, short stories, poetry, or and plays.

SOURCE: Adapted from Jack Faucett Associates, Inc., "Table 2. Attendance Rates at Arts Events by Demographic Group: 1997," in *1997 Survey of Public Participation in the Arts: Summary Report,* Research Division Note # 70, National Endowment for the Arts, Washington, DC, December 1998

somewhat more likely to attend arts events. Higher levels of education and greater income were linked to greater participation and attendance at arts events. (See Table 4.2.)

The *Art Newspaper,* a London-based international monthly magazine, in its annual survey of visitors to art exhibitions in North America, Europe, and Australia, also reports that American art museums are experiencing a boom. The survey finds that "the keenest visitors" to art exhibits during 2000 were Americans. Not only were attendance figures high for museums in New York, Los Angeles, and Washington, D.C., but Boston, Atlanta, Seattle, and Chicago made the top twenty as well.

Free Admission Boosts Attendance at Big City Art Museums

By 2002, museum attendance declined in response to reduced tourism following the events of September 11,

2001, and growing economic uncertainty. The San Jose Museum of Art, located in California's Silicon Valley, chose a novel approach to boost attendance, which had leveled off at about 100,000 visitors annually. In June 2001 the museum eliminated its $7 admission fee, expressing its conviction that every member of the community should be able to attend the museum, regardless of income. One year after instituting the new policy, attendance doubled to 200,000, annual paid membership in the museum increased by 20 percent, and the museum's cafe sales tripled.

The new policy also produced changes in the profile of a typical museum visitor. Through 2000 annual surveys had characterized 75 percent of visitors as white, with women outnumbering men two to one. In 2002 just 50 percent of museum visitors were white, more men visited the museum, and more than 60 percent of museum-goers were first-time visitors, a 20 percent increase from prior years.

TABLE 4.3

Personal participation in the arts, 1997

Arts activity	Private and/or public performance/display		Public performance, display, or publication	
	% of adults doing at least once in last 12 months	Number of adults doing (millions)[1]	% of adults doing at least once in last 12 months	Number of adults doing (millions)[1]
Playing				
Jazz	2.2%	4.3	0.9%	1.8
Classical music	11.0	21.5	1.3	2.5
Singing				
Opera	1.8	3.5	0.3	0.6
Musicals	7.7	15.1	1.7	3.3
Choirs, chorale	NA[2]	NA[2]	10.4	20.3
Dancing				
Ballet	0.5	1.0	0.3	0.6
Other dance	12.6	24.6	2.0	3.9
Acting in non-musical plays	NA[2]	NA[2]	2.7	5.3
Painting/drawing	15.9	31.1	2.9	5.7
Pottery	15.1	29.5	2.4	4.7
Weaving	27.6	54.0	2.7	5.3
Buying art	35.1	68.7	NA[3]	NA[3]
Photography	16.6	32.6	2.3	4.5
Creative writing	12.1	23.7	1.2	2.3
Composing music	3.7	7.2	1.3	2.6

[1] The number of personal participants was computed by multiplying the participation rate by 195.6 million: the U.S. resident noninstitutionalized population, 18 years of age and over.

[2] For these activities, questions were only asked about public performances.

[3] For this activity only questions about "doing" were asked.

SOURCE: Jack Faucett Associates, Inc., "Table 18. Participation in the Arts Via Personal Performance and Creation: 1997," in *1997 Survey of Public Participation in the Arts: Summary Report,* National Endowment for the Arts, Washington, DC, December 1998

Museum director Daniel Keegan considered it a calculated risk to eliminate admission fees, which had generated $200,000 per year for the museum, when the Silicon Valley's economy was at its lowest point. Still, the risk paid off in terms of building a stronger audience and financial support for the museum and may inspire other art museums to consider reducing or eliminating admission fees.

Creating Art

The NEA study also asked respondents about their *doing* of art—that is, personally performing or creating art. The study reveals that the highest rates of personal participation were in photography (17 percent), painting/drawing (16 percent), dance other than ballet (13 percent), creative writing (12 percent), and classical music (11 percent). The survey finds that more than 10 percent of the adult population sang publicly in a choir, chorus, or other ensemble. The lowest rates of participation were in jazz and opera (2 percent each) and in ballet (less than 1 percent). (See Table 4.3.) These low rates were not unexpected since these disciplines are demanding and require extensive training.

Whites and Asians (12 percent each) were more likely to play classical music than Native Americans (9 percent), blacks (8 percent), or Hispanics (7 percent). Greater percentages of blacks bought artwork (43 percent) and sang in groups (26 percent) than Asians (19 percent bought artwork and 9 percent sang in groups), whites (36 percent bought artwork and 8 percent sang in groups), or Hispanics (33 percent bought artwork and 7 percent sang in groups). Native Americans pursued modern dancing (21 percent), pottery (25 percent), and photography (28 percent) more than other races. Asians outnumbered other races in creative writing (21 percent) and drawing (27 percent). In general, active participation in creative artistic endeavors declined with age.

Spending on Art Activities

In addition to increased participation in the arts, Americans are spending more on the arts. According to data released by the Bureau of Economic Analysis, a division of the U.S. Department of Commerce, Americans spent $14.9 billion on admissions to performing arts events in 2001. This included admissions to both nonprofit and for-profit organizations, such as movies, theater, and concerts.

THEATER, CONCERTS, AND OPERAS

Before there were movies, television, and radio, there was live theater. The first American theater, with actors, scenery, and numerous play productions, came to the American colonies from England in 1750. By the beginning of the nineteenth century, every major city had at least one theater company performing plays.

Taking the Show on the Road

As the American population grew and spread westward, so did the number of theaters. From New York City, the leading theater center, hundreds of theater companies took their performers on the road to bring entertainment to new settlers all across the country. Until the early 1900s, the theater—which included opera, drama, comedy, and musical shows—was America's principal form of entertainment. An original American theater type was the showboat, which sailed up and down the Mississippi River entertaining passengers, the gamblers who made a living on the river, and the residents of the towns where the boats docked.

Broadway

The modern period on Broadway began in New York City with the founding of the Theater Guild in 1918. It was the first commercially successful art theater to produce plays of the same caliber and quality as those produced in Europe. Other theaters soon opened and they prospered right up to the stock market crash of 1929. The nation recovered from the Great Depression that followed, but theater did not, because more and more people were going to see motion pictures or staying home to listen to the radio or, later, watching television or renting movies.

It has become extraordinarily expensive to put on a Broadway show. In some instances, the extravagant sets and breathtaking special effects overshadow the play. For example, the show *Sunset Boulevard,* involved two separate stages, and in *Miss Saigon,* a real helicopter lands on the stage. The costs involved in staging a successful theatrical performance on Broadway have become prohibitive. As a result, fewer and fewer shows are produced on Broadway. Financial backers, concerned about minimizing their risks, appear more willing to finance revivals of shows that were successful in years past or stage plays drawn from movies. Examples of recent revivals include classics such as *Kiss Me Kate* and *The Music Man,* as well as revivals of more recent fare such as Lily Tomlin's one-woman show *The Search for Signs of Intelligent Life in the Universe* and *The Rocky Horror Show.*

Thirty-nine venues are designated as Broadway theaters. In 1980 there were sixty-one new Broadway shows, by 1991 just twenty-eight new shows had started, and in 1996 thirty-eight shows opened. At the beginning of 2003, there were thirty-two shows playing on Broadway: seventeen dramas, twelve comedies, one variety show, one musical comedy/drama, and a classical production. In 1996, 9.5 million people spent $436 million to see the shows on Broadway. During the fourth quarter of 2001, the September 11 terrorist attacks on New York City sharply curtailed tourism and theater attendance, producing a temporary, but dramatic 70 percent decline in box office sales.

Nonprofit Theater

According to the Theatre Communications Group's (TCG) annual report *Theatre Facts 2001,* about 363 nonprofit theater companies operated in the United States in 2001, up from 228 in 1996. Theater groups included ensembles, touring companies, children's theater, and small companies. During 2001 they held 81,828 performances of 4,787 different productions: the classics, modern plays, musicals, new plays by American and foreign playwrights, experimental works, and plays aimed at young audiences. In 1980, 14.2 million people attended nonprofit theater productions, in 1994, 20.7 million attended, and in 2001, 21 million attended.

The TCG report, compiled before September 11, 2001, observes that the U.S. economic recession had affected the bottom lines of American nonprofit theaters. Still, nonprofit theaters contributed $923 million to the U.S. economy, employed more than 55,000 people, and attracted more than 12.8 million patrons.

Going to Concerts and Operas

Research conducted by Audience Insight for 15 orchestras and the John S. and James L. Knight Foundation find that in 2002 just 17 percent of adults in the United States reported that they had attended a live classical music performance. Americans attended classical music concerts in a variety of settings, including traditional concert halls (21 percent), school auditoriums and gymnasiums (15 percent), churches and synagogues (14 percent), and outdoor venues (13 percent).

Although less than 4 percent of Americans attend opera performances each year, opera audiences increased by nearly 30 percent between 1980 and 2000 and opera has been the only performing art that has significantly increased its market share (18 percent) of young adults age 18 to 24. In 2000 North America's professional opera companies offered 2,153 performances of 413 fully staged productions and gave 16 world premier performances. According to OPERA America, the 10 most frequently produced North American operas during the 2001–2002 season were: *Little Women, Candide, Of Mice and Men, Porgy and Bess, Susannah, Amahl and the Night Visitors, Street Scene, A Streetcar Named Desire, Dead Man Walking,* and *Therese Raquin.*

MEDIA USAGE

Media experiences have become a part of the fabric of modern life. In their work and personal lives, Americans are bombarded with images and sounds that convey insistent and powerful messages. According to communications expert Marshall McLuhan, the medium is the message, and each medium presents a different type of experience. Listening to music on a compact disc (CD) player is unlike watching television, playing a video game, surfing the Internet, or reading a book.

Multiple contacts with the media are inescapable aspects of daily life. Televisions flicker in kitchens, living rooms, dens, and bedrooms. Children are mesmerized by video game competitions, and families use the computer to budget, bank, and send e-mail, as well as to surf the Internet and make purchases. Music flows from radios, CD players, and tape recorders, while cell phones and pagers connect people to one another and the Internet. Media influence is growing along with the time Americans devote to it.

Americans devote much time to the media, which includes television, radio, recorded music, newspapers, books, magazines, videos/DVDs for rent or purchase, movies in theaters, video games, and online computer services. In general, the less costly a form of consumer media, the greater the media usage. Since broadcast TV and radio are free to consumers, they are the most widely used media, followed by subscription video services, recorded music, and online services. The most expensive media on an hourly basis are movies in theaters and videos/DVDs for rent or purchase.

Veronis, Suhler and Associates, a media industry analyst, predicted that in 2003 Americans would spend nearly 10 hours per day taking in various forms of media, about a half-hour more each day than they devoted to it in 1998. The Internet was anticipated to account for less than 6 percent of the total time spent on media use, and the analysts contended that Internet use would stimulate and reinforce use of other media such as television, recorded music, movies, and books.

Veronis, Suhler and Associates projected that consumer media spending would rise at about 8.2 percent from $118.2 billion in 1998 to $174.9 billion in 2003. Total U.S. spending on media would be about $663.3 billion, and communications, the second fastest-growing industry, would overtake food to become the sixth largest industry in the United States. In 2003 Americans would likely spend more on media than they did on food.

MOVING PICTURES—THE BIRTH OF AN INDUSTRY

In 1891 Thomas Alva Edison, the American inventor best known for the electric light bulb and phonograph, or talking machine, applied for a patent on a "kinetoscopic camera." This camera took motion pictures on a band of film that could be seen by looking or "peeping" into a box, which gave these early pictures the name "peep shows." This invention soon gave rise to movie projectors and screens. In 1893 Edison and his partner, W. K. L. Dickson, built the Black Maria, the first movie studio.

As the United States entered the twentieth century, inventions such as the automobile, radio, telephone, and airplane were beginning to change the way people lived. While not everyone could afford all the modern wonders, almost anyone could pay the price of a ticket to see "mov-

ing pictures" wherever there was a theater and a piano. (The first motion pictures were "silent movies." They had no sound and the actors' words were printed on the screen so the audience could follow the plot. A piano player provided background music to make the movie more exciting.)

The first "blockbuster" movie, *The Birth of a Nation* (also known as *The Clansman*), was released in 1915 and concerned the American Civil War (1861-1865) and the beginnings of the Ku Klux Klan. The film was controversial because some Americans considered it to be racist. World War I (1914-1918) gave filmmakers spectacles that audiences wanted to see, and the American Film Institute Catalog lists 1,175 war films made during that time. The first "talking picture" was 1927's *The Jazz Singer*. The years following World War I were periods of financial growth for the United States, and this prosperity helped the motion picture industry become successful. By the mid-1920s, some 20,000 movie theaters were showing moving pictures in the United States, twice the number of theaters as in 1910.

Movie Business Boom

Motion pictures remained one of America's favorite pastimes throughout the 1930s and 1940s. By 1950 television had become the new developing technology. As televisions grew in popularity, fewer people went to the movies. Weekly movie attendance dropped from about 90 million people in 1947 to an average of 42 million in the 1950s and 1960s. Gross sales fell from an all-time record high of $1.5 billion in 1957 to a yearly average of $1.2 billion in the 1950s and rose only slightly in the 1960s.

To respond to the threat of television, movie producers in the 1950s introduced various types of three-dimensional (3-D) movies to lure people to the movies. Special glasses had to be worn for 3-D movies to make it seem like figures "jumped off" the screen.

In 1945 some 20,355 movie theaters existed; by 1960 that number had dwindled to 11,300. However, 4,700 drive-in movies were built during the 1950s. These outdoor theaters meant families could drive up to speakers and view the movies on giant screens while sitting in the comfort of their own cars. Drive-ins solved baby-sitting problems for parents and were so popular they accounted for 25 percent of movie attendance in the 1950s. As suburbs spread out and property became more expensive, theater companies started to build multiplexes—theaters that could show many movies at the same time. The number of drive-ins began to fall. By 1971 the number of drive-ins had fallen to 3,720, and by 2001 just 663 remained in the whole country.

Personal movie theater attendance remained relatively constant during the 1990s, at about 12 hours per person per year. Consumer spending on movies in theaters rose

TABLE 4.4

Admission receipts for spectator events, 1993–98

	1998 $billions		1997 $billions		1996 $billions		1995 $billions		1994 $billions		1993 $billions	
	Nominal	Real	Nominal	Real	Nominal	Real	Nominal	Real	Nominal	Real	Nominal	Real
Admission receipts to specified entertainments	$88.05	$83.61	$82.92	$80.67	$78.06	$78.06	$73.07	$76.87	$69.92	$76.87	$67.90	$76.43
Performing arts	$34.78	$32.93	$32.49	$31.37	$30.17	$30.17	$28.92	$30.45	$27.66	$29.97	$26.38	$29.87
Motion pictures	$25.16	$24.05	$23.90	$23.16	$21.87	$21.87	$20.93	$22.07	$19.98	$21.90	$19.40	$21.73
Spectator sports	$28.12	$26.64	$26.52	$25.77	$26.02	$26.02	$23.21	$24.36	$22.28	$24.20	$22.11	$24.44

Note: "Real" refers to estimates that are measured in 1996 chained dollars to control for inflation.

SOURCE: "Table 1. Admission Receipts for Performing Arts Events, Motion Pictures, and Spectator Sports: 1993–1998," in *The Arts in the GDP: Consumers Spent $9.4 Billion on Admission Receipts for Performing Arts Events in 1998*, Research Division Note # 75, National Endowment for the Arts, Washington, DC, March 2000

slightly from $19.4 billion in 1993 to $25.2 billion in 1998. (See Table 4.4.) Like spectator sports and the performing arts, motion picture admissions have increased consistently but modestly since 1987.

According to the Motion Picture Association of America (MPAA), total U.S. box office grosses have climbed slowly but steadily, although 2001 receipts of $8.41 billion were 9.8 percent higher than 2000 box office grosses of $7.66 billion. The increased revenues were largely attributable to increased admissions, but increased admission prices—the average ticket price rose more than 25 percent from 1991 to 2001—also contributed.

During 2002 ticket sales reached a record $9.37 billion as Americans sought to escape real world political, economic, and personal woes by watching big screen adventures. The top movie of 2002, *Spider-Man*, earned 17 percent of box office receipts for a total of $405.7 million.

Moviegoers

According to a 2001 Gallup poll, two-thirds of Americans had attended at least one movie during the 12 months preceding the poll. Eighty-six percent of young adults, persons age 18 to 29, had gone to the movies an average of 8 times. Adults age 30 to 49 were also frequent moviegoers—nearly three-quarters had attended four movies. In contrast, just one-third of older adults (age 65 and older) said they had attended a movie.

Stars Attract Moviegoers

A 2001 Gallup poll also finds that more than half of American moviegoers make a special effort to see films featuring their favorite actors. Moviemakers have learned that a particular celebrity's name alone can sharply affect movie attendance and box office receipts. Julia Roberts, Tom Cruise, and Brad Pitt are popular among adult moviegoers age 18 to 29, while Roberts, Tom Hanks, Mel Gibson, and Harrison Ford draw viewers age 50 to 64. (See Table 4.5.)

VIDEOCASSETTE RECORDERS (VCRs) AND DIGITAL VIDEODISC (DVD) PLAYERS

Some industry experts believed that videocassette recorders (VCRs) and digital videodisc (DVD) players, which make it so easy to watch movies at home, would hurt movie box office sales more than television. Many others thought that they would make more money for a film. Moviemakers now know that if a movie makes money at the box office, it will also make money in video/DVD sales/rentals. In fact, sometimes a movie that is not expected to do well in movie theaters will be released directly to video, where it may generate considerable revenue from rentals and purchases. Video/DVD sales have become just as important as domestic and foreign sales to the financial success of a film.

Research conducted by the Consumer Electronics Association (CEA) reveals that by June 2000, 94 percent of U.S. households had VCRs and 22 percent had TV/VCR combinations. Almost 30 percent of households had DVD players, up from just 7 percent two years earlier. (See Table 2.5 in Chapter 2.) A 2001 Gallup poll reports that nearly one-quarter of Americans owned both a VCR and DVD player.

A 2001 Gallup poll also finds that watching movies at home was an increasingly popular way for Americans to spend an evening. Eighty-three percent of all polled respondents and 88 percent of those who owned a VCR or DVD player said they had viewed a movie at home during the month preceding the poll. Nearly all (96 percent) young adults age 18 to 29 reported viewing an average of almost 13 movies per month at home. More than 90 percent of adults age 30 to 49 watched movies at home, but on average they watched about half as many as the younger adults. Rates of home movie viewing as well as the average number of films viewed per month declined with advancing age.

TELEVISION

Television has defined two generations of consumers. It does not, however, possess the unifying power it once had. A TV watcher in decades past could tune in to comedian Milton Berle or the *Gunsmoke* (western) series and know he or she was sharing the moment with nearly every other American. Today, people have many more choices, including cable TV, satellite TV, pay per view, rented videos and DVDs, and computers. The American viewing audience has become fragmented.

A 2000 CEA survey finds that virtually all U.S. households have at least one television and three-quarters of all households have more than one. Nielsen Media Research estimated that by the end of 2002 there would be 106.7 million TV-owning households in the United States, up from 1.2 million in 2001.

Television endures as the most used form of media, which also includes videos/DVDs, radio, CDs/tapes, magazines, newspapers, books, and personal computers/Internet. In 2000 Americans watched more television than ever before—approximately 4.4 hours per day, which tallies to 2 full months of television per year. Many Americans leave the television on even when they are not watching it. During a typical day, the television in American households is on an average of seven hours and forty minutes. Because so many Americans have the television, more than $45 billion is spent each year by TV advertisers.

Although watching television ranked as the second-most popular activity among Americans age 16 and older according to a 2001 survey, when survey respondents were asked how they spent their leisure time the previous day, more than one-third (34.4 percent) reported watching television. TV viewing habits vary by age. While a 2001 Gallup poll finds that more than one-quarter of all respondents named TV viewing as their favorite way to spend an evening, more older adults preferred television. One-third of persons age 50 to 64 and 38 percent of those older than 65 favored watching television, compared to just 16 percent of adults age 18 to 29 and 23 percent of those age 30 to 49. (See Table 1.1 in Chapter 1.)

Effect of the Internet on TV Viewing

There are conflicting opinions about the effect of Internet use on TV viewing. Some data suggest that Americans online view less television, and other data that indicate they may have more time to spend watching television. A 1999 study by the Stanford Institute for the Qualitative Study of Society finds that 60 percent of Internet users said that the Internet had reduced their TV viewing. One-third said that it had reduced the amount of time they spent reading the newspaper. A Nielsen Media Research study conducted during the same year, however, finds only about a 10 percent reduction in the number of hours a television was on in an Internet household, compared to a non-Internet household. During prime time (Monday through Saturday, 8 P.M. to 11 P.M., and Sunday

TABLE 4.5

Actors/actresses Americans make a special effort to see, March 2001

18–to 29–year–olds	%
1. Julia Roberts	24
2. Tom Cruise (tie)	9
2. Brad Pitt (tie)	9
30–to 49–year–olds	**%**
1. Julia Roberts	26
2. Mel Gibson	16
3. Tom Hanks	15
50–to 64–year–olds	**%**
1. Julia Roberts	34
2. Tom Hanks	17
3. Mel Gibson (tie)	9
3. Harrison Ford (tie)	9
Those 65 and older	**%**
1. Julia Roberts	32
2. Tom Hanks (tie)	10
2. George Clooney (tie)	10

SOURCE: Joseph Carroll and Jeffrey M. Jones, "Actors/Actresses Americans Make Special Effort to See," in "Julia Roberts Is Top Current Movie Star, While John Wayne Is All-time Favorite," The Gallup Organization, March 23, 2001 www.gallup.com © 2001 The Gallup Organization, all rights reserved. Reprinted with permission.

7 P.M. to 11 P.M.), there was little difference between Internet and non-Internet households.

Veronis, Suhler and Associates observed that the projected 192 hours per year Americans would devote to Internet use in 2003 was just a fraction of the 1,610 hours they would spend watching television or the 992 hours spent listening to the radio. They forecasted that the time saved using the Internet to perform tasks such as banking, paying bills, and shopping would free up additional hours Americans could devote to other media including television.

Cable and Satellite TV

Cable TV subscribers pay a monthly fee to cable companies to receive not only regular broadcast channels, but also such specialized channels as MTV and VH-1 (music video channels), Nickelodeon (a children's channel), and ESPN (a sports channel). Cable TV subscribers who choose to pay more can also see the latest movies on such premium channels as HBO or Showtime. For the first time, in 1995 basic cable channels drew slightly more total viewers than the three biggest networks (ABC, CBS, and NBC) in homes that had cable. During prime-time hours, however, the major networks still attracted more viewers than the cable channels.

According to a 1999 Nielsen Media Research study, three-quarters of Americans had access to cable or satellite TV. The average home with a cable or satellite system was able to receive 57 channels. People who subscribed to premium services watched, on average, 15 hours per week more television than people who did not subscribe to premium services.

NEWS VIEWERSHIP—REMOTE CONTROL IN HAND

The average American dedicates more than an hour a day to the news. More people read, watch, or listen to the news than exercise or use a personal computer. Although Americans are reading, listening to, and watching the news as often as in the past, technological change and the news climate have affected the way they get their news and information. Fewer and fewer people are watching network broadcasts for news coverage. A 2000 Pew Research Center study finds that Americans were increasingly turning off TV network and local news broadcasts in favor of Internet news coverage. (See Figure 1.1 in Chapter 1.) The proportion of Americans seeking news online tripled from 1995 to 2000.

The number of people watching cable news coverage now approximates the audience for network programming, with nearly half of Americans regularly watching cable news, compared to 57 percent who view network news. The size of the cable news audience swells to 60 percent when specialty programs, such as the Weather Channel and ESPN's Sports Center, are included.

Cable's advantage lies in its immediacy. Americans said they would turn to cable channels first in the event of a major news story. Less than half of Americans only follow national news when a major news event is occurring, and 63 percent react the same way to international news. Only local news attracts a large regular audience that is not event-driven—61 percent of Americans follow it most of the time. The percentage of Americans who viewed only network and local TV news fell from 30 percent in 1993 to 12 percent in 2000.

The Weather Channel and ESPN are very popular. Fully 33 percent of the public watched the Weather Channel regularly, and another 27 percent watched sometimes. Of adults, 20 percent watched ESPN sports regularly.

HOME ELECTRONICS PRODUCTS

America's love affair with consumer electronics shows no sign of waning. Cellular phones and pagers; digital cameras and camcorders; cordless phones; large-screen, flat panel, projection, and high-definition TV sets; mobile navigation devices; and home security systems are high on the wish lists of many Americans.

Americans cannot get enough of consumer electronics. The CEA forecasted that sales of consumer electronics would reach a record $99.5 billion in 2003, up 3.5 percent from 2002. Sales in 2002 of $96.2 billion were 3.7 percent higher than 2001 sales and exceeded the CEA's initial projections.

The CEA credits digital products such as digital televisions (DTVs) and displays as driving industry growth.

More than 2.6 million DTVs were sold in 2002 and by the end of 2003, consumers were expected to spend more than $15 billion on DTV products. Flat panel, plasma, and liquid crystal display TV sales rose in 2002 and were projected to grow as much as 40 percent in 2003. Digital audio sales were also strong, with sales of MP3 players up 56 percent over 2001. Digital camera sales totaled $2.9 billion in 2002 and were projected to rise by more than 25 percent in 2003.

The number of wireless telephone subscribers has skyrocketed, according to the Cellular Telecommunication Industry Association. The CEA predicted that sales of wireless telephones would grow to 6 percent in 2003 to 60 million units, representing $8.8 billion worth of sales.

Sales of personal computers were also expected to rise in 2003 in response to a consumer need to upgrade older systems to accommodate new digital media requirements. The electronic gaming market was forecasted to grow by 17 percent from $9.2 billion in 2002 to more than $12 billion in 2003. Home security systems also projected sales growth of 7 percent from $1.9 billion in 2002 to $2.1 billion in 2003.

RECORDED MUSIC

Americans are the heaviest purchasers of recorded music in the world. The Recording Industry Association of America, a trade association, reports that the total U.S. dollar value of audio recordings grew from $9 billion in 1992 to $13.7 billion in 2001. The dollar value increased every year during the decade, except in 1997 when it decreased slightly compared to 1996 figures and again in 2000 when it dipped slightly from 1999.

In 2001 the most popular category of music was rock, at 24.4 percent. Nonetheless, the popularity of rock has steadily declined since 1995 when 33.5 percent of audio recording consumers purchased rock music. During the same period, interest in country music waned from 16.7 percent in 1995 to 10.5 percent in 2001.

Other categories of music experienced modest growth. Pop music increased by 2 percent between 1995 to 2001, and rap/hip-hop nearly doubled its share of the market rising from 6.7 percent in 1995 to 11.4 percent in 2001. Religious music also more than doubled its market share from 3.1 percent in 1995 to 6.7 percent in 2001. Most other categories were relatively stable throughout the period with the exception of "other"—spoken word, exercise, humor, ethnic, and other types of audio recordings, which increased from 5.4 percent in 1992 to 7.9 percent in 2001.

The form in which Americans purchased music also changed. In 1992 most audio recordings purchased were CDs (46.5 percent) or cassette tapes (43.6 percent). By 2001 cassette purchases had dropped to 3.4 percent. CDs became the format of choice, rising to 89.2 percent in

2001. Sales figures comparing the first half of 2002 with the same period during 2001 reveal that DVDs were the only recording that significantly increased both in units sold and the dollar value of the sales.

Americans over age 45 made almost one-quarter (23.7 percent) of audio recording purchases in 2001, more than twice as many as they made in 1992. The growth in this age group may reflect the enduring interest in music of the aging baby boomer generation. In contrast, young people, once considered the recording industry's strongest supporters, comprised a declining proportion of the market for recordings. Purchases made by consumers age 15 through 19 dropped from 18.2 percent in 1992 to 13 percent in 2001, and among young adults age 20 to 24 the percent of consumers dropped from 16.1 percent in 1992 to 12.2 percent in 2001.

Americans no longer rely as much on record stores to supply their music. In 1992 nearly six out of ten music purchases were made in record stores. By 2001 only 42.5 percent of purchases were made in record stores. More than 40 percent of music purchases were made in stores other than record stores. Only a small percentage of people (2.9 percent) purchased music over the Internet during 2001, but that may reflect the widespread practice of online users sharing and downloading music files or copying CDs without having to purchase the recordings.

During the 1990s gender differences in music purchasing varied little from year to year. In 1992 more music purchases (52.6 percent) were by males. In 2001 females (51.2 percent) made more purchases than males (48.8 percent).

THE INTERNET, CONNECTIVITY, AND CONVERGENCE

An explosion in digital technology coupled with growth of the Internet has combined to produce breathtaking possibilities for media experiences. It is now possible to move seamlessly from one medium to another in the same delivery platform—televisions or personal computers. Along with computer and TV access to the Internet, consumers can gain access via cellular telephones and an expanding array of handheld devices, including personal digital assistants (PDAs).

The recent study *Internet 9: The Media and Entertainment World of Online Consumers,* conducted by Arbitron Edison Research in July 2002, looks at practices and preferences of online consumers. The survey finds that about 83 million Americans, 35 percent of the population over age 12, have on at least one occasion accessed streaming media—that is, listened to audio or watched video online. These online consumers are known as "streamies."

Streamies tend to be male (57 percent) and 43 percent were between the ages of 25 to 44. Nearly three-quarters were white and more than half reported an income in excess of $50,000 per year. Streamies spent an average of two hours and fifty-six minutes per day watching television, two hours and forty-four minutes listening to radio, one hour and fifty minutes accessing the Internet, and thirty minutes reading the newspaper.

Among those who watched streaming video, the most frequently viewed types of content were movie trailers or previews (62 percent), music videos (52 percent), online video weather forecasts (35 percent), video newscasts (35 percent), online video from TV stations (31 percent), and short- or full-length movies (30 percent). Audio users primarily listened to radio station Web casts.

The study also finds that despite a slowing economy, during the 18 months preceding the survey, consumers had flocked to high-speed Internet connections via residential broadband (cable modem or digital subscriber line). Residential broadband Internet access grew to 28 percent, up from 13 percent just 18 months earlier. Consumers with high-speed connections, as opposed to slower dial-up connections, viewed Internet access as much more essential for the activities of their daily life. They also were more inclined to access streaming media, especially video Web casts, than consumers with slower connections.

While the study finds that television (39 percent) and radio (26 percent) are still deemed "most essential" in the lives of more Americans than the Internet (20 percent), the researchers maintain that it is remarkable that such a new medium is already considered "most essential" by one out of five Americans. The higher the educational attainment of consumers, the more essential the Internet was to them. Just 8 percent of persons with a high school education or less said the Internet was "most essential," compared to 30 percent of persons with a college degree.

Children, teens, and young adults viewed the Internet as vitally important to their life. Thirty-four percent of persons age 12 to 24 cited the Internet as "most essential" to their life, more than television (30 percent) and radio (27 percent).

Internet Access—The Digital Divide

Opinions differ about how demographic factors affect access to the Internet. The report from the U.S. Department of Commerce *Falling Through the Net: Defining the Digital Divide* uses data collected by the U.S. Census Bureau between 1997 and 1998 from 48,000 households across the United States. The report finds that people with college degrees were more than 16 times as likely to have Internet access at home as persons with only an elementary education.

High-income households in urban areas were 20 times as likely to have Internet access as low-income, rural households. In low-income households, the report finds, children in white families were three times as likely as children in black households, and four times more likely than children in Hispanic households, to have Internet access.

A 1999 study by the Stanford Institute for the Qualitative Study of Society, however, reaches different conclusions. The Stanford researchers find that income, race, ethnicity, and gender have a statistically insignificant effect on access. The most important factors affecting Internet access, according to the study, were age and education. For example, the study finds that a college education increased rates of Internet access by more than 40 percentage points, compared to the least educated group.

Similarly, a drop of more than 40 percentage points in rate of Internet access was seen for people over age 65, compared to people less than 25 years old.

A more recent study conducted in January 2002 by Arbitron Edison Research suggests that the digital divide is narrowing. More than two-thirds (67 percent) of blacks had Internet access in January 2002, up from 51 percent the previous year. During the same one-year period, the percentage of Hispanics with Internet access rose from 43 percent to 57 percent. The survey also finds that blacks and Hispanics who were online were more likely to access streaming media than whites.

CHAPTER 5

FOOTBALL, BASEBALL, BASKETBALL, AND OTHER POPULAR SPORTS

Americans love sports, and most children grow up playing team and individual sports during their physical education programs at school and simply for pleasure. Many men have played baseball or softball at some time in their lives, and some continue to play in community or neighborhood leagues long after they are finished with school. Today, women are playing sports once played mainly by men, such as soccer, baseball, and basketball. Many men and increasing numbers of women are sports fans.

SPECTATOR SPORTS

Historically, football, baseball, and basketball have been called the "holy trinity" of sports in the United States. They make money not only by filling ballparks and arenas with fans, but also from televised sports events. The start of each new sports season brings hope to millions of sports fans that their teams will be in the championship games at the end of the season. These sports also fill stadiums with fans to watch middle school, high school, and collegiate competitions as well as professional games.

A survey conducted by *USA Today* finds that Americans' favorite spectator sports in 2002 were the National Football League (21.2 percent), Major League Baseball (12.6 percent), the National Basketball Association (NBA) (10 percent), college football (6.3 percent), and college basketball (5.3 percent). For purposes of the survey, spectator sports were defined as those that people attended, watched on television, listened to on the radio, or read about in the media.

In 2002 the Gallup Organization analyzed Americans' spectator sports preferences to determine if their favorite sports to watch had changed from 1994 to 2001. With the exception of a resurgence of interest reported by respondents to a November 1998 poll, enthusiasm for two of the top three spectator sports—football and baseball—steadi-

ly declined throughout the period. The proportion of respondents that named football as their favorite sport to watch dropped from 35 percent in 1994 to 28 percent in 2001. Nine percent fewer respondents cited baseball as their favorite sport in 2001 than the 21 percent that favored it in 1994. (See Table 5.1.)

Of the top three, only basketball had experienced measurable gains among spectators. The proportion of respondents that said basketball was their favorite spectator sport increased from 11 percent in 1994 to 16 percent in 2001, with just one drop in popularity from 1997 to 1998. Other spectator sports that grew in popularity included auto racing and golf. (See Table 5.1.)

In 2001 about 66 million people attended Major League Baseball games. In the NBA, the Philadelphia 76ers set 2002 attendance records by drawing crowds in excess of 20,000 for each of the team's 41 home contests. The 76ers' attendance jumped from 756,929 during the 1999–2000 season to 842,976 in the 2001–2002 season, with many fans coming out to see Allen Iverson, who some fans consider to be among the most exciting basketball players in recent history.

Even more (29.4 million) went to see National Collegiate Athletic Association (NCAA) men's college basketball, and 9.5 million cheered for women's college basketball. More than 20 million fans attended hockey games in the 2000–2001 season.

In 2002 millions of fans around the country watched the Super Bowl victory of the New England Patriots over the St. Louis Rams in one of the country's biggest media events: Super Bowl Sunday. While televised viewing of football may have declined slightly, the proportion of Americans who consider themselves fans has not. In fact, the percent of self-described football fans increased from 56 percent of respondents to a March 1999 Gallup poll to 63 percent just two years later in March 2001.

TABLE 5.1

Public opinion on favorite sports to watch, 1994–2001

QUESTION: WHAT IS YOUR FAVORITE SPORT TO WATCH?

	2001 Mar	2000 Mar	1998 Nov	1997 Apr[1]	1995 Apr	1994 Sep	1994 Aug
	%	%	%	%	%	%	%
Football	28	33	36	30	32	37	35
Basketball	16	16	12	17	15	13	11
Baseball	12	13	16	14	16	16	21
Auto racing	6	5	3	7	2	2	2
Golf	4	5	3	5	4	3	3
Ice/figure skating	4	4	2	2	2	3	3
Ice hockey	3	5	3	3	3	1	3
Soccer	2	2	2	2	1	2	2
Tennis	2	1	2	2	2	3	2
Boxing	2	2	1	2	1	1	1
Gymnastics	1	1	1	1	0	0	*
Motocross	1	—	—	—	—	—	—
Wrestling	1	1	1	1	1	*	1
Volleyball	1	—	—	—	—	—	—
Bowling	*	*	1	*	1	*	*
Fishing	*	*	1	*	1	*	*
Swimming	*	*	—	—	—	—	—
Horse racing	—	—	*	1	0	0	*
OTHER	4	3	6	6	7	5	5
NONE	12	8	9	6	10	12	10
No Opinion	1	1	1	1	2	2	1
	100	100	100	100	100	100	100

*Less than 0.5%
[1]WORDING: What is your favorite sport to follow?

TABLE 5.2

Public opinion on favorite national sporting events to attend, January 15-16, 2000

QUESTION: WHICH OF THE FOLLOWING MAJOR NATIONAL SPORTING EVENTS WOULD YOU MOST LIKE TO GET A TICKET TO — [ROTATED: PRO-FOOTBALL'S SUPER BOWL, BASEBALL'S WORLD SERIES, HOCKEY'S STANLEY CUP FINALS, COLLEGE BASKETBALL'S MEN'S FINALS, PRO-BASKETBALL'S NBA FINALS, (OR) THE COLLEGE FOOTBALL BOWL GAME THAT DETERMINES THE NATIONAL CHAMPION]?

Based on National Adults	2000 Jan 15-16
Pro-Football's Super Bowl	34
Baseball's World Series	20
Hockey's Stanley Cup Finals	7
College Basketball's Men's Finals	11
Pro-Basketball's NBA Finals	11
The College Football Bowl game that determines the national champion	10
No opinion	7

Based on — 613 — Sports Fans; ±4 Pct. Pts.	2000 Jan 15-16
Pro-Football's Super Bowl	40
Baseball's World Series	18
Hockey's Stanley Cup Finals	7
College Basketball's Men's Finals	13
Pro-Basketball's NBA Finals	10
The College Football Bowl game that determines the national champion	11
No opinion	1

Furthermore, a 2002 Gallup poll reveals that professional football's Super Bowl was the sports event Americans would most like to attend. Among surveyed adults, 34 percent said they would prefer Super Bowl tickets to other sports events and 40 percent of sports fans named the Super Bowl as the national sporting event they would most like to see. Baseball's World Series was the second most sought-after sports event, with 20 percent of all surveyed adults and 18 percent of sports fans choosing it as the event they would most like to attend. (See Table 5.2.)

Professional Wrestling—Is It a Sport?

Professional wrestling enjoyed an increase in popularity in the 1990s. A 1999 Gallup poll finds that almost two out of ten Americans (18 percent) considered themselves wrestling fans. Wrestling is no longer limited to regular professional wrestling TV shows. The World Wrestling Federation and World Championship Wrestling make millions of dollars every year from televised pay-per-view events.

Wrestling fans tended to be males with a high school education who earned less than $30,000 per year. The percentage of wrestling fans who were more than 30 years of age or who had a college education was very low. Of blacks, 39 percent considered themselves to be wrestling fans, compared to 16 percent of whites.

Professional wrestling is really athletic entertainment, since the results of the match are usually predetermined, a

TABLE 5.3

Sports participation trends for individual sports, 1987–97

6 yrs. or older, at least once per year (millions)

	1987	1993	1994	1995	1996	1997	Percent change 1996–97	Percent change 1987–97
Archery	8.6	8.6	9.2	8.4	8.5	7.5	-11.7	-11.8
Badminton	14.8	1.9	11.8	11.7	10.8	9.6	-11.2	-35.0
Billiards	35.3	40.3	46.9	42.4	44.5	42.2	-5.2	+19.6
Bowling	47.8	49.0	53.1	53.1	52.2	53.3	+2.1	+11.4
Boxing	NA	1.3	1.8	NA	NA	NA	NA	NA
Golf	22.3	24.2	26.6	24.6	23.7	26.3	+11.0	+18.1
Racquetball	10.4	7.4	7.7	6.3	6.8	6.2	-9.8	-40.7
Roller hockey	NA	2.3	3.7	4.2	4.1	4.0	-3.1	+72.1[3]
Roller skating (traditional)	NA	22.2	21.0	18.5	15.3	15.0	-1.8	-37.6[1]
Roller skating (in-line wheels)	NA	12.6	18.8	22.5	27.5	29.1	+5.6	+848.9[1]
Skateboarding	10.9	5.4	6.0	6.2	6.8	8.2	+22.0	-24.3
Street hockey	NA	NA	5.2	4.8	NA	NA	NA	NA
Tennis	21.1	19.3	17.9	18.5	19.0	17.5	-8.1	-17.3
Table tennis	NA	17.7	20.1	19.5	18.2	17.1	-6.1	-14.8[2]

Note: Percentages based on figures rounded to nearest thousand participants.

[1] Eight-year change
[2] Seven-year change
[3] Four-year change

SOURCE: "Sports participation trends: individual sports," in *Sports Participation Trends Report, 1997,* Sporting Goods Manufacturers Association, North Palm Beach, FL, 1998 www.SGMA.com

fact many Americans formerly did not understand. The 1999 survey finds that eight out of ten Americans believed the outcomes of most wrestling matches were fixed, compared to less than two out of ten who believed that in 1951.

Perhaps, this accounts for the 81 percent of Americans, according to the survey, who said that wrestling was not a sport. True wrestling fans, however, beg to differ. Among persons describing themselves as wrestling fans, 44 percent said that wrestling was, indeed, a sport.

THE WEEKEND WARRIOR— SPORTS PARTICIPATION

Each year, American Sports Data surveys individuals in 25,000 households about their favorite sports and sports activities for the Sporting Goods Manufacturers Association (SGMA). In 2002 the top three activities were recreational swimming, walking, and bowling. Bicycling was the fourth most popular sport. Except for basketball, the other sports in the top ten of popularity were fitness or outdoor activities (with the exception of billiards, which held the ninth spot). (See Table 1.7 in Chapter 1.)

Other Sports Trends

The number of people strapping on in-line skates has grown rapidly. In-line skating was the fastest-growing sport from 1987 to 1997—an 849 percent increase—among both males and females. (See Table 5.3.) In-line skating also made the 2001 list of the top ten sports in which women participate frequently. (See Table 1.9 in Chapter 1.) The SGMA reports that 26 million Americans participated in

in-line skating in 2002, down slightly from the 29 million in 2000. (See Table 1.7 in Chapter 1 and Table 5.4.)

Riding nonmotorized scooters, an activity that was not common enough to be ranked in 2000, was named as one of the top thirty most popular sports in the United States in 2001 with nearly 16 million enthusiasts. Industry observers speculate that some of the decline observed in in-line skating might be the result of people trading their skates in for scooters. Eighty percent of surveyed respondents who said they rode scooters were new to the activity, having participated in it for one year or less. (See Table 5.5.)

However, racquetball lost the greatest share of participants during the 1990s. In 1997, 6.2 million people played racquetball, a 41 percent drop from 1987. (See Table 5.3.) The decline might be due to aging baby boomers switching from this high-speed, high-impact sport to less strenuous sports.

BASEBALL

Baseball participation dropped 12 percent over the ten-year period ending in 1997. (See Table 5.6.) By 2001 participation in baseball had dropped to 10.9 million, but the sport still was named the sixth most popular team sport in the United States and the sixth most popular team sport for youth age 6 to 17. Almost 5 million youth age 6 to 17 played baseball 25 or more days per year. (See Table 1.12 in Chapter 1.) Although children age 6 to 11 have the highest rates of participation, the average age of players was 18.3 years and the number of players over age 35 has risen 18.6 percent since the late 1980s. Industry observers

TABLE 5.4

Sports participation by selected activities, 2000
In thousands

	Total participants	Participants under 18	Participants under 12	Frequent participants
1. Basketball	37,552	20,635	9,183	17,074 (25+)*
2. Running/jogging	33,680	12,679	4,821	9,801(100+)
3. Roller skating (in-line wheels)	29,024	19,421	11,804	9,839 (25+)
4. Volleyball (hard surface/grass)	18,400	8,333	2,394	4,765 (25+)
5. Soccer	17,734	13,792	8,580	8,767 (25+)
6. Softball (slow-pitch)	17,585	6,493	3,279	6,175 (25+)
7. Football (touch)	15,456	9,467	3,784	3,743 (25+)
8. Skateboarding	11,649	9,971	5,756	2,839 (52+)
9. Baseball	10,881	7,240	4,334	5,796 (25+)
10. Roller skating (2x2 wheels)	10,834	6,449	4,071	1,308 (25+)
11. Volleyball (sand/beach)	8,763	2,497	511	952 (25+)
12. Snowboarding	7,151	4,216	1,929	746 (15+)
13. Football (tackle)	5,673	4,031	1,107	3,624 (25+)
14. Softball (fast-pitch)	3,795	1,833	471	2,122 (52+)
15. Roller hockey	3,287	2,188	917	996 (25+)
16. Ice hockey	2,761	1,263	646	1,062 (25+)

* ( ) days per year

SOURCE: "2000 Sports Participation Selected Activities," in *Superstudy of Sports Participation Baseball: Executive Overview 2001,* Sporting Goods Manufacturer's Association, North Palm Beach, FL, 2001 www.SGMA.com

TABLE 5.5

New participants in selected sports activities, 2000

	Percentage of total participants within activity
1. Scooter riding	80
2. Snowboarding	37
3. Skateboarding	31
4. Roller hockey	29
5. Football (touch)	22
6. Ice hockey	22
7. Football (tackle)	22
8. Soccer	21
9. Volleyball (hard surface/grass)	19
10. Roller skating (in-line wheels)	17
11. Volleyball (sand/beach)	17
12. Basketball	16
13. Roller skating (2x2 wheels)	16
14. Softball (slow-pitch)	15
15. Running/jogging	15
16. Baseball	14
17. Softball (fast-pitch)	13

SOURCE: "New Participants," in *Superstudy of Sports Participation Baseball: Executive Overview 2001,* Sporting Goods Manufacturer's Association, North Palm Beach, FL, 2001 www.SGMA.com

attribute this decline to the fact that today's youth are not playing as much casual baseball in sandlots and parks.

While enthusiasm for playing baseball may have waned, the number of Americans who follow the sport has not changed significantly since the 1930s when Gallup pollsters asked Americans whether they were fans of professional baseball. During the late 1930s, about 40 percent of Americans followed big league baseball. In the early 1950s, an average of 43 percent were fans, and polls conducted in 2001–2002 also reported that 43 percent of Americans followed baseball.

Ten percent more women described themselves as baseball fans in 2001–2002 than they did during the 1930s when just 27 percent of polled women said they followed baseball. Among young women, the increase was slight, up just 3 percent to 36 percent of women under thirty in 2001–2002; the increase was greatest among older women. Similarly, there were more baseball fans and followers among older men, along with a decline among men under thirty. Diminishing interest in baseball among younger men suggests that the sport may be less popular in the future.

BASKETBALL

Playing basketball is a tremendously popular activity in the United States. Basketball is the second most popular spectator sport and the most popular participatory team sport. A Gallup poll conducted in June 2002 finds that 45 percent of survey participants identified themselves as basketball fans, up 7 percent from October 2001.

According to a report from the SGMA, an overall decline in basketball participation continued in 2001, dropping to 38.7 million. The SGMA suggests that reasons for a drop in participation might be the increased popularity of other activities, such as in-line skating, computers, and video games. In 1999, 11.2 million persons said that basketball was their favorite activity, an all-time high, indicating that basketball had a core following of participants; however, by 2001 only 9.6 million people named basketball as their favorite sport.

An increasing number of female players, especially at the high school level where girls' varsity teams increased by 18 percent during the 1990s, has made basketball the most

TABLE 5.6

Sports participation trends for team sports, 1987–97

6 yrs. or older at least once per year (millions)

	1987	1993	1994	1995	1996	1997	Percent change 1996–97	Percent change 1987–97
Baseball	15.1	15.6	17.0	16.2	14.7	13.3	-9.7	-12.1
Basketball	35.7	42.1	47.3	46.5	45.6	45.1	-1.0	+26.2
Cheerleading	NA	3.3	3.2	3.2	2.9	NA	NA	NA
Football (touch)	20.3	21.2	23.0	20.0	19.4	18.2	-6.4	-10.5
Football (tackle)	11.7	13.1	13.7	12.2	11.7	12.1	+3.5	+3.6
Soccer	15.4	16.4	18.2	16.8	18.1	18.2	+0.7	+18.4
Softball (fast pitch)	NA	NA	NA	3.5	3.1	3.3	+4.8	-5.7[2]
Softball (slow pitch)	NA	NA	NA	24.5	23.9	20.5	-14.2	-16.5[2]
Softball (total)	31.0	30.1	30.8	26.0	25.3	22.1	-12.6	-28.6
Volleyball (hard surface)	NA	31.7	32.5	28.0	26.4	23.6	-10.8	-27.6[1]
Volleyball (sand/beach)	NA	13.5	14.2	13.3	12.6	10.5	-16.4	+2.3[1]

Note: Percentages based on figures rounded to nearest thousand participants.
[1]Eight-year change
[2]Two-year change

SOURCE: "Sports participation trends: team sports," in *Sports Participation Trends Report, 1997,* Sporting Goods Manufacturers Association, North Palm Beach, FL, 1998 www.SGMA.com

popular high school sport for girls. It's the second most popular sport for high school boys. The Amateur Athletic Union reports that more than three times as many girls (105,000 compared to 29,000) and twice as many boys (98,000 in 1999 and 49,000 in 1990) signed up for basketball competitions in 1999 than they had a decade earlier.

The SGMA study cites the relatively large proportion of adult players—more than 10 million predominantly male players between the ages of 25 and 45—as one of the sport's strengths. Since a growing proportion of adults were parents playing on home courts with their children, the researchers conclude that basketball's role as a family activity bodes well for its long-term popularity.

SOCCER

Increasing numbers of Americans are playing soccer and participation by women and girls is growing. The SGMA analysis of sports participation finds that soccer ranked ninth among the most popular sports for women based on frequent participation. More than 4.1 million women said they played soccer 25 or more days per year. (See Table 1.9 in Chapter 1.)

Soccer was second only to basketball among the most popular sports for youth age 6 to 17, with nearly 7.7 million children and teens who played more than 25 days per year. (See Table 1.12 in Chapter 1.) The U.S. Youth Soccer Association has about 3 million registered players between the ages of 5 and 17 and soccer programs are administered by a network of 45 state associations staffed by more than 300,000 coaches and 500,000 volunteers.

Although soccer has long been popular in Europe, Asia, Central America, and South America, it has only recently captured the imagination of North America. Two Olympic soccer tournaments were held in the United States, in Los Angeles, California, in 1984, and in Atlanta, Georgia, in 1996.

In 1994 U.S. Soccer served as the host federation for World Cup USA 1994, a record-breaking event attended by more than 3.5 million fans, and hosted the most successful women's sporting event in history: the Women's World Cup 1999, which was held in Pasadena, California, and attended by more than 90,000 fans. The U.S. women won the 1999 World Cup by defending against the Chinese team in a zero to zero tie through regulation and overtime and then defeating China five to four in penalty kicks. Their victory provoked soccer hysteria in the United States as the winning team members appeared on television news programs, at the White House, and on the covers of newspapers and magazines. The U.S. women's team continued its winning streak, adding six tournament titles in 2000, capturing the prestigious Algarve Cup in Portugal, and earning a silver medal in the 2000 Summer Olympics.

The *2001 Soccer Participation Survey,* prepared by the Soccer Industry Council of America, finds that 18.2 million people played soccer in 2000, up slightly from 18.1 million in 1996. Those who played frequently—25 or more days a year—rose from 8.5 million to 8.9 million. Almost 60 percent of players were male and more than three-fourths were under the age of 18.

Although the greatest numbers of soccer players were in the more populous states of California, New York, and Texas, in terms of participation rates soccer was most popular in Utah (17.3 percent of residents played), followed by Rhode Island (16.7 percent), Kansas (14.1

percent), Iowa (12.6 percent), and Missouri (12.4 percent). Soccer participation increased 11 percent during the 1990s, and by 2000 participation on high school teams had increased by 73 percent.

BOWLING

Bowling ranks as America's most popular participant sport. According to an SGMA report, the number of bowlers rose from 53.8 million in 2000 to 55.5 million in 2002. (See Table 1.7 in Chapter 1.) Although participation rates increased 17 percent from 1997 to 2000 and the absolute number of bowlers grew 6 percent between 1998 and 2000, when demographic changes and U.S. population growth are considered, actual rates of participation have declined from 22.3 bowlers per 100 people in the United States in 1987 to 21.7 in 2000.

In an attempt to increase participation during the 1990s, many bowling centers upgraded and modernized their facilities and made successful efforts to enhance the image of both the sport and the facilities. Although the overall number of bowling alleys and centers declined, the consolidation of centers resulted in the closing of many antiquated bowling lanes, some of which were replaced by state-of-the-art facilities with attractive decor, updated scoring and playing equipment, quality food service, and other entertainment and located in better locations. Some "megacenters" also provided access to golf driving ranges, basketball, skating, billiards, and even microbreweries.

Other changes were made to reinvigorate the image of bowling and attract the youth market. The industry introduced higher-performance bowling balls at more popular midrange prices and developed products and promotions designed to attract younger players. Centers often included "Rock 'n' Bowl" and "Cosmic Bowling"—bowling under ultraviolet lights with lanes, pins, and bowlers set aglow. Bowlers age 12 to 17 made up 38 percent of America's bowlers according to an SGMA report released in February 2000.

BILLIARDS AND POOL—COMING OF AGE

Despite a slight decline in the number of billiard players since the mid-1990s, billiards remains a favorite participation sport in the United States. In 1999, 36.4 million Americans played billiards at least once, down slightly from 1998 when 39.7 million people played billiards. According to a 2001 SGMA survey, about 9 million Americans played frequently—more than 25 times per year, and the number of people who named billiards as a favorite activity increased 22 percent from 3.6 million in 1990 to 4.4 million in 2000.

The favorable image of billiards is reflected in a changing demographic player profile, one that is younger and more often female than a decade ago. Since 1990 the number of players age 12 to 17 has grown by 20 percent, while the number of female players has risen by 9.4 percent. Growing attention to female players was reflected by the ESPN cable network decision to broadcast 18 hours of the Women's Professional Billiard Association Tour in 2001.

Although the growth of the number of female players (19 percent) has been greater than that of men (17 percent) since 1987, more males (62 percent) than females (38 percent) continued to play billiards in 2000. Whites accounted for about three-quarters of players, Hispanics, 13 percent, blacks, 9 percent, and other minorities, 4 percent.

One of the industry's efforts to boost participation is to try to convert casual players into more frequent, serious players. Billiard leagues are increasing in number. The Billiard Congress of America, the sport's governing body, cultivated a system with more than 450 leagues and 50,000 members and initiated a national tournament system to generate greater frequency of play in poolrooms across the country.

Pool halls are no longer limited to dark and dreary back rooms of bars. Billiard and pool tables are now found in a variety of sites, including upscale multiactivity entertainment centers, which might include video games, basketball hoops, indoor golf, sports bars, satellite-networked trivia games, and restaurants. Billiards and pool are also springing up in food courts, at large military bases, and college student centers. Even traditional pool halls have changed; many are better lighted and more "wholesome" in decor. Some do not serve alcohol. These changes have not only increased the availability of billiards and pool, but also have made the environment in which they are played more appealing to those who might not try the games otherwise.

TENNIS IS ON THE UPSWING

During the 1960s tennis was popular primarily among the affluent. The game became "fashionable" and gained broader participation in the 1970s, but industry experts reported that many tennis players turned to aerobics and other fitness activities in the 1980s. During the 1990s tennis participation grew and the total number of U.S. tennis players, 12 years of age and older, rose from 19.5 million in 1996 to 20.8 million in 1999. During the same period, frequent tennis players, those playing 20 or more times a year, rose from 4.9 million to 5.4 million players.

Research conducted annually by the Tennis Industry Association reveals that tennis began to bounce back in 1995. The number of participants who played at least once in 2001 was just 19.2 million, a slight drop from 2000 and still less than the 22.6 million who played in 1992. However, the sport shows increasing strength among those who play more frequently. The number of participants who played four or more times in 2001, 14.7 million, exceeded the 1992 finding of 13.7 million. The number who played 20 or more times has climbed back to 5.4 million, compared to 5.9 million in 1992.

GOLF

Golf is the fifteenth most popular sport in the United States and according to an American Sports Data report prepared for the SGMA, the total number of golfers grew 5 percent, from 28.9 million to 30.4 million between 1990 and 2000. Professional golf also enjoys a strong following as a spectator sport. A May 2002 Gallup Organization poll finds that nearly one-quarter of Americans described themselves as professional golf fans and an additional 8 percent said they followed the sport.

Golf's popularity among players and spectators has benefited immensely from the remarkable career of golfer Tiger Woods, arguably the greatest golfer who has ever played. The young, talented, and charismatic golfer has encouraged young people to take up the sport and has become a celebrity known throughout the world. A June 2001 Gallup poll finds that public regard for Woods was greater than for practically any other living athlete. Thirty-eight percent of surveyed respondents named Woods the greatest athlete active in the world of sports today. Michael Jordan followed Woods, garnering 6 percent of the respondents, and Allen Iverson was third, chosen by 4 percent of those surveyed. (See Table 5.7.)

Regular golfers, those who play frequently—25 or more times a year—rose from 6.4 million in 1990 to 8.6 million in 2001. The average age of frequent golfers is 48, and three-quarters are males with an average household income of more than $50,000 per year.

The South leads the country as home for golfers, boasting 33 percent of avid players. The north central states are second with more than 2.1 million golfing regulars—25 percent of all frequent players—followed by the West and Northeast, which account for 22 percent and 19 percent of frequent golfers, respectively.

The SGMA also finds that golf appeals to a variety of people with varying educational backgrounds. The largest proportion of frequent players (42 percent) have earned

TABLE 5.7

Public opinion on who is the greatest athlete in the world today, August 2000 and June 2001

	2001 Jun 8-10 %	2000 Aug 24-27 %
Tiger Woods	38	30
Michael Jordan	6	4
Allen Iverson	4	—
Shaquille O'Neal	3	1
Kobe Bryant	1	1
Lance Armstrong	1	1
Jeff Gordon	1	—
Ray Bourque	1	—
Mark McGwire	1	3
Derek Jeter	1	—
Venus Williams	1	1
Andre Agassi	1	—
Cal Ripken	*	2
Sammy Sosa	*	1
Brett Favre	—	1
Troy Aikman	—	1
Pete Sampras	—	1
Michael Johnson	—	1
Deion Sanders	—	1
Ken Griffey Jr.	—	1
Dale Earnhardt	—	1
Cynthia Cooper	—	1
Other	14	13
None	1	4
Don't know	25	30
No opinion	1	1

SOURCE: "In your opinion, who is the greatest athlete active in the world of sports today?" The Gallup Organization, Princeton, NJ, January 4, 2001 www.gallup.com © 2001 The Gallup Organization, all rights reserved. Reprinted with permission.

college degrees and the next largest group (24 percent) have a high school degree or less.

Industry experts believe that the aging of America should benefit golf participation, especially as baby boomers reach retirement age, but that cost and convenience of play are major obstacles to growth. The cost of development and maintaining courses translates into a high fee for play, which discourages people of moderate means and those who are just beginning and not yet regular players. The cost of equipment is more of an impediment than access to golf courses, since 70 percent of the more than 16,000 golf facilities in the United States are open to the public.

CHAPTER 6
GAMBLING IN AMERICA

Historically, gambling has been a popular form of recreation in North America. George Washington liked to play cards, and Benjamin Franklin printed and sold playing cards. Americans were so fond of card games that when the British Stamp Act put a 1-shilling tax on playing cards, people became extremely upset. In fact, anger about the taxes on playing cards and tea was one motivation for the American Revolution. During the colonial period, lotteries (a system of raising money by selling numbered tickets and distributing prizes to the holders of numbers drawn at random) were used to raise money to establish the colony of Virginia. In 1777 the Continental Congress held a $5 million lottery to pay for the Revolutionary War.

By the 1800s Americans were known for their gambling. Visitors to this country said it was impossible to talk to a person from Kentucky without hearing the phrase, "I'll bet you!" Large riverboats that traveled up and down the Mississippi and Ohio Rivers carrying passengers or freight almost always had a casino where gamblers played cards and other games of chance. Along the Mississippi River was New Orleans, a city famous for gambling. After the Civil War, adventurers went searching for gold and silver in the West, and virtually every mining town had a few gambling casinos.

Beginning in the 1870s, however, most forms of gambling and all lotteries were outlawed by states, following a scandal in the Louisiana lottery. This state lottery operated nationwide and the scandal involved bribery of state and federal officials. In 1890 Congress outlawed the use of the mail for lotteries and in 1895 it forbid shipments of lottery tickets across state lines.

Although gambling has always been popular in the United States, many people have opposed it because they believed gambling was immoral and posed a threat to both individuals and the community. Many people become addicted to gambling, and some lose their homes, families,

and careers. Furthermore, during the Prohibition Era (1920–1933), when alcohol was outlawed, organized crime moved into the profitable worlds of alcoholic beverages and gambling. Although legal gambling has gained respectability and is viewed by many Americans as an acceptable activity, the association with organized crime and corruption still taints the activity in the minds of others.

Lotteries began a revival in 1964 when New Hampshire created a state lottery. New York followed suit in 1966. Between 1970 and 1975 ten more states established lotteries. In 2002 thirty-eight states and Washington, D.C., operated lotteries.

TYPES OF LEGAL GAMBLING

There are five primary forms of legal gambling in the United States: bingo, lotteries, pari-mutuel betting, off-track betting, and casinos. Bingo is the most common form of legalized gambling. Lotteries operate in thirty-eight states, Washington, D.C., Puerto Rico, and the Virgin Islands. Forty-three states, Puerto Rico, and the Virgin Islands permit thoroughbred racing. Twenty-two states and Puerto Rico allow casino gambling. Sports gambling is legal in Montana, Nevada, North Dakota, and Oregon. Almost all legal betting on sports occurs in Nevada.

WHERE AMERICANS GAMBLE THEIR MONEY

According to the *U.S. Casino Gaming Market* report, in 2001 Americans bet nearly three-quarters of a trillion dollars on legal gambling in the United States, up from $677.4 billion in 1998. About half of the wagers were made in casinos—mostly in Las Vegas, Nevada, or Atlantic City, New Jersey—and on riverboats. The balance of the wagering took place on Indian reservations, in charitable gaming, and lotteries.

In 2000 the size of the U.S. gaming industry was $64.9 billion. Commercial gaming, largely dominated by

FIGURE 6.1

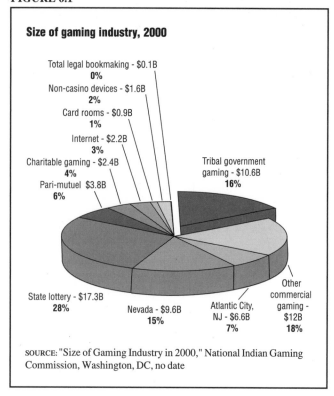

Size of gaming industry, 2000

Total legal bookmaking - $0.1B
0%

Non-casino devices - $1.6B
2%

Card rooms - $0.9B
1%

Internet - $2.2B
3%

Charitable gaming - $2.4B
4%

Pari-mutuel $3.8B
6%

State lottery - $17.3B
28%

Nevada - $9.6B
15%

Atlantic City, NJ - $6.6B
7%

Tribal government gaming - $10.6B
16%

Other commercial gaming - $12B
18%

SOURCE: "Size of Gaming Industry in 2000," National Indian Gaming Commission, Washington, DC, no date

FIGURE 6.2

Number of Indian gaming operations, 1996–2000

Year	Number
1996	232
1997	265
1998	273
1999	252
2000	321

SOURCE: "1996-2000 Number of Indian Gaming Operations," National Indian Gaming Commission, Washington, DC, no date

the Nevada, Atlantic City, and riverboat casinos, accounted for more than 35 percent of the industry. State lotteries were the next largest revenue producers, responsible for 28 percent of the market. Indian tribal government gaming ranked third with 16 percent of the market. (See Figure 6.1.)

CASINO GAMBLING

Technically, a casino is any room or rooms in which gaming is conducted. When most Americans think of casinos, they picture lavish hotel/gambling/entertainment complexes, such as those in Las Vegas or Atlantic City. Before 1990 only Nevada and Atlantic City permitted casinos. In 2002 casinos were legal in 28 states and were operated in various forms. In addition to the Las Vegas resort-type casinos, there were nearly 100 riverboat casinos in 6 states and about 321 casinos on Indian reservations. Nevada had 429 full-scale casinos and nearly 2,000 slots-only casinos.

Riverboat and Cruise Gambling

Some people gamble on riverboats (either seaworthy excursion boats or stationary barges) or on cruises. Riverboats, or "floating casinos," are relatively new, having begun in Iowa in 1991. By 2002 revenues from riverboat gambling totaled more than $6 billion.

Although the cruise lines emphasize that gambling is just one of many attractions to be enjoyed on their cruises, virtually all major cruise lines provide gambling. Many of

the cruises, however, have a limit of $100 to $200 to control losses. "Cruises to nowhere" or "day trips" are gambling opportunities available at coastal ports in Florida, Texas, New York, and Georgia. The ships travel three to twelve miles into international waters, where neither state nor federal gambling laws apply. Since 1985 the day-cruise gambling industry has more than doubled, growing from ten to twenty-five vessels.

Missouri's Riverboats Boost Economy

A survey conducted by the Missouri Riverboat Gaming Association in 2001, which looked at 6,200 Missouri casino workers employed by 9 riverboat casinos, finds that the workers, earning average salaries of more than $31,800, made greater contributions to Missouri's economy than they had before their casino employment. The surveyed workers purchased 2,000 homes, 4,400 automobiles, and 4,500 major appliances in 2000. They also patronized 295,200 restaurants or food take-out facilities with their families in the year prior to the survey.

The surveyed respondents said that working for the casinos offered better health care benefits and enabled them to find and afford more suitable housing in better neighborhoods with better schools for their children. The survey also finds that 1 out of 4 Missouri casino employees no longer needed the assistance of welfare after beginning work at the riverboat casinos, and an additional 3 percent no longer required food stamps or unemployment benefits.

Casino Gambling on Native American Reservations

The Indian Gaming Act of 1988 (PL 100-497) permitted Native American tribes to introduce gambling on their reservations. By 2000 there were 321 Native American

TABLE 6.1

Indian tribal gaming revenues, 1997–2001

Gaming revenue range	Number of operations	Revenues (in thousands)	Percentage of Operations	Percentage of Revenues	Mean (in thousands)	Median (in thousands)
Gaming operation fiscal years ending in 2001						
$100 million and over	39	8,398,523	13%	66%	215,347	158,836
$50 to $100 million	19	1,415,755	7%	11%	74,513	79,083
$25 to $50 million	43	1,528,611	15%	12%	35,549	34,264
$10 to $25 million	57	976,442	20%	8%	17,131	16,328
$3 to $10 million	51	340,019	18%	3%	6,667	6,640
Under $3 million	81	76,029	28%	1%	939	710
Total	**290**	**12,735,379**				
Gaming operation fiscal years ending in 2000						
$100 million and over	31	6,606,284	11%	60%	213,106	141,684
$50 to $100 million	24	1,693,510	8%	15%	70,563	73,314
$25 to $50 million	41	1,360,777	14%	12%	33,190	29,944
$10 to $25 million	50	856,464	17%	8%	17,129	17,335
$3 to $10 million	54	341,062	19%	3%	6,316	6,250
Under $3 million	88	83,519	31%	1%	949	671
Totals	**288**	**10,941,616**				
Gaming operation fiscal years ending in 1999						
$100 million and over	28	5,845,787	10%	60%	208,778	136,897
$50 to $100 million	19	1,323,995	7%	14%	69,684	70,412
$25 to $50 million	33	1,193,049	11%	12%	36,153	35,990
$10 to $25 million	59	1,028,834	20%	11%	17,438	17,562
$3 to $10 million	54	322,268	19%	3%	5,968	5,764
Under $3 million	97	83,700	33%	1%	537	518
Totals	**290**	**9,797,633**				
Gaming operation fiscal years ending in 1998						
$100 million and over	23	4,674,895	8%	55%	203,256	127,972
$50 to $100 million	20	1,354,563	7%	16%	67,728	68,922
$25 to $50 million	31	1,090,227	10%	13%	35,169	34,639
$10 to $25 million	56	948,089	19%	11%	16,930	16,287
$3 to $10 million	55	341,064	19%	4%	6,201	5,746
Under $3 million	112	86,856	38%	1%	776	503
Totals	**297**	**8,495,694**				
Gaming operation fiscal years ending in 1997						
$100 million and over	15	3,298,611	6%	44%	219,907	137,779
$50 to $100 million	22	1,676,320	8%	22%	76,196	73,955
$25 to $50 million	35	1,182,924	13%	16%	33,798	32,695
$10 to $25 million	52	890,465	20%	12%	17,124	17,305
$3 to $10 million	53	311,960	20%	4%	5,886	5,493
Under $3 million	89	91,167	33%	1%	723	644
Totals	**266**	**7,451,447**				

SOURCE: "National Indian Gaming Commission Tribal Gaming Revenues," National Indian Gaming Commission, Washington, DC, 2002

gambling facilities operating in 29 states. (See Figure 6.2.) Tribes in California, Montana, Oklahoma, Washington, and Wisconsin operated 178 of the gaming facilities—more than half of the total. The revenue has provided employment for Native Americans and monies for investment in housing, education, health care, and other reservation needs. Data from the National Indian Gaming Commission shows that tribal gaming revenue increased from $10.9 billion in 2000 to $12.7 billion in 2001. (See Table 6.1.)

WHO IS GAMBLING?

Harrah's Entertainment, Inc., operates 25 casinos in the United States and commissions an annual survey to identify characteristics and preferences of casino gamblers. The most recent survey results, in *Profile of the American Casino Gambler: Harrah's Survey 2002,* are based on 2 nationwide studies, the Roper Reports, conducted by Roper ASW, and the U.S. Gaming Panel, conducted by the NFO World Group, Inc.

The survey finds that 27 percent of the U.S. population aged 21 and older gambled at a casino in 2001. (See Table 6.2.) Gamblers were characterized as sharing many of the same leisure-time preferences as other Americans, but they tended to be more active during their leisure time—traveling on weekends, attending cultural events, eating out, and reading more than most American adults. They made an average of almost 6 trips to a casino per year.

Compared to the average American, the typical casino gambler was middle-aged, more likely to be female, and slightly better educated with a higher average household income. (See Table 6.3 and Figure 6.3.) The median household income for casino gamblers was a full 20 percent higher than that of the average American; and 5 percent more casino gamblers held white-collar jobs. (See Figure 6.4.)

Casino gambling was most popular among adults aged 51–65; and this group accounted for more than 30 percent of persons who had gambled during the 12 months prior to

TABLE 6.2

Number of adults who gambled in a casino in the last 12 months, 2001

U.S. adult population (age 21+)	**196.9 million**
Casino gamblers	53.2 million
Casino participation rate	27%
Average trip frequency	5.7 trips/year
Casino trips	303.3 million

SOURCE: "Adults who gambled in a casino in the last 12 months," in *Profile of the American Casino Gambler,* Harrah's Entertainment, Inc., Las Vegas, NV, 2002. Reproduced by permission.

TABLE 6.3

Age, income and gender of casino gamblers vs. national average, 2001

Demographics	U.S. population	U.S. casino gamers
Median age - age 21+	45	46
Median household income	$41,343	$49,753
Male/female ratio	48/52%	45/55%

SOURCE: "Age, income and gender of casino gamblers vs. national average," in *Profile of the American Casino Gambler,* Harrah's Entertainment, Inc., Las Vegas, NV, 2002. Reproduced by permission.

FIGURE 6.3

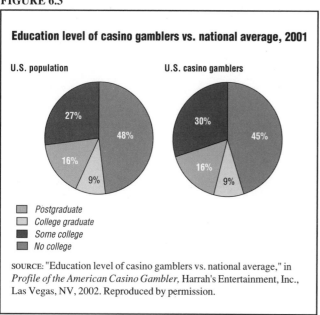

Education level of casino gamblers vs. national average, 2001

SOURCE: "Education level of casino gamblers vs. national average," in *Profile of the American Casino Gambler,* Harrah's Entertainment, Inc., Las Vegas, NV, 2002. Reproduced by permission.

FIGURE 6.4

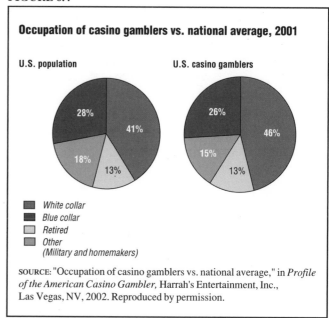

Occupation of casino gamblers vs. national average, 2001

SOURCE: "Occupation of casino gamblers vs. national average," in *Profile of the American Casino Gambler,* Harrah's Entertainment, Inc., Las Vegas, NV, 2002. Reproduced by permission.

the survey. The second most frequent casino gamblers were persons over age 66. (See Table 6.4.) One reason that casino gambling was more popular among older adults was that they had more free time and discretionary income (funds they could choose to use for recreation as opposed to life's necessities) than younger adults.

Casino participation rates increased with increasing income. Less than one-quarter of adults with annual household incomes of less than $35,000 gambled in casinos, while 35 percent of those earning more than $95,000 per year said they were casino players. (See Figure 6.5.)

There were geographic variations in casino participation: the rates were highest in the West and Northeast and lowest in the South. The higher participation in the West may in part be due to the proximity of Las Vegas with its many casinos. Similarly, residents of the Northeast may more easily travel to Atlantic City casinos. (See Figure 6.6.) In 2001 more than half of all trips to casinos were made by residents of 10 states, with California at the top of the list (15 percent). Of the top 10 states, only 3—

Nevada, Missouri, and Louisiana—were not among the top 10 states in population. (See Figure 6.7.)

Favorite Casino Games

According to the 2002 survey by Harrah's Entertainment, Americans loved slot machines and other electronic gaming devices, preferring them to table games, such as blackjack, roulette, and craps. Nearly three-quarters of the games played were slots or video poker, and quarter slots were the most popular denomination to play. (See Table 6.5.) The preference for slots and electronic gaming machines increased with age: more than three-quarters (78 percent) of casino players older than 66 favored machines over table games. Surprisingly, younger players who grew up playing video games were not the biggest fans of slots and electronic gambling games, as they were more likely than older adults to prefer table games. (See Table 6.6.)

Women were far more likely to play slot machines and other electronic games than men: 80 percent favored slots and electronic gaming and just 8 percent played table games. Although more men played slots and machines than table games (66 percent versus 20 percent), men were more than twice as likely as women to play blackjack, roulette, or craps. (See Table 6.7.)

BINGO AND OTHER CHARITABLE GAMES

Charitable gambling is permitted in all states except Arkansas, Hawaii, Tennessee, and Utah. In 2000 it constituted about 4 percent of the total amount wagered on legalized gambling in the United States. (See Figure 6.1.) Of this total, bingo accounted for approximately half. Charity games include bingo, raffles, casino nights, "pull tabs," lucky 7s, pickle cards, and jar tickets. Bingo ses-

sions are a common form of fund-raising by charitable organizations, such as churches, synagogues, and service clubs. It is a relatively inexpensive social and recreational pursuit; however, industry observers believe that bingo is declining in terms of both popularity and revenues.

TABLE 6.4

Casino participation rate by age, 2001

21 – 35 years old	26%
36 – 50 years old	25%
51 – 65 years old	31%
66 and above	27%

SOURCE: "Age differences in casino participation," in *Profile of the American Casino Gambler,* Harrah's Entertainment, Inc,. Las Vegas, NV, 2002. Reproduced by permission.

FIGURE 6.5

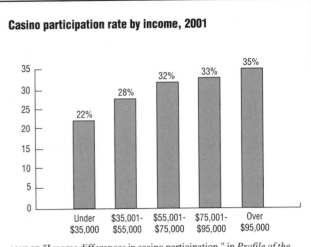

Casino participation rate by income, 2001

SOURCE: "Income differences in casino participation," in *Profile of the American Casino Gambler,* Harrah's Entertainment, Inc., Las Vegas, NV, 2002. Reproduced by permission.

FIGURE 6.6

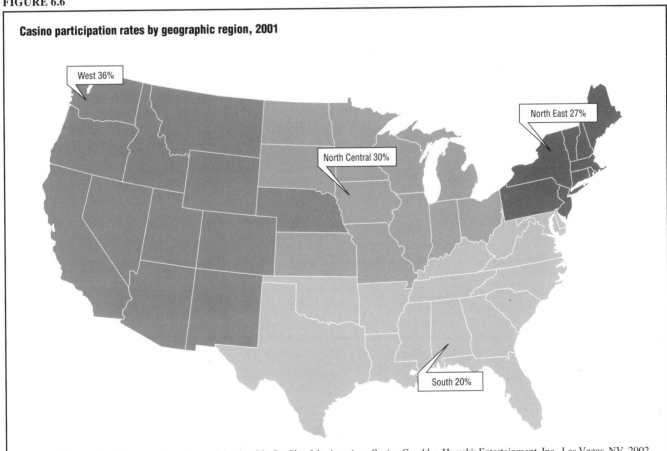

Casino participation rates by geographic region, 2001

SOURCE: "Geographic differences in casino participation," in *Profile of the American Casino Gambler,* Harrah's Entertainment, Inc., Las Vegas, NV, 2002. Reproduced by permission.

FIGURE 6.7

Top states generating casino trips in the last 12 months, 2001

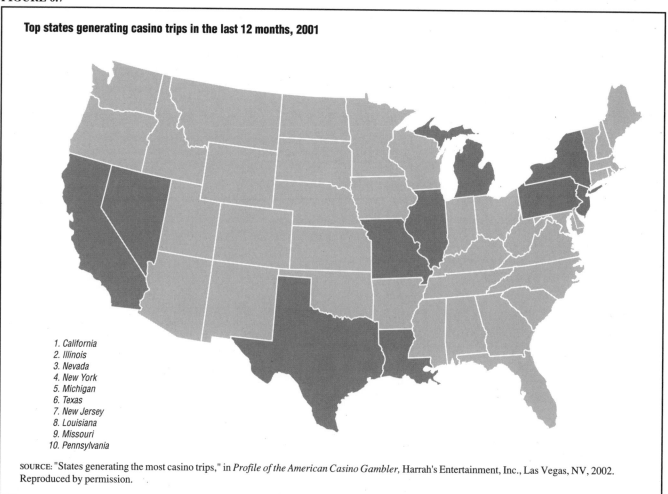

1. California
2. Illinois
3. Nevada
4. New York
5. Michigan
6. Texas
7. New Jersey
8. Louisiana
9. Missouri
10. Pennsylvania

SOURCE: "States generating the most casino trips," in *Profile of the American Casino Gambler,* Harrah's Entertainment, Inc., Las Vegas, NV, 2002. Reproduced by permission.

PARI-MUTUEL WAGERING

Pari-mutuel wagering combines wagers into a common pool. Sports in which pari-mutuel wagering takes place are horse racing, greyhound racing, and jai alai. Winners are paid according to odds calculated with reference to the amounts bet on each contestant. In 2000 pari-mutuel wagering represented 6 percent of the gaming industry. (See Figure 6.1.)

From 1974 to 2000 the overall trends in pari-mutuel wagering included an increase in horse racing and decreases in greyhound racing and jai alai.

Horse Racing

The largest sector in pari-mutuel wagering is horse racing. Horse racing has a long history in America. The first American horse race took place in New York in the late 1660s. Several larger tracks, such as Churchill Downs, in Louisville, Kentucky, have been in operation since the 1800s.

Many Americans enjoy going to the racetrack for entertainment, some to enjoy the beautiful animals, many more to gamble. Horse racing is a popular spectator sport,

although it has declined significantly in popularity relative to other forms of gambling.

Even though the amounts wagered grew between 1974 and 2000, when the dollars wagered were adjusted for inflation, there was a noticeable decline. Although there are 150 racetracks in America, today most betting takes place elsewhere. In 1991 more than half of horse racing wagers were made at the track, but by 2000 less than 20 percent of the $16 billion handled were live bets. Satellite broadcasting makes it possible to simultaneously broadcast races between racetracks or at off-track betting sites where there are no races. In addition, at-home pari-mutuel betting is now possible and several companies provide 24-hour racing channels. There are even Internet simulcasts. It is estimated that off-track and simulcast betting, which are permitted in 38 states, now account for more than three-quarters of pari-mutuel wagering.

Account wagering is also possible in 9 states. Patrons are permitted to set up accounts at racetracks and, in 8 of those states, can phone in their bets from anywhere. Pari-mutuel wagering on horse races is legal in 43 states and generates about $3.8 billion in gross

TABLE 6.5

Casino games played most often, 2001

Slots/video poker (net)	74%
$.01 - .02	1%
$.05 - .10	16%
$.25 - .50	46%
$1.00 - 4.00	10%
$5.00 +	1%
Table games (net)	14%
Blackjack / 21	9%
Roulette	2%
Craps	2%
Other	4%
Don't know	8%

SOURCE: "America's favorite casino games," in *Profile of the American Casino Gambler,* Harrah's Entertainment, Inc., Las Vegas, NV, 2002. Reproduced by permission.

TABLE 6.6

Casino games played most often by age, 2001

	Age			
	21 - 35	36 - 50	51 - 65	66 +
Slots/video poker (net)	69%	74%	76%	78%
$.01 - .02	1%	0%	1%	1%
$.05 - .10	16%	15%	15%	18%
$.25 - .50	42%	47%	49%	50%
$1.00 - 4.00	9%	10%	11%	9%
$5.00 +	1%	1%	1%	1%
Table games (net)	18%	14%	11%	9%
Blackjack / 21	13%	10%	7%	6%
Roulette	3%	2%	1%	1%
Craps	3%	2%	2%	1%
Other	4%	4%	4%	4%
Don't know	8%	8%	8%	8%

SOURCE: "Favorite games by age," in *Profile of the American Casino Gambler,* Harrah's Entertainment, Inc., Las Vegas, NV, 2002. Reproduced by permission.

TABLE 6.7

Casino games played most often by gender, 2001

	Male	Female
Slots/video poker (net)	66%	80%
$.01 - .02	0%	1%
$.05 - .10	11%	20%
$.25 - .50	42%	50%
$1.00 - 4.00	11%	9%
$5.00 +	1%	1%
Table games (net)	20%	8%
Blackjack / 21	14%	6%
Roulette	2%	1%
Craps	4%	1%
Other	5%	4%
Don't know	10%	7%

SOURCE: "Favorite games by gender," in *Profile of the American Casino Gambler,* Harrah's Entertainment, Inc., Las Vegas, NV, 2002. Reproduced by permission.

revenue, according to a study reported by the National Indian Gaming Commission.

There are three major forms of horse racing: thoroughbred, harness, and quarter horse. In the United States, thoroughbred is, by far, the most popular form of horse racing, followed by harness and then quarter horse racing. For example, in 2000 nearly half (4,032) of the 8,475 live races run in California were thoroughbred, while in Florida, more than half the races were thoroughbred.

Greyhound Racing—The Sport of Queens

Once a favorite pastime of Queen Elizabeth I of England, dog racing became known as the "Sport of Queens." Originally, a hare would be released and a pair of greyhounds set in pursuit. In the early 1900s a mechanical lure replaced the hare, eliminating the killing of a rabbit.

The first American greyhound racetrack opened in Emeryville, California, in 1919. In 2002 there were 46 tracks operating in 15 states, but dog racing is in a decline and many tracks have closed due to low attendance. During 2000, 14,403 races took place, down from 15,151 races in 1996. About 30 percent of races were held in Florida. Almost 16 million people attended dog racing events in 1996; by 2000 only about 7 million went.

Like horse tracks, dog tracks have turned to simulcasting and off-track betting. The total amount wagered on greyhounds in 2000 was $2.1 billion, down from $2.3 billion in 1996.

The animal rights movement protests the sport, claiming the dogs are mistreated. Although the claims have led many track owners to improve conditions, animal rights activists have persuaded some legislators to ban racing or rescind existing permits. The declining financial condition of many tracks is, however, the primary reason that so many have closed.

Jai Alai

Jai alai is a fast-paced game in which the players, using a large curved basket strapped to their arms, whip a small ball made of goatskin against the three walls and floor of a huge playing court (fronton). Jai alai was invented in the seventeenth century in Spain and France. Although the game is popular in Latin America, its popularity has been declining in the United States. At the start of 2001, it was legal in only three states: Florida, Rhode Island, and Connecticut.

The popularity of jai alai peaked during the 1980s when more than $600 million was bet annually. By 2000 the amount bet had fallen below $196 million. During 2000 there were 2,034 jai alai events, down from 2,542 in 1996.

Florida once had ten frontons; it now has only six. The future of the sport in the United States is uncertain. Cruises, many of which offer casino gambling and lotteries, have taken considerable money from the frontons. Most jai alai frontons now offer simulcasting of horse races, which offer gamblers an additional wagering opportunity.

Problems for Pari-Mutuels

Because of the increased availability of other forms of gambling, pari-mutuels are facing hard times. Off-track betting and simulcasting has helped, but many owners of racetracks and frontons say more is needed for them to stay competitive. Track owners want to install electronic gambling devices (EGDs) as an additional source of revenue. As of 2002 Delaware, Rhode Island, South Carolina, and West Virginia permitted EGDs at racetracks. This is a highly controversial issue: according to the National Coalition Against Legalized Gambling, attempts to legalize EGDs at racetracks have been defeated in twelve states since 1995.

LOTTERIES

A lottery is a game in which people purchase numbered tickets in hopes of winning a prize. A person wins if the number on his or her ticket is the one drawn from a pool of all the tickets purchased for that event. In the case of instant lotteries, a bettor wins if the ticket contains a predetermined winning number. Raffles are a form of lottery in which the prize is usually goods rather than cash.

Lotteries are created and run by government. In 2002 thirty-eight states; Washington, D.C.; Puerto Rico; and the Virgin Islands had operating lotteries. Lottery revenues may go into the general fund of the state or may be earmarked for particular purposes, such as education, parks, or police pension funds. Developments in technology and communications have created many possible ways to conduct lotteries. There are five principal types of lottery games:

- Instant games, in which the player scratches off the ticket to find out whether and what he or she has won

- Daily numbers games, in which the player picks a combination of numbers

- Lotto, or a variation of it, in which numbers are chosen from a large set of possibilities with winners selected periodically—Powerball is a popular lottery of this type

- Video keno, in which the player chooses numbers with drawings held very frequently—sometimes as often as several times an hour

- EGDs, which allow bettors to play a game, such as video poker, and receive an immediate payout

As more and more states have introduced lotteries to raise money for government, people have had the opportunity to do more gambling. State lottery tickets are sold in grocery stores, convenience stores, gas stations, and many other places. When the winnings become unusually large or when 2 or 3 states get together for a big lottery jackpot, the lines to buy lottery tickets can be long. According to the North American Association of State and Provincial Lotteries, in 2001 Americans bet $38.9 billion on lotteries. Per capita sales grew from $150 in 1997 to $157 in 2001.

In general, poor people play lottery games less frequently than middle- and high-income groups. The lottery appeals to young people more than to older people. Most people who play the game report playing it regularly.

A number of studies show that while the poor tend to spend a higher percentage of their income on lotteries than do middle- or high-income persons, the lotteries tend to benefit high-income persons because they make greater use of the sporting and cultural organizations that receive lottery funds. Critics of lotteries observe that even when lotteries are considered as a tax they are unfair, taxing the poor disproportionately for the benefit of the better-off.

Furthermore, detractors also contend that lotteries are generally inefficient. Less than 40 percent of the funds they generate are returned to the causes they are meant to support, and about 47 percent is distributed as prize money. The remainder is used up for administration and promotion. Despite their inefficiency and relatively modest returns, governments favor lotteries because those who buy the tickets do so voluntarily.

Electronic Gambling Devices

EGDs include stand-alone slot machines, video poker, video keno, and other types of gambling games. Because EGDs are portable, they make gambling possible at locations that, unlike racetracks or casinos, are not dedicated to the business of gambling. Bars, truck stops, convenience stores, and other locations that did not formerly offer gambling may now feature EGDs. Some states, such as Louisiana, Montana, and South Carolina, permit private businesses to operate EGDs. In other states, such as Oregon and California, EGDs are operated by the state lottery.

In addition to legal EGDs, in other states there are many illegal EGDs, or "gray machines," so called because they exist in a gray area of the law. Basically, if such a machine is used for amusement and no proceeds are paid out, then gambling laws have not been broken. Nevertheless, according to the 1999 *National Gambling Impact Study Commission Report,* many establishments with these machines surreptitiously pay winners. Gray machines are common in bars and fraternal organizations in many states. It is estimated that there are 15,000 to 30,000 gray machines in West Virginia, 10,000 each in New Jersey and Alabama, and as many as 65,000 in Illinois.

Opponents of EGDs are concerned that the easily accessible devices may encourage the unhealthy gambling practices that can result in addiction. They caution that EGDs provide immediate, intense, and potentially prolonged gambling experiences and that consumers unfamiliar with gambling may be encouraged to wager recklessly.

SPORTS GAMBLING

It is legal to bet on sports in only two states. Nevada has 142 legal sports books that permit wagering on professional and amateur sports. Oregon has a game associated with the Oregon lottery that permits betting on professional football games.

Almost all the money wagered legally on sporting events, such as football and basketball games, is bet in Nevada. Championship games, such as the Super Bowl or the World Series, are some of the most popular sporting events on which people bet.

In addition, an unknown number of people participate in illegal gambling, such as office or social "pots," on sports events. Estimates of illegal sport betting range from $80 billion to $380 billion annually. Furthermore, some Americans cross the Mexican border to gamble or travel to the Caribbean or Central America, where sports gambling is legal.

Does Gambling Threaten College Athletics?

Wagering on college sports is a hotly contested issue. A poll conducted by the Gallup Organization in March 2002 finds that Americans were divided about whether gambling on college athletics should be made illegal throughout the country. Nearly half the surveyed respondents (49 percent) thought betting on college sports should be illegal and 47 percent felt it should not be illegal.

The National Collegiate Athletic Association (NCAA) is staunchly opposed to sports wagering because the organization contends that it attracts organized crime and has the potential to undermine the integrity of college sports contests. In its position paper, the NCAA states that "sports wagering demeans the competition and competitors alike by a message that is contrary to the purposes and meaning of sport. Sports competition should be appreciated for the inherent benefits related to participation of student-athletes, coaches and institutions in fair contests, not the amount of money wagered on the outcome of the competition."

INTERNET GAMBLING

Internet gambling first appeared on the World Wide Web in the summer of 1995. By May 1998, according to the 1999 *National Gambling Impact Study Commission Report,* there were 90 online casinos, 39 lotteries, 8 bingos, and 53 sports books. A year later, that had increased to 250 online casinos, 64 lotteries, 20 bingo games, and 139 sports books. Sebastian Sinclair, a gambling industry analyst for Christiansen Capital Advisors LLC (CCA),

estimated that the Internet gambling industry would increase from $3.1 billion in 2000 to $6.3 billion in 2003.

Industry observers estimate that more than 2 million Americans regularly place bets at casino Web sites, despite the fact that none are based within the United States. Such sites are usually located in the Caribbean and Australia. The number of visitors to casino-operated sites, as well as to other Internet gambling sites, has grown significantly. In December 2002, for example, Jupiter Media Matrix, a Web analysis firm, calculated there were 13.6 million visitors to online gambling Web sites—up significantly from the previous year.

Gambling experts contend that there are two major obstacles to the growth of Internet gaming: the 1961 Interstate Wireline Act (18 U.S.C. section 1084) and the Internet Gambling Prohibition Act, which seeks to criminalize both the operator and customer of an Internet gaming facility. The Interstate Wireline Act makes it illegal to offer or take bets from gamblers over phone lines or through other wired devices unless otherwise authorized by a particular state.

The Internet Gambling Prohibition Act, introduced in 1997, was passed by the Senate in 1998 but was held up in the House during 1999 because some legislators felt it might adversely affect other forms of e-commerce. By 2000 the bill that was originally intended to simply ban Internet gambling had been rewritten and included so many exceptions, exemptions, immunities, loopholes, and clarifying clauses that political observers thought it would be more appropriate to call it the Federal Internet Gambling Regulatory Code. Despite the many revisions and amendments, the House rejected the act on July 18, 2000. Operators of online gambling businesses were elated by this outcome.

Many countries, as well as the U.S. Department of Justice, are concerned about the enforceability of any kind of Internet gambling prohibition. Most Internet gambling businesses operate offshore and are licensed by foreign governments.

As of 2002, 55 global jurisdictions had provisions for Internet wagering. In the United States, several states have passed or are considering laws prohibiting Internet gambling. Some attorneys general have brought lawsuits against Internet gambling businesses. The Department of Justice has arrested or caused arrest warrants to be issued for more than 50 Internet gambling operators; and several have been indicted.

Nevertheless, Internet gambling is growing. A report published jointly by the CCA and the River City Group, *Wagering on the Internet,* estimates that in 2001, 19 million Americans were gambling on the Internet. In 2000 more than 700 Web sites offered gambling in the form of sports betting or casino-style games. Projections of revenue from Internet gambling vary widely, but one study predicted revenues of $1.5 billion in 2000 and $3 billion or more by 2002.

Sinclair opines that the future of this industry is bright: "E-gambling continued to grow at an astounding pace and despite the threats of limited moratoriums, potential prohibitions, and actions taken by credit card issuers. Technologies are now being developed to effectively regulate new media gambling and an increasing number of nations and states are exploring and enacting legislation to regulate the industry. E-gambling is quickly becoming a mainstream activity."

WHEN RECREATION BECOMES ADDICTION

Although gambling is simply one form of recreation and fun for many people, for 4 to 6 percent of gamblers it can become a compulsion or addiction. This behavior may cause them to gamble away their paychecks and go deeply into debt. It may harm marriages and relationships with children, other relatives, and friends.

The overwhelming majority of problem gamblers are male and most are bright, scoring well above average or high on intelligence quotient tests. For many, gambling began during the early teen years. They usually excel at trading stocks, commodities, futures, options, and bonds and at games requiring skill, such as black jack and poker. Problem gamblers are described as controlling, risk-taking, self-involved, sociable, and in need of approval, affirmation, and confirmation.

A review of 14 U.S. and 6 Canadian gambling studies on adolescents finds that between 1990 and 2000 the number of teens aged 12–17 reporting serious gambling problems increased from 10 percent to 15 percent. Teens' involvement in gambling is believed to be greater than their use of tobacco, hard liquor, and marijuana. Furthermore, gambling affects children as well as teens. In 2000 a majority of 12-year-olds had had at least 1 experience with gambling.

Problem gambling is not new—the first Gamblers Anonymous group was started in 1949. In 1972 the National Council on Problem Gambling (NCPG) was founded and in 1975 the first nationwide study was conducted to determine the scope of the problem. Maryland opened the first state-funded treatment program in 1979.

In 1980 the American Psychiatric Association accepted pathological gambling as a "disorder of impulse control." It is an illness that is chronic and progressive, but it can be diagnosed and treated. There are three phases in the progression of gambling addiction:

- The winning phase—Gamblers experience a big win or a series of wins that give them unreasonable confidence and optimism that their winning streak will continue.

During this phase they often increase the amounts of their wagers.

- The losing phase—When they are losing, gamblers often start to gamble alone, borrow money, and become irritable and withdrawn, especially when they are unable to pay off debts. Many accelerate their gambling in an effort to win back their losses.

- The desperation phase—During this phase, more time is spent gambling. The gamblers often blame others for their problems and alienate family and friends. Some may even engage in illegal activities to finance their gambling. They may feel hopeless, attempt suicide, abuse alcohol and/or other drugs, or suffer an emotional breakdown.

A national survey conducted by the NCPG finds that during 1998 about $20 million in public and private funds was spent on problem gambling programs. The programs included prevention, employee education and training, research, and treatment. In 2000 the NCPG established the National Problem Gambling Helpline (800-522-4700) and received almost 116,000 calls. The Fifteenth National Conference on Problem Gambling attracted 425 attendees from 10 countries to a conference held in Seattle, Washington, in 2001.

Does Internet Gambling Encourage Addiction?

Some researchers and industry observers believe that the Internet may attract problem gamblers, especially those who are trying to hide their gambling addiction. Others are concerned because the anonymity offered by the Internet creates the potential for children and teens, posing as adults, to gamble.

George T. Ladd and Nancy M. Petry, in "Disordered Gambling Among University-Based Medical and Dental Patients: A Focus on Internet Gambling" (*Psychology of Addictive Behaviors,* vol. 16, no. 1, March 2002), determine that while Internet gambling was the least common activity (reported by about 8 percent of problem gamblers), persons with Internet gambling experience had the most severe problems with gambling addiction.

Only 22 percent of the participants without any Internet gambling experience had problems, compared to 74 percent of those who used the Web. Internet gamblers were younger, more likely to be unmarried, and tended to have less education and income than persons who did not use the Internet to gamble.

Ladd and Petry caution that "the availability of Internet gambling may draw individuals who seek out isolated and anonymous contexts for their gambling behaviors. Accessibility and use of Internet gambling opportunities are likely to increase with the explosive growth of the Internet."

CHAPTER 7

VACATIONS AND TRAVEL

Millions of Americans love to vacation. Their vacation destinations vary from a trip to a national park for camping, fishing, boating, or hiking, to a theme park such as Disneyland. A vacation can also be a flight to Egypt, a cruise to the Virgin Islands, a romantic three-day weekend, or staying home to read a book. The way Americans vacation and travel and their expectations of vacation time have been changing as U.S. society has evolved. Unchanged, however, is Americans' conviction that travel and vacationing improves the quality of their lives.

The perception that Americans work more and have less vacation time than people in other countries around the world is accurate. Data gathered by the World Tourism Organization on nine countries find that Americans, who averaged just thirteen days per year, had the least vacation time. Italians enjoyed the most vacation with an average of forty-two days per year, followed by the French with thirty-seven days, Germans with thirty-five days, and Brazilians with thirty-four days. Residents of the United Kingdom and Canada both averaged nearly one month's vacation time and both the Koreans and Japanese averaged twenty-five days per year, nearly twice as many vacation days as Americans.

DOMESTIC TRAVEL

Where Do Americans Travel?

The U.S. Department of Transportation periodically conducts the *American Travel Survey,* which collects information about trips of 100 or more miles taken by American household members. The most recent survey for which data have been analyzed reports that Americans took nearly 685 million long-distance trips in 1995. About 96 percent of these trips—656 million trips, totaling 1 billion person trips (a person trip is one person traveling on a trip, fifty miles or more, one-way, away from home; for example, if three people from the same household go together on a trip, the trip is counted as one household trip and three

person trips)—were to destinations in the United States. Only 4 percent of trips were outside the United States. Approximately 55 percent of trips were to locations outside the traveler's home state (interstate). (See Table 7.1 for selected characteristics of domestic travelers.)

The South was the destination in 38 percent of all trips. The south Atlantic division of the South accounted for one out of five (20 percent) of all person trips. The east north central division of the Midwest attracted the next largest number of travelers, approximately 15 percent, and the Pacific division in the West drew over 13 percent. Less than 5 percent of trips were to locations in the New England division of the Northeast. (See Figure 7.1.)

According to more recent data collected by the Travel Industry Association of America (TIA), a nonprofit organization representing all components of the $537 billion travel industry, the total domestic miles traveled by U.S. citizens increased from 968 million in 1994 to more than 1 billion in 2001. More than three-quarters of these miles were described as leisure travel—that is, trips made for pleasure or personal reasons. The most miles of U.S. travel logged in 2001 occurred in summer (33 percent), followed by spring and fall, with 24 and 23 percent, respectively. Traditionally, more vacation travel occurs in the summer months because of favorable weather and because school generally is not in session during the summer, so families are able to take children on vacations.

Means of Travel

The *American Travel Survey* (1995) finds that three out of four trips within the United States were taken in a personal vehicle, resulting in over 280 billion vehicle miles of travel on U.S. highways. Personal vehicles were the favorite means of travel for shorter trips. (See Figure 7.2.) Travelers used commercial air travel for 19 percent of all trips; 72 percent of those trips were 1,000 miles or more, round-trip, with a median distance of 1,732 miles.

TABLE 7.1

Travel in the United States by selected characteristics, 1995

(Trips of 100 miles or more, one way. U.S. destinations only. Data based on a sample and subject to sampling variability)

Trip characteristic	Household trips Number (thous.)	Household trips Per-cent	Person trips Number (thous.)	Person trips Per-cent	Person miles Number (mil.)	Person miles Per-cent	Personal use vehicle trips Number (thous.)	Personal use vehicle trips Per-cent	Personal use vehicle miles Number (mil.)	Personal use vehicle miles Per-cent
Total	**656,462**	**100.0**	**1,001,319**	**100.0**	**826,804**	**100.0**	**505,154**	**100.0**	**280,127**	**100.0**
Principal means of transportation:										
Personal use vehicle	505,154	77.0	813,858	81.3	451,590	54.6	505,154	100.0	280,127	100.0
Airplane	129,164	19.7	161,165	16.1	355,286	43.0	NA	NA	NA	NA
Commercial airplane	124,884	19.0	155,936	15.6	347,934	42.1	NA	NA	NA	NA
Bus	17,340	2.6	20,445	2.0	13,309	1.6	NA	NA	NA	NA
Intercity bus	2,755	0.4	3,244	0.3	2,723	0.3	NA	NA	NA	NA
Charter or tour bus	11,890	1.8	14,247	1.4	9,363	1.1	NA	NA	NA	NA
Train	4,200	0.6	4,994	0.5	4,356	0.5	NA	NA	NA	NA
Ship, boat, or ferry	391	0.1	614	0.1	1,834	0.2	NA	NA	NA	NA
Other	213	—	243	—	429	0.1	NA	NA	NA	NA
Round trip distance:										
Less than 300 miles	194,098	29.6	306,433	30.6	74,658	9.0	185,418	36.7	45,159	16.1
300 to 499 miles	174,389	26.6	274,045	27.4	106,007	12.8	159,743	31.6	61,779	22.1
500 to 999 miles	140,046	21.3	214,006	21.4	146,631	17.7	106,846	21.2	72,114	25.7
1000 to 1999 miles	76,110	11.6	108,331	10.8	153,316	18.5	36,722	7.3	49,953	17.8
2000 miles or more	71,819	10.9	98,503	9.8	346,192	41.9	16,425	3.3	51,123	18.3
Mean (miles)	872	NA	827	NA	NA	NA	555	NA	NA	NA
Median (miles)	438	NA	425	NA	NA	NA	368	NA	NA	NA
Calendar quarter:										
1st quarter	130,963	19.9	200,331	20.0	155,603	18.8	99,549	19.7	50,801	18.1
2nd quarter	168,669	25.7	258,400	25.8	208,266	25.2	130,135	25.8	72,421	25.9
3rd quarter	193,913	29.5	304,542	30.4	261,463	31.6	152,862	30.3	90,558	32.3
4th quarter	162,917	24.8	238,047	23.8	201,471	24.4	122,607	24.3	66,346	23.7
Main purpose of trip:										
Business	192,537	29.3	224,835	22.5	212,189	25.7	125,036	24.8	61,929	22.1
Pleasure	372,586	56.8	630,110	62.9	506,971	61.3	305,571	60.5	177,698	63.4
Visit friends or relatives	195,468	29.8	330,755	33.0	264,769	32.0	159,981	31.7	92,190	32.9
Leisure*	177,119	27.0	299,355	29.9	242,201	29.3	145,590	28.8	85,508	30.5
Rest or relaxation	65,017	9.9	115,154	11.5	100,838	12.2	53,780	10.6	33,598	12.0
Sightseeing	24,272	3.7	42,649	4.3	50,781	6.1	18,069	3.6	14,654	5.2
Outdoor recreation	39,899	6.1	65,418	6.5	41,620	5.0	35,987	7.1	19,407	6.9
Entertainment	37,456	5.7	58,757	5.9	42,929	5.2	27,920	5.5	14,531	5.2
Personal business	91,319	13.9	146,338	14.6	107,621	13.0	74,532	14.8	40,490	14.5
Other	19	—	36	—	23	—	16	—	9	—
Vacation or weekend trips:										
Vacation trip	301,197	45.9	515,383	51.5	484,144	58.6	236,055	46.7	154,167	55.0
Weekend trip	270,231	41.2	441,385	44.1	325,864	39.4	216,743	42.9	118,290	42.2
1 or 2 nights away from home	151,377	23.1	252,581	25.2	132,782	16.1	133,147	26.4	60,906	21.7
3 to 5 nights away from home	118,854	18.1	188,804	18.9	193,083	23.4	83,597	16.5	57,384	20.5
Travel party type and size:										
One adult, no children under 18	386,479	58.9	386,510	38.6	352,350	42.6	275,034	54.4	144,795	51.7
Two or more adults, no children under 18	155,148	23.6	299,485	29.9	248,762	30.1	133,163	26.4	79,273	28.3
One adult, 1 or more children under 18	29,436	4.5	67,959	6.8	48,083	5.8	24,879	4.9	13,827	4.9
Two or more adults, 1 or more children under 18	66,086	10.1	225,875	22.6	158,334	19.2	60,497	12.0	34,758	12.4
No adult, 1 or more children under 18	19,313	2.9	21,489	2.1	19,275	2.3	11,581	2.3	7,472	2.7
Mean travel party size (household members)	1.6	NA	2.2	NA	NA	NA	1.7	NA	NA	NA
Nights away from home:										
None	164,032	25.0	239,727	23.9	104,444	12.6	140,914	27.9	49,619	17.7
1 to 3 nights	321,227	48.9	502,465	50.2	331,504	40.1	259,354	51.3	131,559	47.0
4 to 7 nights	121,279	18.5	184,766	18.5	243,546	29.5	76,380	15.1	61,317	21.9
8 or more nights	49,924	7.6	74,361	7.4	147,309	17.8	28,506	5.6	37,631	13.4
Mean excluding none (nights)	4.5	NA	4.3	NA	NA	NA	4.0	NA	NA	NA
Type of lodging at destination:										
One or more nights at destination	486,305	100.0	751,958	100.0	709,097	100.0	359,745	100.0	226,001	100.0
Friend's or relative's home	211,832	43.6	345,506	45.9	290,428	41.0	170,271	47.3	103,180	45.7
Hotel, motel, or resort	201,264	41.4	282,929	37.6	318,323	44.9	126,160	35.1	82,447	36.5
Rented cabin, condo, or vacation home	17,607	3.6	30,648	4.1	31,161	4.4	14,631	4.1	10,809	4.8
Owned cabin, condo, or vacation home	20,205	4.2	38,572	5.1	26,269	3.7	18,103	5.0	9,819	4.3
Camper, trailer, recreational vehicle, tent	11,944	2.5	22,208	3.0	15,836	2.2	11,663	3.2	8,204	3.6
Other type of lodging	23,452	4.8	32,095	4.3	27,080	3.8	18,917	5.3	11,542	5.1
Nights at destination:										
Mean nights at destination	4.2	NA	4.0	NA	NA	NA	3.8	NA	NA	NA
Friend's or relative' home	4.3	NA	4.0	NA	NA	NA	3.6	NA	NA	NA
Hotel, motel, or resort	3.0	NA	3.0	NA	NA	NA	2.8	NA	NA	NA

— Represents zero or a value too small to report.   * Includes other leisure purposes not shown separately.   NA Not applicable.

Note: Numbers and percents may not add to totals due to rounding.

SOURCE: "Table 1. Travel in the United States by Selected Trip Characteristics: 1995," in *1995 American Travel Survey: Profile*, U.S. Department of Transportation, Bureau of Transportation Statistics, Washington, DC, October 1997

Recreation: Having a Good Time in America

FIGURE 7.1

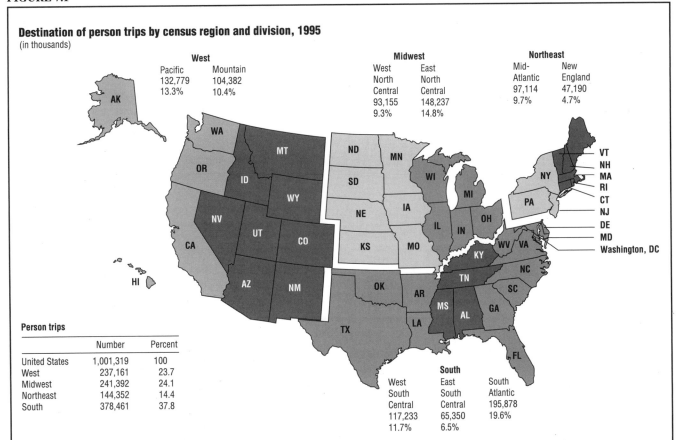

Destination of person trips by census region and division, 1995
(in thousands)

SOURCE: "Figure 2. Destinations of Person Trips by Census Region and Division: 1995," in *1995 American Travel Survey: Profile,* U.S. Department of Transportation, Bureau of Transportation Statistics, Washington, DC, October 1997

Tour or charter buses were used for only 2 percent of trips. Intercity bus and train travel accounted for less than 1 percent of trips. Intercity bus and train trips were more likely to be taken by persons sixty-five and over, females, minorities, those less educated, and those living in households with incomes under $25,000.

The TIA study finds that ground transportation—personal automobile, truck, recreational vehicle (RV), bus, and rental car—was used for nearly 80 percent of domestic U.S. travel in 2001. Airplane travel accounted for 17 percent of domestic transportation.

AIR TRAVEL TAKES A NOSEDIVE. The entire travel industry, as well as hospitality and other tourism-dependent businesses, declined sharply following the September 11, 2001, terrorist attacks. Air travel was hardest hit, and by late 2002 one major airline and several smaller ones had filed for bankruptcy.

A 2002 TIA consumer poll, the *Air Travel Survey,* considered possible reasons for the continued declines in air travel. Sponsored by the Bureau of Transportation Statistics, the survey was based on a representative sample of 4,000 travelers who had traveled by air at least once in the past year.

Thirty percent of all air business travelers reported traveling less by air in the twelve months preceding the survey, compared to only 21 percent who said they traveled more. Nearly 30 percent of business travelers said they planned to travel more by air in 2003 and 55 percent said they would travel the same amount. The majority (80 percent) of leisure air travelers reported traveling the same amount or more in 2002 than they had in the past and only 14 percent predicted they would travel less or not at all by air during 2003.

Concern about the U.S. economy as well as their personal or business finances may have affected Americans' outlook about travel and the airline industry. Just 16 percent of business and leisure air travelers said they were satisfied with the current cost of air travel, a surprising finding in view of the fact that in 2002 airfares were at their lowest level since 1988.

Reasons for Travel

The TIA study finds that of the 1 billion person trips Americans took in 2001, more than three-quarters of the trips were for pleasure. Of the remaining trips, 13 percent were for business, 8 percent combined business and pleasure, and 3 percent were for personal or other reasons.

FIGURE 7.2

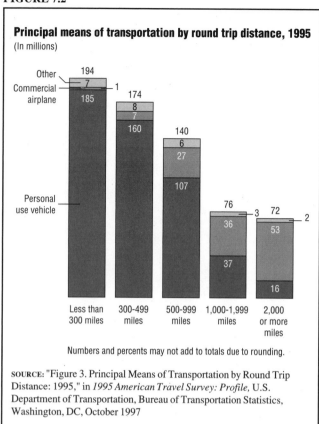

Principal means of transportation by round trip distance, 1995
(In millions)

SOURCE: "Figure 3. Principal Means of Transportation by Round Trip Distance: 1995," in *1995 American Travel Survey: Profile*, U.S. Department of Transportation, Bureau of Transportation Statistics, Washington, DC, October 1997

The TIA also reports that shopping was a favorite activity of travelers during 2001. Thirty-four percent of travelers shopped during a trip. Other popular trip activities included spending time outdoors (17 percent), visiting historical sites or museums (14 percent), going to the beach (11 percent), attending cultural events/festivals (10 percent), and visiting national and state parks (10 percent). Other trip activities engaged in by less than 10 percent of travelers were visiting theme or amusement parks (9 percent), gambling (8 percent), nightlife/dancing (8 percent), attending sporting events (6 percent), and golf/tennis/skiing (4 percent).

Weekend Travel

The growing number of two-career families often makes it difficult for families to schedule long trips. Weekend trips, especially three-day weekends, have become the practical, if not ideal, solution for such couples.

According to the TIA, most travelers in 2001 made short trips involving either no overnight stay at their destinations (17 percent) or short stays of one to two nights (38 percent). Less than one-third of domestic travelers took three- to six-night trips and just 14 percent were away for seven or more nights.

Weekend trips have increased dramatically. The TIA reports that weekend trips by Americans increased by 70 percent during the 1990s. Weekend trips now account for more than half of all U.S. travel.

Not all travel is planned in advance. In 2001 more than 83 million American adults took last-minute trips. Most last-minute travelers (70 percent) used their own cars, 15 percent used air transportation, and 8 percent took RVs. About one-third of these trips involved overnight stays of three to four days, just 12 percent were longer than eight days, and 9 percent of last-minute travelers made day trips.

Type of Lodging

Of travelers who spent one or more nights away from home, 41 percent stayed with friends or family, while more than half (51 percent) stayed in a hotel, motel, or bed and breakfast. Seven percent stayed in RVs or tents, 5 percent found lodging in condos or time-shares, and 8 percent found other accommodations.

Who Travels?

The TIA reports that baby boomers (aged thirty-five to fifty-four) generated the highest volume of domestic travel in 2001, and the average age of the head of household of domestic travelers was forty-eight. About two-thirds of domestic travelers were married, 19 percent were single or never married, and 18 percent were divorced, widowed, or separated. More than a third (36 percent) of the travelers had children in their households.

Fifty-seven percent of the heads of household that traveled held college degrees and 42 percent were employed in managerial or professional occupations. Seventeen percent of travelers were retirees. The average annual household income of travelers increased from $61,500 in 1999 to $68,800 in 2001.

TAKING THE KIDS ALONG. According to the TIA, more adults traveled with children during 2001 than they had during 2000—more than 180 million adults said they included a child or children on a trip during 2001. The percentage of adults traveling with children was up from almost 18 percent from 1994. Not surprisingly, children accompanied adults on more pleasure trips than business trips, however, the percentage of adults who brought children along on business trips grew by more than 20 percent between 1994 and 2001.

PLANNING AND ENJOYING FAMILY TRAVEL. A family travel survey commissioned by Avis, the car rental company, in 2002 looked at how American families prepare for car trips and summer road vacations. Along with travel planning, the 1,000 American parents who participated in the survey were asked about passenger concerns, automobile maintenance, and entertaining children while on the road.

The survey finds that many families (46 percent) planned summer vacations that would enable them to spend quality time with one another. Other motivations for planning family trips included visiting family and friends (25 percent) and exploring new parts of the country (14 percent).

Vacation destinations were most often determined by mothers (49 percent), compared to fathers who decided just 24 percent of travel plans. Children were named as influences by 10 percent of the surveyed respondents and grandparents by 4 percent.

More than three-quarters of the families surveyed used information obtained from the Internet and road atlases as their primary source of maps and directions to plan trips. Other less widely used sources were friends and family (50 percent), clerks at gas stations or convenience stores (20 percent), or rental car maps (7 percent).

Nearly half of parents surveyed said they would prefer to take several short trips during the summer, as opposed to one long trip. When families took to the road, fathers typically handled more of the driving (62 percent), while mothers drove just 33 percent of the time.

Rather than relying on digital videodisc (DVD) and videocassette recorder (VCR) players to amuse children, as they might when they were at home, respondents said they preferred to entertain children during car trips by engaging them in traditional pastimes, such as sing-a-longs, reading, and made-up games. Only 14 percent of parents used DVD and VCR players to entertain children in the car.

THE NATURE TRAIL

National parks are one of America's biggest tourist attractions. The United States has set aside 80 million acres of land for national parks. The National Park System (NPS) includes parks, monuments, historical and military areas, parkways, recreation areas, nature preserves, rivers, seashores, and lakes.

In 2001 the majority of national park and state forest visits were made by baby boomers (adults aged thirty-five to fifty-four) who were married (62 percent) and nearly half (47 percent) had children. National parks offer many opportunities for families to enjoy activities together or individually, and because visitors' fees are low, a trip to a national park is a popular summer vacation choice for many families with children.

The TIA reports that 10 percent of U.S. domestic travelers visited a national or state park in 2001. Participating in outdoor activities, including visits to national or state parks, was the second most popular activity cited by American travelers.

THE LURE OF SAND, SURF, AND OCEAN BREEZES

Americans flock to the beach in the summer. The TIA reports that in 2001, nearly 110 million person trips were made to beaches, up 7 percent from the year before. Near-

TABLE 7.2

Annual cruise ship passengers, 1980–2001

	Passengers (in thousands)
1980	1,431
1981	1,453
1982	1,471
1983	1,755
1984	1,859
1985	2,152
1986	2,624
1987	2,898
1988	3,175
1989	3,286
1990	3,640
1991	3,979
1992	4,136
1993	4,480
1994	4,448
1995	4,378
1996	4,656
1997	5,051
1998	5,428
1999	5,894
2000	6,882
2001	6,906
Average annual growth rate 1980-2001	8.40%

SOURCE: Adapted from "The Big Picture," in *Cruise Industry Overview,* Cruise Lines International Association, New York, NY, Spring 2002

ly four out of ten (37 percent) beach trips were family vacations that included a child and the average beach trip with at least one overnight stay lasted 5.9 nights.

Travel to the beach involves air transportation more often than other travel (21 percent versus 17 percent), probably because of the distances involved for visitors who live far from the U.S. coasts. Beach travelers do more than swim, sunbathe, and stroll along the shores—nearly half of beach trips involve shopping, almost one-quarter of beachgoers visit historical sites or museums, 20 percent enjoy national or state parks, and 17 percent include a visit to an amusement or theme park.

GOING ON CRUISES—NEW PORTS AND OPTIONS

A New Generation of Cruisers

For many travelers, few experiences compare to sailing to exotic destinations on a cruise ship. According to the Cruise Lines International Association (CLIA), an organization of twenty-three member cruise lines, since 1980, when 1.4 million Americans took cruises, the cruise industry has grown by an average of more than 8 percent each year. (See Table 7.2.) About 7.4 million people cruised during 2002. The CLIA asserts that cruising appeals to Americans seeking to be pampered and to enjoy fine dining, as well as to those who wish to visit several destinations. Cruising is also considered better than other vacations in terms of ease of planning, being a good value, and offering quality entertainment.

TABLE 7.3

Demographic profile of cruisers

		Ever cruised	Past 5 year cruisers	Cruise prospects	Non-vacationers
Gender:	Male	49%	51%	50%	50%
	Female	51%	48%	49%	50%
Age:	25-under 40 years	27%	28%	43%	35%
	40-59 years	42%	42%	44%	43%
	60 years or older	32%	30%	13%	22%
	Average	51 yrs.	50 yrs.	43 yrs.	47 yrs.
	Median	51 yrs.	51 yrs.	42 yrs.	47 yrs.
Marital status:	Married	76%	78%	69%	65%
	Not married	24%	22%	31%	35%
Household composition:	Have children under 18	37%	35%	54%	51%
	Adults only	63%	65%	46%	49%
	Occupants	3	3	3	3
Education:	Some college or less	42%	36%	54%	76%
	College graduate or more	58%	64%	46%	24%
Household income:	$20,000-$29,999	8%	5%	13%	32%
	$30,000-$39,999	12%	10%	17%	26%
	$40,000-$59,999	32%	31%	31%	27%
	$60,000-$99,999	28%	30%	29%	11%
	$100,000 or more	20%	25%	9%	4%
	Average	$72,600	$79,100	$60,400	$44,200
	Median	$58,500	$64,500	$51,800	$36,900

* Repercentaged without refusal/no answer

SOURCE: "Demographic Profiles," in *Cruise Industry Overview,* Cruise Lines International Association, New York, NY, Spring 2002

In 2001 the cruise industry created 268,000 American jobs and contributed $20 billion to the U.S. economy. Although the North American cruise industry suffered in the aftermath of the events of September 11, 2001, according to the CLIA, the industry had rebounded by February 2002. Several of the CLIA's member cruise lines reported record numbers of reservations made in the first three weeks of January 2002, the period known in the cruise industry as the "Wave Period" because it usually provides a good indication of booking activity for the balance of the year.

Historically, most cruise passengers were over the age of sixty. Today's cruise vacationers are younger, active, and adventurous. (See Table 7.3.) Almost half of the people who cruised during 2000 were first-timers, and eight out of ten of them reported they would cruise again. The CLIA reports that current cruisers (those who had cruised during the past five years) were:

• Nearly evenly distributed among all age ranges. The average age was fifty years. Twenty-eight percent were under forty years, 42 percent were forty to fifty-nine, and 30 percent were over the age of sixty.

• Almost equally male (51 percent) and female (48 percent).

• Predominantly married (78 percent).

• Less likely than the average vacationer to have children under eighteen in the family.

• Spread among all income ranges, with a median income of $64,500. One-quarter earned more than $100,000 a year and 15 percent earned less than $40,000 per year.

According to the CLIA, from 1997 to 2002 cruises sailed, in general, at about 90 percent of capacity. In 2001 the average length of cruises was 6.4 days. (See Table 7.4.) Cruises ranged in cost from $75 to more than $500 per day per adult, depending on cabin choices, upgrades, and other features, but nearly all included meals and entertainment. Children often traveled free or at reduced cost. Growth is predicted in all types of cruises, especially short cruises (one to five days).

Cruisers Run the Gamut

The CLIA describes the market of recent cruisers as containing basically six different types of people. Understanding the distinctions is important to the cruise lines because it enables them to customize cruise itineraries, programs, and promotions to appeal to the various market segments. Figure 7.3 shows the percentage of the six types of consumers in the current cruiser market:

• Restless Baby Boomers—New to cruising, they are cost-conscious but are also open to trying different vacation experiences. The CLIA estimates that this segment represents 33 percent of total cruising days and 59 percent are first-timers.

• Enthusiastic Baby Boomers—Wild about cruising, they lead intense, stressful lives and seek vacations

TABLE 7.4

Average length of cruises, 1981–2001

	Average length of cruise (days)	Percentage of total passengers in 2-5 day category
1981	6.7	29.6%
1982	6.9	25.3
1983	6.9	21.6
1984	6.9	22.3
1985	6.8	26.3
1986	6.4	35.1
1987	6.4	32.8
1988	6.4	32.9
1989	6.4	33.8
1990	6.2	38.3
1991	6.1	37.4
1992	6.2	35.2
1993	6.4	36.7
1994	6.3	38.0
1995	6.5	33.7
1996	6.4	35.9
1997	6.5	33.6
1998	6.7	34.7
1999	6.6	35.8
2000	6.5	36.9
2001	6.4	37.2

SOURCE: "Average Length of Cruise" in *Cruise Industry Overview,* Cruise Lines International Association, New York, NY, Spring 2002

FIGURE 7.3

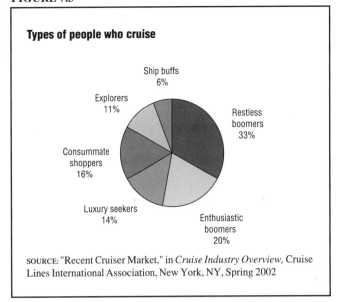

Types of people who cruise

Ship buffs 6%
Explorers 11%
Restless boomers 33%
Consummate shoppers 16%
Luxury seekers 14%
Enthusiastic boomers 20%

SOURCE: "Recent Cruiser Market," in *Cruise Industry Overview,* Cruise Lines International Association, New York, NY, Spring 2002

TABLE 7.5

Number of cruise passengers, by length of cruise, 1980–2001

	1980 (Thousands)	2001 (Thousands)	Growth (in percent)
2-5 days	347	2,566	639.5
6-8 days	846	3,549	319.5
9-17 days	221	757	242.5
18+ days	17	34	100
Total	1,431	6,906	382.3

SOURCE: "Growth by Length of Cruise," in *Cruise Industry Overview,* Cruise Lines International Association, New York, NY, Spring 2002

that offer opportunities for escape and relaxation. This segment accounts for 20 percent of total cruising days and 46 percent are first-timers.

- Luxury Seekers—Are able and willing to spend money for deluxe accommodations and pampering. This segment represents 14 percent of total cruising days and 30 percent are first-timers.

- Consummate Shoppers—Seek the best value in a cruise. This segment represents 16 percent of total cruising days and 20 percent are first-timers.

- Explorers—Are highly educated, well-traveled consumers with a keen interest and curiosity about their destinations. This segment represents 11 percent of total cruising days and 20 percent are first-timers.

- Ship Buffs—Are seasoned cruisers who find the on-board experience of cruising satisfying and comfortable. This segment represents 6 percent of total cruising days and 13 percent are first-timers.

Unprecedented Cruise Options

Short cruises are extremely popular, with many Americans favoring long weekend getaways. In 2001, 37 percent of those who cruised took short, two- to five-day cruises. (See Table 7.5.) Among the most popular destinations for short cruises were the Bahamas, the Caribbean, the west coast of Mexico, the Mediterranean, the Mississippi River, Hawaii, Canada/New England, the West Coast, and Bermuda. (See Table 7.6.) Transatlantic cross-

ings and party cruises were also available in shorter trips. Theme cruises included "big band" cruises, arts and crafts, wine and food festivals featuring famous chefs, Civil War trips, and jazz and film festivals. Many people enjoyed day trips, which often included gambling.

CLIA-member lines visit 1,800 ports of call around the world. From Antarctica to the Caribbean, and Africa to the Mississippi, cruises reach virtually all waters of the world. Cruise ship passengers can visit ancient Buddhist temples in Indonesia, sip cappuccino in Venice, watch whales on the Pacific Coast, scuba dive in the Caribbean, or shop in Turkey. For passengers who prefer relaxing, as opposed to exhilarating vacations, the opportunity to simply lounge in a deck chair or read is enjoyable. Cruise ship cuisine is legendary, as is the pampering most cruisers experience.

In an effort to attract families, many ships offer extensive youth facilities and programs that include kids-only shore excursions. The CLIA reports that about 15 percent of people going on cruises traveled with children. Cruise lines such as Disney's Big Red Boat were designed and outfitted to appeal to families.

TABLE 7.6

Cruise destinations, 1987–2002

Destination	1987 total bed-days	1995 total bed-days	1998 total bed-days	1999 total bed-days	2000 total bed-days	2001 total bed-days	2001 %	2002 total bed-days	2002 %	Percentage change 2001–02
Caribbean	8,828,791	15,254,551	17,117,659	16,666,328	21,510,142	21,833,347	36.64%	26,741,052	42.06%	22.48%
Mediterranean	841,051	3,477,729	5,092,530	5,898,948	6,277,064	7,546,816	12.67%	6,497,444	10.22%	-13.90%
Alaska	1,715,197	3,008,146	3,790,816	4,086,620	4,197,332	4,698,538	7.89%	5,052,907	7.95%	7.54%
Bahamas	1,922,386	2,761,224	2,891,352	3,060,866	3,200,346	4,698,724	7.89%	2,876,295	4.52%	-38.79%
Trans Canal	970,191	2,277,201	2,612,788	3,036,208	2,573,444	2,396,424	4.02%	2,092,723	3.29%	-12.67%
Mexico West	1,131,462	1,754,312	2,421,126	2,529,106	2,680,934	1,166,756	1.96%	3,386,475	5.33%	190.25%
Europe	357,516	1,582,589	3,714,437	3,475,922	3,744,693	4,837,375	8.12%	6,922,608	10.89%	43.11%
Bermuda	1,141,121	1,094,707	1,094,982	1,482,573	988,391	1,269,952	2.13%	1,226,806	1.93%	-3.40%
Transatlantic	339,388	658,928	725,040	961,213	1,015,625	1,129,669	1.90%	1,005,665	1.58%	-10.98%
Hawaii	602,728	601,542	745,216	885,268	857,390	1,557,438	2.61%	1,903,302	2.99%	22.21%
South Pacific	352,983	574,218	369,507	947,382	1,155,217	1,158,004	1.94%	835,454	1.31%	-27.86%
South East Asia	272,592	430,123	157,705	150,107	244,620	429,550	0.72%	346,196	0.54%	-19.40%
Africa	0	347,432	291,850	184,373	502,773	401,011	0.67%	259,962	0.41%	-35.17%
Canada/New England	283,714	334,735	527,530	681,689	1,107,689	1,138,975	1.91%	1,150,950	1.81%	1.05%
Far East (Orient)	465,608	327,009	218,988	188,038	201,582	215,022	0.36%	360,022	0.57%	67.43%
Mississippi	231,392	286,228	353,510	353,088	347,140	403,956	0.68%	0	0.00%	-100.00%
World	0	272,425	545,242	565,824	414,342	613,046	1.03%	582,314	0.92%	-5.01%
South America	620,396	255,83	943,392	657,992	825,670	1,422,755	2.39%	1,394,808	2.19%	-1.96%
U.S. Coastal West	64,444	108,092	136,198	65,108	217,518	1,944,752	3.26%	216,338	0.34%	-88.88%
Indian Ocean	0	84,009	90,159	40,572	120,698	227,483	0.38%	93,708	0.15%	-58.81%
Unclassified	0	69,560	119,158	86,890	108,676	239,774	0.40%	233,258	0.37%	-2.72%
Trans Pacific	17,904	42,610	99,814	86,150	52,400	67,120	0.11%	143,020	0.22%	113.08%
U.S. Coastal East	132,794	42,840	50,648	113,387	1,402,429	80,312	0.13%	147,422	0.23%	83.56%
Antarctica	0	12,240	63,603	53,179	48,499	48,517	0.08%	73,176	0.12%	50.83%
Party Cruises	85,336	3,602	67,462	59,846	68,203	56,010	0.09%	43,296	0.07%	-22.70%
	20,376,994	35,661,526	44,240,712	46,316,587	53,862,817	59,581,366	100.00%	63,585,211	100.00%	6.72%

Note: Current destination classifications were established in 1994. Prior to 1985, Bermuda was included in Bahamas/Caribbean, Mississippi and Coastal East were not reported. Prior to 1992, Indian Ocean and Africa were part of unclassified. In 1993 Mexico East was changed to Western Caribbean.

SOURCE: "Geographical Destination/Application," in *Cruise Industry Overview*, Cruise Lines International Association, New York, NY, Spring 2002

ECOTOURISM

"Green" (advantageous to the environment) travel is important to many travelers. The Vermont-based Ecotourism Society defines this kind of tourism as "responsible travel to natural areas which conserves the environment and sustains the well being of local people." The TIA reports that 83 percent of travelers supported green travel companies and claimed they were willing to spend an average of 6.2 percent more for travel services and products provided by environmentally responsible travel vendors and suppliers.

The Ecotourism Society reports survey data that reveals considerable interest in nature-based activities among vacationers. Nearly half (48.1 percent) of the more than 3,340 surveyed participants indicated a degree of enthusiasm for activities such as biking, hiking, canoeing, and visiting parks, as well as observing animals and other wildlife when they vacation. Of these nature enthusiasts, more than 30 percent were termed either "heavy users" (who planned trips that involved nature-based recreation the majority of the time) or "moderate users" (who planned trips that entailed some time spent pursuing nature-based activities).

The Ecotourism Society characterizes the typical ecotourist as between the ages of thirty-five and fifty-four, a college graduate, and as likely to be male as female. Experienced ecotourists preferred trips of longer duration, from eight to fourteen days, and were willing to spend more on travel than general tourists. The activities ecotourists favored included visiting parks, hiking, exploring preserved areas, and wildlife viewing.

During the 1990s a large number of ecotourism companies sprang up, promoting vacations that were claimed to conserve the environment and directly benefit local and indigenous (native) people. While some operators succeeded in achieving their ambitious ecological objectives, a few unscrupulous operators may have used the "eco" label as a marketing device for tours that exposed fragile regions, such as the Amazon River, to tourism without regard for their preservation.

CULTURAL AND HERITAGE TOURISM

Heritage tourism seeks to draw visitors to historic and cultural sites. Although historic and cultural destinations are not as popular with leisure travelers as cities, visits to friends and family, beaches, and lakes, a significant number of travelers choose educational experiences.

According to the TIA report *The Historic/Cultural Traveler, 2001 Edition*, nearly 93 million Americans attended at least one cultural, arts, heritage, or historic activity or event while traveling in 2001. Many travelers prolonged their trips solely to participate in cultural or historic events and activities. Almost one-third (32 percent) of historic/cultural travelers (29.6 million) said they added extra time to their trips to enable them to attend a cultural, arts, heritage, or historic activity or event.

The TIA finds that these travelers spend more—an average of $631 per trip, compared to $457 for all U.S. travelers, excluding transportation to their destinations. The report also distinguishes historic/cultural travelers from other travelers, describing them as inclined to take longer trips (5.7 nights versus 5.1 nights), and more likely to use air travel. Travelers interested in arts and history were more willing to participate in a variety of activities while traveling and frequented hotels, motels, and bed and breakfast establishments more often. Historic/cultural travelers were also observed to:

- Add extra time to their trip because of that activity. Part of a day was added by 43 percent, one night by 31 percent, two extra nights by 19 percent, and three or more nights by 74 percent.

- Travel in June, July, and August. Twice as many historic/cultural travelers (6 percent) took group tours, compared to other travelers (3 percent). More than 20 percent reported primarily using air travel.

- Be older than other U.S. travelers (forty-eight versus forty-six years old), have a postgraduate education (23 percent versus 20 percent), and participate in four or more activities while traveling (17 percent versus 5 percent).

- Shop more than other U.S. travelers (44 percent versus 33 percent) and make more visits to national and state parks, outdoor venues, beaches, and theme parks.

- Choose south Atlantic and Pacific destinations for travel more frequently than other travelers.

Consumer interest has led many corporate sponsors to invest in programs promoting heritage tourism. Travel services companies have invested in projects by the National Trust for Historic Preservation to help communities develop and maintain their historic and cultural sites. Some hotels and car rental agencies have contributed to school programs to educate children about historic sites across the United States.

Civil War Reenactments—Mock Combat

A growing number of people participate in reenactments of the U.S. Civil War. Estimates of the number of these hobbyists vary. In 1996 a reenactment of the Battle of Antietam drew 13,000 costumed people to Maryland. In 1997 almost 20,000 costumed soldiers and civilians went to Gettysburg for the 134th anniversary of that battle. The *Camp Chase Gazette,* a trade publication, estimates that in 2000 there were between 20,000 and 25,000 active Civil War reenactors. When they attended a reenactment, they were often accompanied by their families.

Reenactors visit school classrooms, march in parades, teach seminars, hold public demonstrations, and participate in weekend battle games. Groups also meet in a number of overseas countries, including England, Germany, Taiwan, France, Belgium, Spain, Japan, Sweden, and Norway. The hobby has also spread to areas of the country that never experienced the war. About 100 reenactment groups have Internet sites. In California, the American Civil War Association grew from 6 member groups in 1995 to 500 in 1998. One of the biggest groups, the North-South Alliance, is based in Nashville, Tennessee, and includes the 3,500-member First Federal Division and the 5,000-member First Confederate Division.

Reenactments began during the 1960s at the time of the Civil War's centennial. A love of history and a desire to educate are the primary motivations mentioned by reenactors. Interest in reenactments often grows after mass-market films about the war are shown on television or at the movies.

Civil War reenactments are not for everyone. Just getting started requires buying period clothes, boots, a tent, mess equipment, and a gun, at a cost of $1,000 to $1,500. The cost can reach $2,000 for members of groups that strive for authenticity. These groups are so exacting that they do not allow members to use modern speech or eyeglasses. An estimated 200 businesses have grown to satisfy the need for authenticity in costumes, including "great coats" and brogans (heavy, ankle-high shoes), and equipment. Participating in reenactments requires physical strength, vigor, and endurance. Young men serve as soldiers since the average age of soldiers fell from twenty-five in 1862 to eighteen in 1864. Some older adult enthusiasts remain involved in the activity as spectators when marching long distances in inclement weather becomes too physically demanding.

ROMANTIC VACATIONS

Many Americans dream about romantic getaways with a spouse or other love interest to ignite or rekindle romantic feelings in the relationship. According to the January 2002 *TIA Travel Poll,* more than 42 million American adults said they had taken a romantic vacation in the year preceding the poll. Many of these reported romantic vacations were honeymoons or anniversary celebrations.

Not surprisingly, the periodic TIA surveys find that Americans without children in their households took more romantic vacations than parents with children. The 2002 poll reveals that romance-related travel was most popular among baby boomers—four out of ten (41 percent) romance travelers were aged thirty-five to fifty-four. One-third (33 percent) of these travelers were Generation X and Y travelers (aged eighteen to thirty-four). The majority (67 percent) of romance-related travelers were married. Many of these travelers (38 percent) had above-average annual household incomes of $50,000 or more.

Residents of the South (35 percent) were more likely than those living in the West (24 percent), Midwest (26 percent), and Northeast (15 percent) to have taken romance-related trips during 2001.

SHOPPING TRIPS TO OUTLET MALLS

Outlet shopping malls are becoming major attractions for American travelers. According to the *TIA Travel Poll*, out of all travelers on trips of 100 or more miles away from home, almost 40 percent visited a discount outlet mall in 2000. Of the visitors, 46 percent were men and 54 percent were women. One out of ten respondents cited outlet-shopping as the primary reason for the trip. Most said it was the secondary reason, and about 10 percent said it was not an original reason for the trip, although they did visit the malls.

FAMILY REUNIONS

Family reunions were popular with about one-third of Americans, according to the January 2002 *TIA Travel Poll*. Thirty-four percent of U.S. adults (72 million) had traveled to a family reunion during the three-year period preceding the poll and one in five had traveled to a family reunion in the year preceding the poll.

Married people were more likely to take a trip to attend a family reunion than unmarried people (38 percent versus 30 percent). Similarly, adults with children under eighteen were more inclined than those without children to take a family reunion trip (39 percent versus 32 percent). There is a widespread willingness to travel great distances to reconnect with far-flung family members: 34 percent of surveyed respondents reported traveling 500 or more miles one way away from home. Another 34 percent traveled between 150 and 499 miles, while 32 percent traveled less than 150 miles to attend reunions.

Family reunions were most often held in a private home (52 percent). The TIA poll finds that other popular locations for reunions were city or town parks (12 percent) and national or state parks or forests (6 percent).

COMBINING BUSINESS AND PLEASURE TRIPS

According to the TIA report *Business and Convention Travelers, 2001 Edition,* almost one out of five Americans took a business trip during 2001. More than one-third (36 percent) of all business travel included some time for pleasure, and most business travel (84 percent) included an overnight stay. When travelers stayed overnight, their trips lasted an average of five nights. Most stayed at hotels, motels, or bed and breakfasts. One-third of combined overnight household trips (more than one person traveling) involved a stay at homes of friends or family. On average, combined business and pleasure travelers spent $639 per household trip.

Half of combined business and pleasure household trips were taken by solo travelers, one-third were taken by multiple adults from a household, and one in five included a child. Baby boomers were the most likely to take combined business and pleasure trips, and households with at least one college degree took two-thirds of combined trips. About half of combined travelers were professionals or employed in managerial capacities and their median household income was $57,800. One-third of combined business and pleasure trips were taken by households with children who lived at home.

In an effort to attract and better serve business travelers, during the 1990s many hotels installed in-room fax machines and high-speed Internet access. These accommodations were important to business travelers since, based on 2001 TIA survey data, nearly half of all business travelers went online when they traveled and about one out of three traveled with a laptop computer.

Business Travel Declines

A 2000 TIA report documents a 2.4 percent decline in the volume of business person trips since 1999. By 2000 business-related travel had already slowed. The events of September 11, 2001, and an uncertain economy resulted in a sharper decline in the frequency of business travel. A TIA survey of air travelers conducted during 2002 finds that 30 percent of all air business travelers reported traveling less by air in the twelve months preceding the survey.

According to the TIA, nearly 80 percent of all companies have established or recently revised business travel policies and one-third of surveyed respondents reported that some of these policies were implemented at some point during the year preceding the survey. Some of the new restrictions on corporate travel included limiting the class of air service that can be used (14 percent), permitting U.S.-only travel (31 percent), limiting travel per diems (19 percent), restricting the number of employees traveling (25 percent), and requiring or recommending that employees drive rather than fly (34 percent). Other new policies aimed at containing costs were restricting the number of trips taken (39 percent), limiting trip duration (25 percent), and restricting the class of hotel (14 percent).

Surveyed corporate travelers said weakened business conditions, reduced travel budgets, the unstable economy, and the high cost of travel have reduced the need for travel. The TIA attributes some of the decline in business

FIGURE 7.4

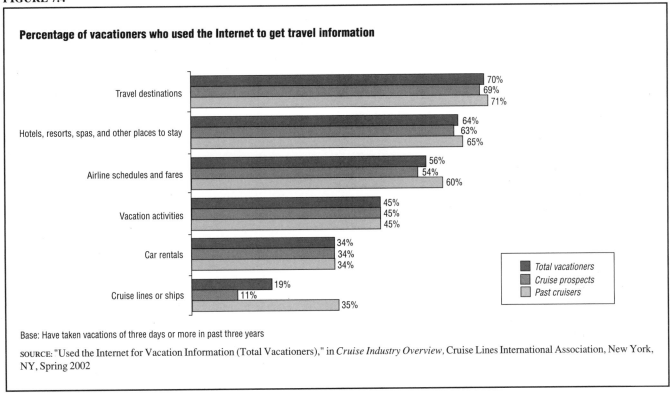

Percentage of vacationers who used the Internet to get travel information

Travel destinations — 70% / 69% / 71%

Hotels, resorts, spas, and other places to stay — 64% / 63% / 65%

Airline schedules and fares — 56% / 54% / 60%

Vacation activities — 45% / 45% / 45%

Car rentals — 34% / 34% / 34%

Cruise lines or ships — 19% / 11% / 35%

Total vacationers
Cruise prospects
Past cruisers

Base: Have taken vacations of three days or more in past three years

SOURCE: "Used the Internet for Vacation Information (Total Vacationers)," in *Cruise Industry Overview*, Cruise Lines International Association, New York, NY, Spring 2002

travel to enhanced online business communications and the use of technology as alternatives to taking business trips. Teleconferencing was used by 42 percent of all air business travelers in the year preceding the survey as a substitute for taking a business trip. Video conferencing and Web casting or conferencing were used instead of taking trips by 17 percent and 15 percent, respectively, of business travelers. The use of alternatives increased with respondents' reported frequency of travel. One-quarter of frequent air travelers (eight or more trips per year) substituted some business travel with alternative communication techniques, compared to only 15 percent of infrequent travelers. Two-thirds of all air business travelers deemed alternative technologies more efficient in terms of the time and money spent on travel, however, only 20 percent considered them more effective.

ARRANGED TRIPS FOR OLDER ADULTS

Elderhostel, a nonprofit organization that arranges trips that combine learning and recreation for people 55 and older, has grown from 240 participants in the 1980s to 10,000 programs attended by more than 250,000 people a year. Along with exotic travel adventures around the world, Elderhostel has developed intergenerational programs that pair grandparents with their grandchildren in a range of learning adventures. It has turned ships and barges into floating classrooms and created service programs that offer participants the chance to volunteer for worthy causes around the world.

TECHNOLOGY AND TRAVEL

The TIA reports in its *Travelers' Use of the Internet* that 64 million travelers used the Internet in 2002. Use of the Internet for travel planning has skyrocketed since 1997, when just 12 million Americans planned and researched travel online. The rate of growth in the online travel planning market slowed from 2000 to 2001 in response to the slower rate of growth of "wired" (Internet-connected) households.

Although the overall number of online travel planners did not increase from 2000 to 2001, consumers were doing more travel research and planning online than ever before. Forty-two percent of surveyed respondents said they did all or most of their trip research and planning online, up from 29 percent from the previous year. During 2002 more than 39 million people booked travel using the Internet, an increase of 25 percent from 2001. The Internet was also used more frequently to make reservations—more than two-thirds of respondents (70 percent) did at least half of their travel booking online, up from 56 percent in 2001.

A 2002 CLIA study finds even greater use of the Internet for vacation planning—more than half of all vacationers reported that they had gone online to seek information about travel destinations, hotels, and airlines. Nearly two-thirds of respondents said they went online to obtain information about lodging (hotels, resorts, spas, and other places to stay) and well over half looked at airline schedules and fares. (See Figure 7.4.) Fewer CLIA surveyed respondents said they had actually done their vacation

FIGURE 7.5

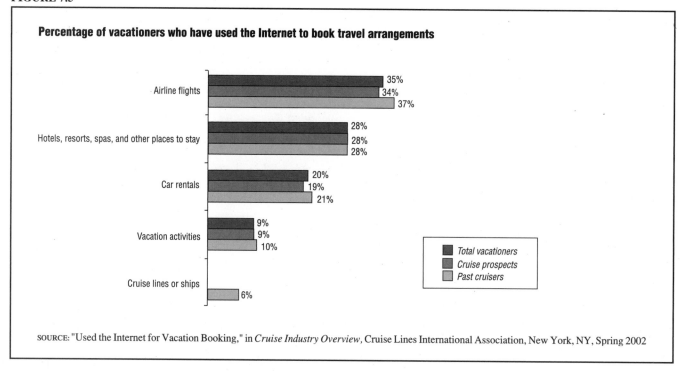

Percentage of vacationers who have used the Internet to book travel arrangements

Airline flights — Total vacationers 35%, Cruise prospects 34%, Past cruisers 37%

Hotels, resorts, spas, and other places to stay — Total vacationers 28%, Cruise prospects 28%, Past cruisers 28%

Car rentals — Total vacationers 20%, Cruise prospects 19%, Past cruisers 21%

Vacation activities — Total vacationers 9%, Cruise prospects 9%, Past cruisers 10%

Cruise lines or ships — Past cruisers 6%

- Total vacationers
- Cruise prospects
- Past cruisers

SOURCE: "Used the Internet for Vacation Booking," in *Cruise Industry Overview,* Cruise Lines International Association, New York, NY, Spring 2002

booking online—just over one-third had booked air travel online—compared to the more than 50 percent of TIA surveyed respondents who booked online. (See Figure 7.5.)

The TIA report speculates that the Internet was responsible for changing booking patterns—more consumers booked later to take advantage of low prices on last-minute travel and specials available exclusively online. Airline tickets were the most frequently purchased travel products online, reported by 77 percent of all online travel bookers, followed by accommodations (57 percent) and rental cars (37 percent). About 25 percent of online consumers bought tickets for cultural events and almost as many (21 percent) purchased travel packages. More than 30 percent of online buyers reported spending $2,500 or more in the year preceding the survey on travel booked online.

Business travelers shopped online for the best airline ticket prices, with almost half of all business air travelers personally purchasing their tickets online at least once in the year preceding the survey. Underscoring the impact of the Internet on business travel habits is the fact that 35 percent of online business travelers said they planned to use the Internet much more frequently in 2003 to book business flights.

WORLD TOURISM

During 2000 international tourism increased by 45 million arrivals. Although for the first time since 1982 international arrivals dipped by 0.6 percent in 2001, the year was still very successful in terms of tourism and the decline was much less than had been anticipated follow-

ing the events of September 11, 2001. According to *Tourism Highlights, 2002,* a publication of the World Tourism Organization (WTO), the world's top tourist destinations were France (76.5 million), Spain (49.5 million), the United States (45.5 million), Italy (39.1 million), China (33.2 million), the United Kingdom (22.8 million), Mexico (19.8 million), Canada (19.7 million), and Austria (18.2 million). Tourists spent $463.6 billion in 2001, down 2.8 percent from $477 billion in 2000.

The WTO predicts that China, where tourism increased more than 6 percent from 2000 to 2001, will likely be the top destination for international travel in 2020. The organization projects that China, excluding Hong Kong, will receive 137.1 million visitors, while Hong Kong will receive 59.3 million. The United States, the second most popular future destination point, will receive 102.4 million visitors in 2020. France will get 93.3 million visits, followed by Spain, with 71 million. China (8 percent) will experience the largest rate of increase annually; U.S. arrivals are expected to grow an average of 3.5 percent per year. In its 2002 report, the WTO cites China as an example of the fact that the economic success of a country positively influences both inbound and outbound tourism.

The WTO Tourism Recovery Committee contends that recent events in the world have temporarily set back the pace and scale of international travel recovery. However, the organization expresses optimism that consumers will still seek to travel, even if they must occasionally change their destinations or postpone their trips.

CHAPTER 8

THE ROLE OF RECREATION IN AMERICAN SOCIETY

A CHANGING ROLE

The expectations of free time have shifted and expanded over time. Eric Miller, in *At Our Leisure* (EPM Communications, Inc., New York, 1992), depicts recreation and leisure in the United States in the 1950s as an expression of comfort; it rounded out lives and reaffirmed the importance of home and family. During the 1960s it acquired an identity of its own apart from "traditional values." In the 1970s free time became an expression of an individual's identity; it pushed work into secondary importance. During the 1980s many Americans began to work at having fun—they were intent on working hard and "playing hard."

Americans spent wildly on material necessities, pleasures, and extravagances. Shopping was elevated to a form of recreation; American leisure included unabashed consumerism. At the turn of the twenty-first century, Americans demanded more of their free time—recreation had to provide personal satisfaction. Aging baby boomers, poised to become the largest group of older Americans in the country's history, exert tremendous influence over societal views and values about work, life, and leisure. As the members of this generation begin to recognize there is a limit to the quantity of life, they are turning their attention to improving the quality of their life.

American culture's structuring of leisure is relatively new. The five-day workweek was institutionalized as a part of President Franklin D. Roosevelt's New Deal (1938), and Americans settled into "nine-to-five" workdays (or slight variations) after World War II. When free time became a national institution, no corresponding leisure industry existed. Since then, leisure has developed into a huge industry. According to the U.S. Department of Labor, in 2001 Americans spent about 5 percent of their annual expenditures on entertainment, just slightly less than the 5.5 percent they spent on health care.

SEEKING FULFILLMENT

The work world has also changed greatly. More and more people work in structured, hierarchical environments where they perform highly specialized, repetitive tasks. Many workers report they are fulfilled less than previously by the actual work they do—they feel less creative and they say they have little input. Some workers report their jobs involve constant monitoring and little or no autonomy. In addition, employees often fear that they lack job security or loyalty from their employers. During an economic downturn, these fears may become reality as employers fire, downsize, or lay off workers in efforts to reduce their costs.

Consequently, studies suggest that many workers derive job satisfaction primarily because they feel their compensation—salaries and benefit packages—is adequate. When compensation is the principal source of fulfillment from work, then recreation assumes increasing importance as a contributing factor to an individual's quality of life. During the past two decades, research demonstrates that work stress is related to health, well-being, and longevity. The kind of work stress that causes the greatest harm to physical and mental health is effort-reward imbalance—that is, when great effort is made and the effort is neither recognized nor rewarded. Although women appear more vulnerable to job stress, men's health seems more dependent on the availability of social relationships and emotional support.

Many of Americans' favorite forms of recreation are popular for three reasons: they are convenient, possible to do alone or with others, and able to be performed for pleasure rather than for competition. For example, treadmills and resistance machines are popular because they can be performed almost anywhere, at anytime, and alone or with others.

Americans Want More Time

The perception of Americans as hardworking, stressed, and lacking leisure time is often supported by the observa-

TABLE 8.1

Public opinion on hobby interests, December 6–9, 2001 vs. February 20–25, 1948

DO YOU HAVE ANY HOBBY THAT YOU ARE PARTICULARLY INTERESTED IN? WHAT?

	2001 Dec 6-9	1948 Feb 20-25
None	19	42
Athletics and sports — bowling, fishing, hunting, riding horses	33	10
Handiwork — knitting, sewing, woodwork, model aviation, restoring antiques, autos	17	15
Reading	12	1
Art and music — play, listen, see, produce, paint	9	3
Rural arts and domestic arts — farming, planting, gardening, canning, cooking	8	2
Computers— programming, Internet, games	4	—
Collections — antiques, stamps, buttons, old coins, records, etc.	3	5
Movies, radio, going out to dinner, plays, bingo, games	3	2
Amateur craftsmen — photography, ham radio, television, carpentry, activities that have a professional counterpart, not otherwise specified	3	6
Family activities	3	—
Social endeavor — Red Cross, teaching, politics, church work	2	2
Crosswords, puzzles	2	—
Traveling	1	—
Writing	1	—
Shopping	1	—
Miscellaneous	5	2
No answer	1	3

SOURCE: Lydia Saad, "Do you have any hobby that you are particularly interested in? What?" in "There's No Place Like Home to Spend an Evening, Say Most Americans," The Gallup Organization, January 10, 2002 www.gallup.com © 2002 The Gallup Organization, all rights reserved. Reprinted with permission.

tion that Americans routinely work more hours per day and more days per year than residents of many other countries. For example, the World Tourism Organization finds that Americans averaged just thirteen vacation days per year, compared to Italians with an average of forty-two days per year, followed by France with thirty-seven days, Germany with thirty-five days, and Brazil with thirty-four days.

Americans themselves feel time-strapped and increasingly starved for leisure time. The poll by the Shell Oil Company "Time's Up: Many Americans Indicate That Work, Leisure Aren't in Sync" (*The Shell Poll* vol. 2, no. 2, Spring 2000) finds that given the choice between an extra day off every two weeks or an extra day's pay, more employed adults would rather have extra time (58 percent) than extra money (40 percent). Furthermore, the Shell poll observes that while 60 percent of working-age (thirty-five to sixty-four) Americans said they were satisfied with their leisure time, a Gallup poll conducted in 1963 reported 74 percent of Americans felt satisfied with the amount of leisure time in their life.

About half (53 percent) of the respondents in the Shell poll said they had two hours or less of leisure time per weekday and nearly 30 percent claimed they only had an hour or less of leisure time. Employed parents felt the most deprived of leisure time. The Shell poll finds that less than half of working mothers were satisfied with their leisure time and only one-quarter of working parents with children living at home said they were very satisfied with the free time they had to themselves. When compared to a 1963 Gallup poll finding of 70 percent of working mothers reporting satisfaction with their free time, these numbers reflect a sharp decline in satisfaction with leisure time.

The decline in both the actual leisure time available to working adults and their relative satisfaction with their free time is somewhat surprising in view of the technological advances, such as fax machines, cell phones, and e-mail, that many observers believed would free up more time for working Americans. The Shell poll finds that more than half of Americans felt they had less free time as a result of these advances. Just 36 percent said fax machines, cell phones, and the Internet had increased their leisure time.

HOW WILL THEY SPEND IT? A Gallup Organization poll published in 2002 compared 1948 and 2001 data about Americans' interest in hobbies and other leisure-time activities. In February 1948 more than 40 percent of respondents said they had no hobby that interested them, but by December 2001 the proportion fell to just 19 percent. Interest in athletics and sports jumped from 10 percent in 1948 to 33 percent in 2001. Similarly, interest in reading grew from just 1 percent to 12 percent and the percent of respondents who were interested in art and music grew threefold. (See Table 8.1.)

Interest in handiwork, such as knitting, sewing, model building, and restoring antiques, remained about the same, as did enthusiasm for movies, plays, bingo, and dining out. By 2001 there were half as many respondents who were amateur craftsmen, but there was a fourfold increase in interest in rural and domestic arts, such as gardening and cooking. (See Table 8.1.)

Public support for the arts and appreciation of their importance was confirmed by the results of a 2001 public opinion survey conducted by the California Arts Council. The survey was designed to assess Californians' attitudes about the arts, public participation in the arts, the role and value of arts education, and public funding of the arts. Rather than viewing the arts as a "frill or a luxury," the survey reveals that fully 55 percent of respondents felt the arts were extremely important to them personally, while only 5 percent felt they were not at all important. Another surprising survey finding was that 91 percent of those surveyed considered the arts as important or more important than sports.

Recreation as Socialization

Many forms of recreation are popular because they offer opportunities to socialize and interact with others.

Many young people enjoy sports as an inexpensive dating practice, believing they can get to know another person well from an afternoon spent in-line skating or bicycling together. Billiards in modern, upscale parlors has become a "hip" couples' activity and bowling has regained popularity. Gyms, health clubs, and sporting activities have been touted as great ways to simultaneously improve health and fitness, engage in recreation, and meet people.

There is mounting evidence that socialization and recreation hold important health benefits. Family, friends, active interests, and community involvement may do more than simply help people enjoy their life. Social activities and relationships may actually enable people to live longer by preventing or delaying development of many diseases, including dementia (impaired mental function). Furthermore, social activities seem to protect against disease and increase longevity even when the activities do not involve physical exercise. C. F. Mendes de Leon et al., in "Social Networks and Disability Transitions Across Eight Intervals of Yearly Data in the New Haven EPESE" (*Journals of Gerontology Series B: Psychological Sciences and Social Sciences* vol. 54, no. 3, May 1999), tracked the health and longevity of 2,761 older adults living in New Haven, Connecticut. After thirteen years, the researchers determine that "social and productive activities that involve little or no enhancement of fitness lower the risk of all cause mortality as much as fitness activities do."

A CHANGING MARKET

The gaming industry reports in "Boomers Are a Tough Target" (*International Gaming and Wagering Business* May 1998) that along with other entertainment industries, the next wave of megaresorts and vacation destinations will target a new group: affluent baby boomers. Industry experts predict that:

- Boomers will demand holistic experiences—that is, locations that allow them to nurture their mind, body, and spirit. Learning will increasingly be a desirable aspect of the vacation experience.

- Vacation resorts will offer entertainment for the whole family. In two-income families, parents will consider vacations as a way of reconnecting with children rather than escaping from them, as in the past.

- Authenticity is important. People will visit places that are fabricated once because they are new and exciting, but they will not often return. Visitors will seek locations that are genuine in a particular setting, for example, a cabin in the woods or at the seashore.

- Boomers want recreation to be hassle-free. In their already complicated lives, they will seek vacations that are well programmed so that they can enjoy them and do not have to think.

- Technology will be essential to a boomer getaway. If boomers can work while on their vacations, they will stay longer. They will require high-speed Internet access and business services on the premises. Many will consider a vacation hotel an extension of their office.

In order to survive, leisure activities and vacation destinations will have to evolve to attract and retain the changing market.

Preferred Vacation Destinations

The Shell poll also compares its findings about Americans' vacation preferences to those expressed by respondents to a 1965 Gallup poll. For example, in 1965 just 13 percent of Americans thought they would travel overseas during the next five years and a scant 6 percent said they were very likely to travel overseas. In contrast, the Shell poll finds that nearly half of Americans felt it was likely that they would take an overseas trip during the next five years and almost one-third considered it very likely that they would travel overseas.

Still, Americans' preference to stay at home was relatively unchanged from a 1968 Gallup poll to the 2000 Shell poll. In 1968 more than one-third (38 percent) of respondents said they had taken a weeklong vacation away from home. The Shell poll finds just 4 percent more Americans (42 percent) had taken a vacation that kept them away from home for at least six nights during the year preceding the poll.

More Americans may vacation at home, or at least in the United States, during 2003 than in previous years. The Shell poll was conducted prior to the downturn in the U.S. economy and the terrorist attacks of September 11, 2001. Together, these events have sharply curtailed both Americans' desire to travel overseas as well as their ability to pay for such travel.

The Shell poll reports that when they do think about a vacation, Americans dream of taking a cruise (31 percent), visiting an outdoor attraction, such as the Grand Canyon or the Yellowstone National Park (29 percent), and going to a major theme park (17 percent).

Another survey, conducted by the Cruise Line International Association (CLIA) in 2001, finds that among persons who had taken cruises in the past five years, more than one-third (34 percent) said they were extremely satisfied with cruise vacations. Approximately the same number of past cruisers were also extremely satisfied with vacation house rentals (30 percent), visits to friends or relatives (29 percent), and package tours (25 percent). (See Table 8.2.)

SPORTS—AN EXPRESSION OF NATIONAL VALUES

A Brief History of American Sports

From ancient times, sports played a role in defining manhood. Powerful men displayed their status and wealth

TABLE 8.2

Percentage reporting themselves to be "extremely satisfied" with their vacation, by type of vacation

	Extremely satisfied (percentage)
Cruise	34
Vacation house rental	30
Visit to friends/relatives	29
Package tour	25
Resort vacation	24
Land-based escorted tour	24
Trip using individual reservations	23
Vacation as part of a business trip	19

SOURCE: "Satisfaction with Vacations Taken in Past 5 Years," in *Cruise Industry Overview*, Cruise Lines International Association, New York, NY, Spring 2002

by building horse racing tracks or sponsoring sporting events, while humbler ones gained a sense of power, prowess, masculinity, and sometimes wealth as participants or spectators in games. Despite differences in social rank, sports united men in a shared patriarchal culture. Athletics encouraged men to display their competitiveness and physical abilities and motivated them to think in terms of winning and losing. Sports generally helped to support a vision of masculinity that emphasized aggression and physicality.

In the late 1800s the advent of daily sports pages and telegraph lines to transmit baseball scores contributed to a growing sporting culture. The expansion of cities spurred the growth of sports, which developed most rapidly in urban areas, where a burgeoning manufacturing economy was producing huge amounts of wealth. As cities grew, recreation was increasingly transformed into entertainment, an amusement to be purchased with earnings.

Despite events that drew many thousands of fans and hundreds of newspaper reporters, professionalism in sports was still unusual, profits were secondary to pleasure, organizations were informal, and scheduling was irregular. Sports continued to be voluntary associations based on class, ethnic, or occupational background. Sports, like religion, politics, and business, became threads binding the tapestry of American culture.

Not only were sports changing and growing, but also many Americans were beginning to view sports as a moral force. Taking charge of one's physical condition became a prerequisite for a virtuous, self-reliant, spiritually elevated life. Moral improvement, self-mastery, and godliness were invoked in the name of sports. By the mid-1800s, even clergymen, intellectuals, and reformers "took up the cause." As Henry David Thoreau declared, "The body existed for the highest development of the soul."

The Profit Motive Emerges—Professionalization and Commercialization

In an era of urban overcrowding and strict labor discipline, leisure activities had the potential to blunt workers' rebelliousness. Reformers argued that sports refreshed workers' spirits, improved their productivity, and alleviated class tensions. If these benefits were insufficient motivation to participate, sports advocates claimed a moral high ground, contending that sports built character. Other people found they could earn money by teaching a game or hustling other players.

Sports became part of a new consumerism. New technologies led to better sports gear and equipment, and as a result, improved performance. A sports team became an employer with a "bottom line." Unlike athletes who earlier participated because they believed it would improve their body or their character, players now threw a ball to earn a living. By the close of the twentieth century, professional sports were generally recognized as commercial endeavors. Sports were big business and those who did not compete in sports could pay to see other people compete or wager on the outcomes of competitions.

Amateur Sports

Following the lead of professional sports, amateur sports have also become big business. Some critics believe that the status of amateur sports, even at the middle school and high school levels, is threatened by an increasing emphasis on commercialization. They cite scandals involving recruiting, redshirting (holding a player back a year until he or she grows bigger, gets better, or a player in his or her position graduates; although the player attends school, he or she does not use up a year of athletic eligibility), phony courses, and inflated or bogus grades. There is even fear that the scandals plaguing professional and Olympic sports, such as steroid and drug use, sexual misconduct, and corruption, will derail the careers of promising high school and college athletes.

Looking Good

When Americans participate in a sports activity, they often buy the best equipment and gear. During the 1980s and 1990s the robust economy produced many Americans with a considerable amount of discretionary income, and many used it to support their varied sports and fitness interests. Sporting goods is a thriving market, with new technologies and products arriving on the shelves weekly.

Many Americans not only participate in a sport or fitness activity, but they also increasingly compete against others. While many people still jog or run for health, growing numbers do so competitively—in marathons. A biker may not necessarily ride his or her bike to the grocery store, but he or she may enter (with a racing bike costing thousands of dollars) bike races or weekend group rides. Some cyclists take biking holidays or biking day trips.

National Values

Labor and play once overlapped more freely than they do today because leisure time and work time were not so rigidly delineated. For example, sports were not necessarily played according to standardized rules—they were often a part of local culture, passed on by word of mouth, with rules varying from place to place. Today's sports include multiple layers of communication, transportation, professionalism, regulating bodies, records, statistics, and media coverage.

Sports respond to, and reflect, American values. It would be very easy to confuse a Super Bowl presentation with a Fourth of July celebration, with its veneration of nationalism, racial and ethnic integration, "rugged individualism," and hard work. Yet, some see the Super Bowl as more than just a big game celebrating athletic skill; they view it as an enormous commercial undertaking intended to sell advertisements and generate huge profits for owners, players, and television networks.

Violence in the Sports Arena

Although physical prowess has a place in American society today, it competes with an appreciation of, and need for, other qualities, such as intellect and cooperation. Furthermore, valuing and rewarding physical aggression in a civil society sometimes presents serious challenges. When athletes and others are trained and encouraged to excel at physically aggressive pursuits, they are sometimes unable to harness those tendencies outside the sports arena. Hitting an opponent so hard that he has trouble getting up is a positive act loudly applauded on the playing field, while the same action in the parking lot after the game may send an athlete—or spectator—to jail.

The Deification of Sports Figures—Who Are the Heroes?

The sudden flowering of a "mass culture" brought about by the growth in media and communications produced a wealth of new sports heroes. Increasingly, the public world became populated by sports celebrities with national reputations and appeal—heroes such as Joe Louis, Jackie Robinson, Babe Didrikson Zaharias, Muhammad Ali, Joe DiMaggio, Babe Ruth, Sandy Koufax, and Billie Jean King.

The Gallup Organization conducted a poll and reported in January 2000 that Michael Jordan, by an enormous margin, was considered to be the top athlete of the twentieth century. A sampling of adults, aged eighteen and older, were asked "what man or woman living anytime this century do you think was the greatest athlete of the century, in terms of their athletic performance?" Jordan was chosen by 23 percent. By June 2001 Jordan was toppled from supremacy as polled Americans named Tiger Woods as the greatest athlete active in the world of sports today. (See Table 5.7 in Chapter 5.)

Are They What They Seem?

Celebrity athletes serve as role models for young people and aspiring athletes, and they can exert powerful marketing effectiveness. Advertising and public relations professionals quickly understood the benefit of linking these icons to products. The public's fascination with fame and glamour enabled heroes to mold the taste of their fans. Sports heroes gained widespread recognition and became known as marketing images rather than real human beings.

As a result, many people have come to revere sports figures, to regard them as heroes, and to credit them with attributes they may not possess. The American public holds its sports figures in high esteem, puts them on pedestals, and appears truly shocked when heroes demonstrate they are mortals who share the weaknesses of others. Although sports have always had their share of misbehavior, in recent years the media has been able to publicize the indiscretions, such as allegations of substance abuse and domestic violence, of a number of sports figures. Famous athletes who earned reputations as models of athletic prowess and success have sometimes disappointed and disenchanted admiring fans.

RECREATION FOR HEALTH

Americans are living longer and are generally healthier. More people are able physically and, increasingly, financially to participate in recreational activities. Older adults are a growing market in the sales of many consumer items, including recreation vehicles, sporting goods, books, and computers.

Active Recreation Prevents Disease

Lack of physical exercise not only contributes to the risk of heart disease, but also increases the risk of colon cancer, diabetes, high blood pressure, osteoporosis, and arthritis. Regular physical activity is also linked to improved mental health by reducing mild anxiety and depression. Health professionals agree that even moderate amounts of exercise, such as walking thirty minutes a day, five times a week, as opposed to strenuous physical activity, such as running, provides substantial health benefits. Despite unassailable evidence demonstrating its potent disease prevention and health promotion benefits, the Centers for Disease Control and Prevention finds that 60 percent of American adults do not exercise enough to reap health benefits and 25 percent do not exercise at all during their leisure time.

Physical activity is the first leading health indicator of *Healthy People, 2010,* the source document that serves as a blueprint for improving the health status of Americans. *Healthy People, 2010* defines regular leisure-time physical activity as performing light to moderate physical activity for thirty or more minutes, five or more times per week, or vigorous physical activity for twenty or more minutes, three or more times per week. National health surveys that offered respondents this definition of regular leisure-time activity find a slow, steady increase in the percent of adults aged eighteen and older who engaged in regular leisure-time physical activity, from 29.9 percent in 1998 to 32.1 percent in 2001. The percent of adults who obtained regular leisure-time physical activity declined with advancing age, and women in every age group reported less physical activity. When the survey results were adjusted for age and sex, regular leisure-time physical activity was highest among white (35 percent) followed by black (25.3 percent) and Hispanic (21.1 percent) adults (*Physical Activity and Good Nutrition: Essential Elements to Prevent Chronic Diseases and Obesity, 2002,* Centers for Disease Control and Prevention, 2002).

THE PRESIDENT MAKES PHYSICAL FITNESS A TOP PRIORITY. Concern about Americans' inactivity prompted President George W. Bush to announce a federal effort to improve fitness levels among adults and children on June 20, 2002. In a campaign that recalled the one launched by President John F. Kennedy four decades earlier, President Bush appointed a presidential council and issued an executive order along with twelve pages of recommendations about how Americans could improve their health and fitness. The president urged Americans to follow his example of running three miles a day and lifting weights to stay fit.

RECREATION FOR HEALING

Ancient teachings are replete with claims of the benefits of recreational experiences: "A merry heart doeth good like a medicine" (Proverbs) and "You can learn more about a man in an hour of play than in a lifetime of conversation" (Plato). But beginning in the nineteenth century, such principles were beginning to be applied in health care settings in a purposeful, organized manner.

Increasingly, medical professionals are applying recreation to healing. Therapists research the effects of aquatic therapy on the treatment of multiple sclerosis. Others find that horseback riding, for as yet unknown reasons, produces a remission in some patients suffering from multiple sclerosis. Mental health facilities now recognize the importance of bright, healthy surroundings and pleasant diversions for sufferers of mental and emotional conditions, unlike the harsh penal atmosphere generally accorded to patients in early mental facilities.

Many people find that the presence of animals helps the recovery of the ill and improves the health and well-being of residents in nursing homes. Some studies document the relaxation response and resulting reduction in blood pressure from simply observing an aquarium. Almost everyone understands that engaging in satisfying forms of recreation and pleasurable leisure-time pursuits is vital for maintaining overall health.

IMPORTANT NAMES AND ADDRESSES

American Theatre
Theatre Communications Group
520 Eighth Ave., 24th Fl.
New York, NY 10018-4156
(212) 609-5990
FAX: (212) 609-5901
E-mail: tcg@tcg.org
URL: http://www.tcg.org

Association of American Publishers
71 Fifth Ave., 2nd Fl.
New York, NY 10003
(212) 255-0200
FAX: (212) 255-7007
URL: http://www.publishers.org

**Association of Racing
Commissioners International**
2343 Alexandria Dr., Suite 200
Lexington, KY 40504
(859) 224-7070
FAX: (859) 224-7071
E-mail: support@arci.com
URL: http://www.arci.com

Book Industry Study Group, Inc.
19 W. 21st St., Suite 905
New York, NY 10010
(646) 336-7141
FAX: (646) 336-6214
E-mail: bisg-info@bisg.org
URL: http://www.bisg.org

Consumer Electronics Association
2500 Wilson Blvd.
Arlington, VA 22201-3834
(703) 907-7600
FAX: (703) 907-7675
E-mail: cea@ce.org
URL: http://www.ce.org

Hobby Industry Association
319 E. 54th St.
Elmwood Park, NJ 07407
(201) 794-1133

FAX: (201) 797-0657
E-mail: hia@hobby.org
URL: http://www.hobby.org

Motion Picture Association of America
15503 Ventura Blvd.
Encino, CA 91436
(818) 995-6600
URL: http://www.mpaa.org/

Motorcycle Industry Council
2 Jenner St., Suite 150
Irvine, CA 92618
(949) 727-4211
FAX: (949) 727-3313
E-mail: aftmgr@mic.org
URL: http://www.mic.org

Museum of Television and Radio
25 W. 52nd St.
New York, NY 10019
(212) 621-6600
URL: http://www.mtr.org

National Association of Theatre Owners
4605 Lankershim Blvd., Suite 340
North Hollywood, CA 91602
(818) 506-1778
FAX: (818) 506-0269
E-mail: nato@mindspring.com
URL: http://www.natoonline.org

National Collegiate Athletic Association
700 W. Washington St.
P.O. Box 6222
Indianapolis, IN 46206-6222
(317) 917-6222
FAX: (317) 917-6888
URL: http://www.ncaa.org

National Endowment for the Arts
1100 Pennsylvania Ave., NW
Washington, DC 20506-0001
(202) 682-5400
URL: http://arts.endow.gov

**National Marine
Manufacturers Association**
200 E. Randolph Dr., Suite 5100
Chicago, IL 60601
(312) 946-6200
URL: http://www.nmma.org

National Park Service
1849 C St., NW
Washington, DC 20240
(202) 208-6843
FAX: (202) 219-0910
URL: http://www.nps.gov

National Sporting Goods Association
1601 Feehanville Dr., Suite 300
Mt. Prospect, IL 60056-6035
(847) 296-6742
FAX: (847) 391-9827
URL: http://www.nsga.org

National Trust for Historic Preservation
1785 Massachusetts Ave., NW
Washington, DC 20036
(202) 588-6000
FAX: (202) 588-6038
URL: http://www.nthp.org

Newspaper Association of America
1921 Gallows Rd., Suite 600
Vienna, VA 22182-3900
(703) 902-1600
FAX: (703) 917-0636
URL: http://www.naa.org

Office of Travel and Tourism Industries
International Trade Administration
U.S. Department of Commerce
1401 Constitution Ave., NW, Rm. 7025
Washington, DC 20230
(202) 482-0140
FAX: (202) 482-2887
E-mail: info@tinet.ita.doc.gov
URL: http://www.tinet.ita.doc.gov

Recording Industry Association of America
1330 Connecticut Ave., NW
Washington, DC 20036-1704
(202) 775-0101

Recreation Roundtable
American Recreation Coalition
1225 New York Ave., NW, Suite 450
Washington, DC 20005
(202) 682-9530
FAX: (202) 682-9529
E-mail: arc@funoutdoors.com
URL: http://www.funoutdoors.com

Recreational Vehicle Industry Association
1896 Preston White Dr.
P.O. Box 2999
Reston, VA 20195-0999
(703) 620-6003
FAX: (703) 620-5071
URL: http://www.rvia.org

Sporting Goods Manufacturers Association
200 Castlewood Dr.

North Palm Beach, FL 33408-5696
(561) 842-4100
FAX: (561) 863-8984
E-mail: info@sgma.com
URL: http://www.sportlink.com

Toy Industry Association, Inc.
1115 Broadway, Suite 400
New York, NY 10010
(212) 675-1141
FAX: (212) 633-1429
E-mail: info@toy-tia.org
URL: http://www.toy-tia.org

Travel Industry Association of America
1100 New York Ave., NW, Suite 450
Washington, DC 20005-3934
(202) 408-8422
FAX: (202) 408-1255
URL: http://www.tia.org

U.S. Department of Labor
Frances Perkins Bldg.
200 Constitution Ave., NW, Room S-1093
Washington, DC 20210
(202) 693-4650

(866) 4-USA-DOL
URL: http://www.dol.gov

U.S. Fish and Wildlife Service
U.S. Department of the Interior
1849 C St., NW
Washington, DC 20240-0001
(202) 208-4717
E-mail: contact@fws.gov
URL: http://www.fws.gov

U.S. Forest Service
U.S. Department of Agriculture
P.O. Box 96090
Washington, DC 20090-6090
(202) 205-8333
URL: http://www.fs.fed.us

World Trade Organization
Centre William Rappard
rue de Lausanne 154, CH-1211
Geneva 21, Switzerland
(41-22) 739.51.11
FAX: (41-22) 731.42.06
E-mail: enquiries@wto.org
URL: http://www.wto.org

RESOURCES

The U.S. Department of Transportation periodically conducts its *American Travel Survey* on the travel patterns of Americans. The U.S. Travel and Tourism Administration of the U.S. Department of Commerce gathers and analyzes data about travel within the United States and overseas travel to and from the United States. The Travel Industry Association of America and the World Trade Organization also provide information about travel, including the number of trips, people's activities during trips, and demographic data about American travelers.

The National Park Service of the U.S. Department of the Interior published the *National Park Service Statistical Abstract 2001,* with information about the national parks, their facilities, services, accommodations, hours of operation, costs, and utilization. The U.S. Fish and Wildlife Service of the U.S. Department of the Interior published the *2001 National Survey of Fishing, Hunting, and Wildlife-Associated Recreation.* Information about nature-based recreation and ecotourism was gleaned from Visit Florida publications.

The U.S. Bureau of Labor Statistics report *Consumer Expenditures in 2000: The U.S. General Accounting* and the U.S. Department of Commerce, Bureau of Economic Analysis Data contributed information about consumer spending. The International Association of Amusement Parks and Attractions provided helpful statistics about amusement parks and other attractions.

The National Endowment for the Arts provided important information about trends in attendance of performing arts, motion pictures, and spectator sports. Ipsos-NPD Reports provided valuable information about book purchases in its *Ipsos Book Trends* (Uniondale, NY, 2002). The Association of American Publishers provided sales data in its *2001 Industry Statistics Report* (New York, 2002). The Book Industry Study Group and the American Booksellers Association shared the results of their research on reading and purchasing behavior in the United States.

The National Organization of Theatre Owners is a source of statistical data about theater admissions, ticket prices, and number of movie screens. MPAA Worldwide Market Research offered economic data about U.S. theatrical box office receipts and revenues.

The Toy Manufacturers of America and the NPD Group reported on the toy industry in *2001 vs. 2000 State of the Industry,* which offers an overview of the toy industry and product safety, as well as marketing and advertising. The Hobby Industry Association, in its *2001 Nationwide Craft and Hobby Consumer Usage and Purchases Study,* supplied information about hobbies, crafts, and collecting.

The National Sporting Goods Association provided important information on the sporting goods market and participation in sports, such as walking, fishing, football, baseball, basketball, bicycle riding, bowling, and running. The National Collegiate Athletic Association collected information on student athletes. The Sporting Goods Manufacturers Association supplied many useful publications and charts from its *Superstudy of Sports Participation* (2002), *Recreation Market Report* (2001), and *SGMA Market Report* (North Palm Beach, FL, 2002). The American Recreation Coalition publication *Outdoor Recreation in America, 2001* (Washington, DC, 2001) provided data about recreational activities by age.

Gallup Poll, Gallup News Service, and Roper Starch Worldwide supplied public opinion research cited in this book. Information from *International Gaming and Wagering Business,* a monthly trade magazine devoted to the gaming industry that contains data about every aspect of the industry and special reports on particular types of gambling activity, such as lotteries and casino gambling, was also helpful.

The Association of Racing Commissioners International provided material from its *Pari-mutuel Racing* (Lexington, KY, 2000). Harrah's Entertainment *Profile of the American Casino Gambler* (Las Vegas, NV, 2002) described American gambling preferences and habits. The National Indian Gaming Commission provided a wealth of information about tribal gaming.

Materials and information were supplied by a number of private organizations and associations. The Leisure Trends Group provided data and insight into how Americans spend their leisure time. Independent Sector's *Volunteering in the United States, 2000* and *Giving and Volunteering in the United States* (Washington DC, 2002) provided data about American volunteerism. The findings of a survey about road trips, commissioned by the Avis car rental company, were cited in this book, as were data from the Shell Oil Company's "Time's Up: Many Americans Indicate That Work, Leisure Aren't in Sync" (*The Shell Poll* vol. 2, no. 2, Spring 2000), about how Americans view their leisure time. Cruise Lines International Association provided information about cruise lengths, destinations, consumers, and industry trends.

Data on heritage and historical tourism were received from the National Trust for Historic Preservation. The Pew Research Center provided analyses of American media use in the Pew Internet and American Life Project (2002) and the Pew Research Center for People and the Press (Washington, DC, 2000). The Recording Industry Association of America's *2002 RIAA Mid-year Statistics* and *2001 Consumer Profile* provided valuable information, as did the Recreational Vehicle Industry Association and the Motorcycle Industry Council. The National Marine Manufacturer's Association and Consumer Electronics Association also provided source material for this publication.

INDEX

violence in, 85
See also Individual sports
Sports Participation in America, 6
States, 28(*t*3.3)
   casino gambling, 62
   casino gambling participation rates, 63(*f*6.6), 63(*f*6.7)
   electronic gambling devices (EGDs) in, 66-67
   participation in hunting, by, 35*f*
   soccer participants, 55-56
   sports gambling, 67
   visits to National Park Service areas, by, 28(*t*3.3)
   wildlife-related recreation, by, 30*t,* 31
   wildlife watching, by, 36*f,* 37*f*
   See also Individual states
Statistical information
   age of moviegoers preferring certain actors/actresses, 47*t*
   annual expenditures of all consumer units, 13*t*
   arts, participation in, 43
   athletes, public opinion on best, 57*t*
   athletic footwear shipments, 20*t*
   attendance at arts activities, 41*t,* 42*t*
   average annual expenditures, 14*t*-15*t*
   boats sold, 21*t*
   book selection methods, 2(*t*1.2)
   camping in National Park Service areas, 28(*f*3.2)
   casino gamblers, education level of, 62(*f*6.3)
   casino gambling and occupation, 62(*f*6.4)
   casino gambling, by age, 62(*t*6.4), 65(*t*6.6)
   casino gambling, by games played, 65(*t*6.5)
   casino gambling, by gender, 65(*t*6.7)
   casino gambling, by income, 62(*f*6.5)
   casino gambling participation rates, by region, 63(*f*6.6.)
   casino gambling participation rates, by state, 63(*f*6.7)
   casino gambling profile, 62(*t*6.2), 62(*t*6.3)
   cruise ship passengers, 73*t,* 74*t,* 75(*f*7.3), 75(*t*7.5)
   cruises, 75(*t*7.4), 76*t*
   electronics, factory sales of, 16*t*
   electronics, household penetration of, 17*t*
   expenditures, personal consumption, 15 (*t*2.3)
   extreme sports, 9(*t*1.14)
   finance and investment news on the Internet, 6(*t*1.6)
   fishing, participation in, 32(*f*3.4), 33(*f*3.6), 33(*t*3.6)
   gambling industry, 60(*f*6.1)
   hobby interests, public opinion on, 82*t*
   hunting, days, trips and expenditures for, 34*t*
   hunting, participation in, 32(*f*3.4), 35*f*
   Indian gambling operations, 60(*f*6.2), 61(*t*6.1)
   Internet activities, survey of, 4-5(*t*1.4)
   Internet activities of parents, 3*t*-4*t*
   leisure time pursuits, by age, 2(*t*1.1)

   men's sports participation, 7(*t*1.8)
   National Park Service area visits, 27*t,* 28(*t*3.3), 29*f*
   new participants in sports, by activity, 54(*t*5.5)
   news sources, 5*f*
   news use, by age, 6(*t*1.5)
   outdoor activities, participation rates in, 26*f*
   outdoor activities, by age, 8(*t*1.10)
   recreation market report, 19*t*
   spectator events, admission receipts for, 46*t*
   spectator sports, 52(*t*5.1)
   spectator sports attendance, 52(*t*5.2)
   sporting goods, costs of, 17-20
   sports and fitness activities for older adults, 9(*t*1.13)
   sports and fitness activities for teens, 9(*t*1.12)
   sports participation, 7(*t*1.7), 26*t,* 53*t,* 54(*t*5.4)
   team sports, participation in, 55*t*
   travel, by selected characteristics, 70*t*
   travel, by type of transportation, 72*f*
   travel destinations, by region, 71*f*
   travel information from the Internet, 79*f,* 80*f*
   vacations, public opinion on, 84*t*
   wildlife-related recreation, expenditures on, 23(*f*2.3), 31*t*
   wildlife-related recreation, by state, 30*t*
   wildlife-watching, 32(*f*3.5)
   wildlife-watching, by gender and age, 33(*t*3.7), 38*t*
   wildlife-watching, by state, 36*f,* 37*f*
   women's sports participation, 7(*t*1.9)
Streaming video, 49
Super Bowl Sunday, 51-52

T

Table gambling games, 62-63
TCG (Theatre Communications Group), 44
Teenagers
   Internet usage, 5
   sports preferred by, 9(*t*1.12)
Telephone products, 16*t,* 17*t*
Television, 45, 46-48
   compared to Internet, 49
   factory sales of, 16*t*
   satellite systems, 15, 17, 47
Tennis, 56-57
Theater, 43-44
Theatre Communications Group (TCG), 44
Theme parks, 20, 24, 38-39
Therapeutic benefits of recreation, 86
Thoreau, Henry David, 84
TIA (Toy Industry Association), 20
TIA (Travel Industry Association of America), 20, 69
Time, 81-83
   favorite ways to spend, 2
   free, 1
Tomlin, Lily, 44
Tourism, 20, 37*f,* 42
   See also Traveling
Toy Industry Association (TIA), 20

Toys, 18*t,* 20-21
Trail running, 25
Travel Industry Association of America (TIA), 20, 69
   business and pleasure trips, 78-79
   cultural and heritage tourism, 76
   ecotourism, 76
   reasons for traveling, 71-72
   romantic vacations, 77-78
   on travel destinations, 73
Traveling, 20, 69-80, 70*t*
   by air, 71
   cruise destinations, 76*t*
   cruise ship passengers, demographic profile of, 74*t*
   cruise ship passengers, number of, 73*t,* 75(*t*7.5)
   cruises, 73-76
   cultural and heritage tourism, 76-77
   domestic, 69-73
   ecotourism, 76
   family reunions, 78
   Internet, 79-80
   profile of travelers, 72-73
   reasons for, 71-72
   by region, 71*f*
   romantic vacations, 77-78
   shopping, 78
   transportation while, 69, 71, 72*f*
   vacations, public satisfaction with, 84*t*
   weekend, 72
   wildlife-watching, 37*f*
   world tourism, 80

U

U.S. Fish and Wildlife Service, 31
U.S. Parachute Association, 39

V

Vacations, 69-80
   See also Traveling
Values, 85
VCRs (Video cassette recorders), 46, 73
Vegetable gardening, 29
Veronis, Suhler and Associates, 45, 47
Video products, 15, 17
   video cassette recorders (VCRs), 46, 73
   streaming, 49
Violence, 85
Volunteering, 1, 10-11
   number of people and hours, 10*t,* 11*t*
   when asked, 11*f*

W

Wagering on the Internet, 67
Washington, George, 59
Weather Channel, 48
Weekend travel, 72
Whale watching, 34
Wildlife-related recreation, 22*f,* 23, 30-35
   "canned hunting," 34-35
   expenditures, 32-33
   fishing, 34
   by gender and age, 33
   hunting, 33-34
   participation rates in, 33